Entrepreneurship
and New Value Creation

Why do some individuals decide they want to create businesses and then actually do so? Why do others decide against this course of action, even though they appear to have what it takes to succeed? These two questions were among the first that researchers in the field of entrepreneurship tried to answer. Today, it seems that the problem is much more difficult to solve than it first appeared thirty years ago. The venture creation phenomenon is a complex one, covering a wide variety of situations. The purpose of this book is to improve our understanding of this complexity by offering both a theory of the entrepreneurial process and practical advice on how to start a new business and manage it effectively. *Entrepreneurship and New Value Creation* is a highly original, research-driven book that will appeal to graduate students, researchers and reflective practitioners concerned with the dynamics of the entrepreneurial process.

ALAIN FAYOLLE is Professor and Director of the Entrepreneurship Research Centre at EM Lyon, France.

Entrepreneurship and New Value Creation

The Dynamic of the Entrepreneurial Process

ALAIN FAYOLLE

CAMBRIDGE
UNIVERSITY PRESS

CAMBRIDGE
UNIVERSITY PRESS

University Printing House, Cambridge CB2 8BS, United Kingdom

Cambridge University Press is part of the University of Cambridge.

It furthers the University's mission by disseminating knowledge in the pursuit of education, learning and research at the highest international levels of excellence.

www.cambridge.org
Information on this title: www.cambridge.org/9780521855181

First published 2007
First paperback edition 2011

A catalogue record for this publication is available from the British Library

Library of Congress Cataloguing in Publication data
Fayolle, Alain.
Entrepreneurship and new value creation: the dynamic of the entrepreneurial process / Alain Fayolle.
    p.   cm.
Includes bibliographical references and index.
ISBN 13: 978 0 521 85518 1 (hardback)
ISBN 10: 0 521 85518 7 (hardback)
1. New business enterprises.   2. Entrepreneurship.   3. New business enterprises – Management.   I. Title.
HD62.5.F39   2007
658.1'1 – dc22   2007013269

ISBN 978-0-521-85518-1 Hardback
ISBN 978-1-107-40290-4 Paperback

Contents

Figures

Tables

Foreword

WILLIAM B. GARTNER
Clemson University

I am delighted to write this Foreword to Alain Fayolle's *Entrepreneurship and New Value Creation: The Dynamic of the Entrepreneurial Process*. The book offers a portal into the breadth and depth of entrepreneurship scholarship and provides many avenues for understanding entrepreneurship and the entrepreneurial process. As Professor Fayolle points out, there is a long history of thought and scholarship about entrepreneurship. The word entrepreneur is, appropriately (given the author is French), French, with roots in sixteenth- and seventeenth-century ideas about the accomplishment of tasks, risk bearing, undertaking to do something, and the organising, operating and assumption of risk for a business. While the idea of the entrepreneur and entrepreneurship has evolved to include the attributes of innovation, opportunity discovery (or construction) and value creation, my sense of the basic gist of the term continues to focus on this facet of human behaviour: *initiative taking*. The process of entrepreneurship invariably involves an individual or individuals investing effort into something they had not previously done before. As this book points out, there are many ways in which initiative taking may occur. I have tended to think of the entrepreneurial process as involving 'organising' (Weick 1979) in a general sort of way, and more specifically, as 'organisation creation' as the phenomenon where entrepreneurship might be more likely to occur and to be ascertained (Gartner 1985; 2001). As this book points out, entrepreneurship, as a phenomenon, is theoretically and empirically much more complicated than either 'organising' or 'organisation creation'.

What *Entrepreneurship and New Value Creation* makes an excellent job of doing is taking the reader on a journey through the many different worlds in which entrepreneurship has been conceptualised and studied. The scholarship of entrepreneurship is somewhat like the phenomenon of entrepreneurship itself. Just as Schumpeter (1934) suggests that entrepreneurship involves undertaking 'new combinations', the scholarship of entrepreneurship constantly combines new theories, new evidence and ideas from other disciplines (and the phenomenon of entrepreneurship itself), into new approaches to understanding what entrepreneurship is. Keeping up with the various ways that entrepreneurship has been studied as well as how it is currently studied is, then, a daunting challenge in so far as an entrepreneurship scholar has to grapple with such a diverse set of disciplines and approaches. This book more than meets this task.

Entrepreneurship and New Value Creation provides the reader with various concepts and perspectives about entrepreneurship; describes and outlines how entrepreneurship can be understood as a system; demonstrates the characteristics of the process of entrepreneurship; and suggests how entrepreneurship can be seen through process dynamics. As Professor Fayolle points out, there are so many ways that an exploration of the nature of entrepreneurship can be approached that any attempt appears to be a daunting task. He begins this attempt by centring the phenomenon of entrepreneurship as an individual/new value creation dialogic, which links the individual (entrepreneur) to the project (the new value creation potential) as a process. Implicit in this exploration, then, is the sense that the nature of entrepreneurship is not static but ongoing, so that observing the phenomenon of entrepreneurship at one particular moment in time is inadequate. A recognition of the dynamic properties of individual/new value creation dialogic is critical, but often difficult to encompass, particularly as one reviews prior scholarship.

The first part of the book provides a broad overview of the various ways that entrepreneurship can be approached. As a social and economic phenomenon, entrepreneurship has been considered as an engine of economic development and renewal, transformation and growth; a way to generate jobs; a way to organise firms; a set of individual skills; and a way of being and learning. As a phenomenon subject to research, entrepreneurship has been considered as having its disciplinary origins in economics, which continues to overshadow how other disciplines might approach this topic. Scholars have often focused on entrepreneurship as an individual level phenomenon, and have explored a variety of social and psychological factors, as well as process-based approaches that consider how the environment, organisational context and process of entrepreneurship impact this phenomenon. Entrepreneurship scholars have more recently focused on the nature of opportunity, and the process of emergence, from Fayolle's point of view, through the lens of value creation, which he suggests has a wider and more useful application than other approaches. Finally, entrepreneurship can be considered as an academic subject, so that what entrepreneurship is taught as, how it is taught and the reasons for teaching it impact our understanding of what entrepreneurship is.

The second and third parts of the book explore entrepreneurship as a system: the individual/new value creation dialogic. As mentioned earlier, the critical aspect of this system approach is to consider seriously the impact of process, that is, that entrepreneurship as a phenomenon always involves change, and therefore, to consider also how events unfold over time. The author considers how other scholars have dealt with concepts of entrepreneur and with value creation, and then develops a framework for exploring the evolutionary nature of the individual/new value creation system dynamic. I find that the core of the book centres on this exploration of the nature of the process of entrepreneurship. The questions of what we mean by process, what the theories of process are and how process is modelled are explored, and then synthesised into a generic model of the entrepreneurial process that considers individual, organisational and environmental factors in an evolving dynamic system. This framework suggests that the evolution of the system involves a trigger that initiates the entrepreneurial process, a commitment to the process, and an unfolding of this process to survival (or failure) and subsequent development.

The last part of the book provides details of the three phases of this entrepreneurial dynamic. The process trigger is elaborated by identifying prior theoretical approaches for explaining the factors that influence why some individuals decide to engage in entrepreneurial activity. Various intention and displacement theories are evaluated and a synthesis of these models is applied to two real situations. The fulcrum of the entrepreneurial dynamic is in the process of entrepreneurial commitment. The evolution of commitment in the individual/new value creation dynamic is not simple to describe: it is complicated and multidimensional. I am intrigued with how the book uses catastrophe theory as a metaphor and heuristic for modelling the dynamics of commitment over time. I believe there is some necessity for a coagulation of favourable events to occur in order for entrepreneurial situations to emerge successfully, and that process of emergence is not inherently linear in nature (Lichtenstein *et al.* 2007). Complexity dynamics or other models, such as catastrophe theory, are likely to be the pathways for understanding entrepreneurial processes. The book then explores the entrepreneurial process through the survival/development stage, using, primarily, structuration theory (Giddens 1979; 1984b). While most Europeans will be familiar with Giddens' ideas, many North American entrepreneurship scholars would be wise to explore further the value of using structuration theory in entrepreneurship research.

The last chapter of the book is a call to conduct research on entrepreneurship in a manner that is honest to the phenomenon: recognising multidimensional complexity in real time, over time.

Overall, what I found most valuable in this book was the close reading the author undertakes of various books and articles that seem to constitute the core ideas in entrepreneurship scholarship. Professor Fayolle's ability to pay careful attention to the meanings and nuances that other scholars bring to their work is sorely missing from many overviews and analyses of the entrepreneurship field.

In addition, the book introduces a number of new conversations about entrepreneurship that scholars who only read work in English will probably not be familiar with. In a somewhat random sample of citations in this book, I found that about 25 per cent of the references are to works that appear in French. It is apparent, in Professor Fayolle's analysis of entrepreneurship scholarship, that French scholars have been involved in a deep and wide-ranging discussion of this topic, and that this conversation brings to the forefront important new perspectives on the nature of entrepreneurship. The inability to read French has become for many of the 'only English' readers, then, a barrier to grasping a more nuanced view of entrepreneurship. I am really pleased to be introduced to this new literature, as well as guided to how it is related and applied to other entrepreneurship scholarship.

Entrepreneurship, then, is not solely the providence of American scholars, or that of an American way of acting entrepreneurially. Indeed, as this book demonstrates, entrepreneurship is a phenomenon that has deep historical roots based in European culture, ideas and sensibilities, and a more comprehensive and thoughtful understanding of entrepreneurship will only occur when we recognise and use these past and current perspectives.

Acknowledgements

While I am the sole author of this book, the project behind it would not have emerged without the discussions and exchanges with my colleagues. I feel strongly that I am part of a community of researchers who have been working for many years in the emerging field of entrepreneurship. When I first became interested in this field, at the beginning of the 1990s, I was lucky to meet pioneers and people who were convinced of the social and economic importance of this new field of research and education. I have learnt a lot from them and I have the feeling that, with this book, I continue to pass on their message and echo the works and approaches that they largely contributed to initiating.

I especially wish to thank Philippe Albert who, in 1984, created the Centre des Entrepreneurs (Centre for Entrepreneurs), in the institution within which I pursue my academic activities today. He has worked untiringly to promote the entrepreneurial spirit in French society and higher education institutions. He, along with Stéphane Marion, convinced me of the interest to focus my research on entrepreneurship.

For this book, I am also greatly indebted to my colleague Christian Bruyat, whose contribution has been invaluable in helping French-speaking teachers and researchers better understand this complex and heterogeneous field. I feel privileged to have been engaged in a meaningful discussion with him for over ten years and I believe that I continue to make progress through this continued exchange. This work is also a way to spread some of his ideas and works.

On a different level, as this type of work can only be made possible by the combination of many different skills, I wish to express my most sincere thanks to Karen Bruneaud for the quality of her translation and the professionalism she has shown throughout a year-long collaboration.

Lastly, I would also like to thank all the people who provided the raw material for this book, the individuals who explore new territories, who innovate, who contribute to making people and things evolve, those who take risks to pursue their passions and make their ideas happen.

Introduction

Why and how is it that some individuals decide they want to create businesses and then actually do so? Why and how is it that others do not, even though they appear to have what it takes to succeed in business? These two questions were among the first that researchers in the field of entrepreneurship tried to answer. Today, it seems that the problem is much more difficult to solve than it first appeared thirty years ago. It is not enough for someone to have a strong desire for achievement or a high tolerance for risk in order to choose an entrepreneurial career path. The venture creation phenomenon is a complex one, covering a wide variety of situations. We can no longer expect multiple criteria, or additive and linear models, to be wholly predictive, although they may have a 'here and now' probabilistic predictive power.

The main purpose of this book is to present a **generic model and a theoretical framework of the entrepreneurial process in order to improve our understanding of its complexity.** The qualitative model developed here is based on numerous research findings in the field of entrepreneurship and my own research programme which began in the 1990s. Therefore, this work is based on hundreds of new business creation cases that I have observed and supported over this period.

Before presenting the contents and positioning of this book, I feel it is important to give a dual historical perspective in this introduction. The first perspective addresses the notion of 'entrepreneur' which is so often used and misused that it has lost most of its meaning, while the second focuses on research in this field and aims at highlighting some of its shortcomings.

The notion of 'entrepreneur' over time

The conception of the 'entrepreneur' has evolved over time, just as economic activities have become more complex too. At the dawn of

1

the industrial revolution, entrepreneurs were sorts of intermediaries; they were seldom the 'producers'. They were characterised by their aptitude to take risks. Then they became the cornerstone of economic development, starting to produce and innovate, while still taking the risk.

In the Middle Ages, the French word 'entrepreneur'[1] designated a person who performed a task. Later, it referred to a bold individual, keen on taking economic risks. In the sixteenth and seventeenth centuries, the entrepreneur was an individual who engaged in speculative activities. The term did not yet refer to the manufacturer, nor to the seller or the trader, but generally to a person who had a contract with the king to undertake the construction of a public building or ensure the provision of supplies to the army (Vérin 1982).

In short, 'the entrepreneur was a person who was under contract to the government for a service or the supply of goods'.[2] Hence, the risks taken were essentially financial, as the amount allocated for this service was arranged prior to the execution of the contract.

The general meaning of 'entrepreneur' in the seventeenth century was 'a person who undertakes to do something', or even a very active individual. The *Dictionnaire universel du commerce*, published in 1723 in Paris, gives the following definitions for the French word:

entrepreneur: he who undertakes to do a particular piece of work. We say: 'entrepreneur in manufacture' to mean 'manufacturer', 'entrepreneur in masonry' to mean 'a mason'.

In 1735, *L'Encyclopédie* of d'Alembert and Diderot defines the entrepreneur as somebody who is in charge of a job.

In Emile Littré's *Dictionnaire de la langue française*, published in 1889, the definition also refers to the act of 'undertaking': 'he who undertakes to do something is an entrepreneur'. In the *Century Dictionary* (1889–91),[3] the entrepreneur is 'one who undertakes a large industrial enterprise, a contractor'.

---

[1] Entrepreneur comes from the French: 'from old French enterprise, from past participle of entreprendre, to undertake: entre-, between (from Latin inter-) + prendre, to take (from Latin prehendere)', *The American Heritage Dictionary of the English Language*, 4th edn, Boston: Houghton Mifflin, 2000. Accessible online at www.dictionary.com.

[2] Definition from the *Dictionnaire universel* of A. Furetière (1690), vol. 1, p. 951.

[3] William Dwight Whitney and Benjamin Eli Smith (eds.), *The Century Dictionary*, rev. edn 1911 (first published 1889–91).

Today *Le Petit Robert* gives three definitions of the word 'entrepreneur'. The first definition is exactly the same as that given in the *Dictionnaire de la langue française* previously mentioned. The second sees the entrepreneur as a 'person in charge of performing a job'. Finally, in a more economic perspective, the entrepreneur is 'any person who manages an enterprise of their own, and implements the various factors of production (land, labour, and capital) in order to sell goods or services'. The *American Heritage Dictionary*'s definition[4] is in the same vein: 'a person who organizes, operates, and assumes the risk for a business venture'.

Although the definitions of the entrepreneur proposed through the ages vary slightly in meaning and precision, there remains a constant in them: the entrepreneur and risk-taking are closely linked,[5] and this from the very first time the notion was mentioned in written form (Cantillon 1755). At the beginning of the nineteenth century, Jean-Baptiste Say (1803) associated the entrepreneur with innovation, a notion later made popular in the Anglo-Saxon world by Schumpeter (1934).

Moreover, in the economic literature, the entrepreneur is presented with multiple facets and combines the roles of capitalist, innovator, opportunist, and even coordinator and organiser of resources.

In continuity with the works of Joseph Alois Schumpeter, former Minister of Finance of the Austro-Hungarian Empire who established himself at Harvard University in 1932, Anglo-Saxons, and more particularly Americans, have often identified the entrepreneur as a creator of new ventures. Schumpeter wrote extensively about the relationship between the entrepreneur and innovation as well as the entrepreneur's role in identifying opportunities. He saw in the entrepreneur an individual capable of revitalising existing businesses rather than a simple company creator. This led Harvard teachers in administrative science to associate innovation with the aptitude to identify business opportunities. They realised how hard it was to teach how to innovate, which led them to introduce a lot of creativity in their teaching of management.

---

[4] *American Heritage Dictionary*, 4th edn.
[5] See also the following definitions: 'Someone who organizes a business venture and assumes the risk for it', *Wordnet* 2.0, 2003, Princeton University; or 'A risk-taker who has the skills and initiative to establish a business', in David L. Scott, *Wall Street Words: An A to Z Guide to Investment Terms for Today's Investor*, Boston: Houghton Mifflin, 2003.

This approach, introduced in the 1960s and 1970s, still constitutes one of the main differentiating assets of the Harvard Business School teachings over those of other schools of management.

One of the first to speak of the entrepreneur in terms of a creator was Jeffrey A. Timmons in several pedagogical works, and in particular in his book *New Venture Creation*. This book, first published in 1977, then re-edited several times featuring various co-authors, has become a classic in venture creation in the United States (Timmons and Spinelli 2004). All the editions of this book include a chapter devoted to the identification of opportunities, which is exceptional for a book on business plans, as this theme, though of crucial interest for entrepreneurs, generally receives little attention in such works.

Howard Stevenson, former entrepreneur and tenured professor of the Sarofim-Rock Chair of Business Administration at Harvard Business School, has synthesised this approach, which was already present in the teachings of his institution. He proposed a concise definition of the entrepreneur, which clearly associates the entrepreneur with his or her aptitude to identify business opportunities.

This definition is often cited and endorsed by researchers: that entrepreneurship is a field that is interested in the identification of business opportunities by individuals and organisations, and their pursuit and exploitation, independently of the directly controlled resources. This conception of entrepreneurship assumes that in an entrepreneurial situation there is always a significant tension between the available controlled resources and the resources necessary to transform the opportunity. The entrepreneurial capacity amounts to the actor's capacity to identify a favourable situation and exploit it by using a minimum of resources.

Filion (1990) suggested that the entrepreneur, more than any other economic actor, is a person who develops systemic thinking; in other words, entrepreneurs organise their activities in order to achieve the goals and objectives they wish to reach in the future. The study of entrepreneurs, compared with studies of other organisational actors, reveals individuals who have further developed forward thinking. They think more about the future and the long term, and organise their activities according to the goals and objectives they want to achieve.

This perspective leads to the following definition by Filion (1991): 'an entrepreneur is an individual who conceives and develops visions'. The author sees the vision as 'a space to occupy in the market and the type of organisation required to achieve this'. This implies that entrepreneurs define the strategic contexts in which they will structure their activities (which requires good differentiation skills), whereas other organisational actors evolve within contexts defined by others.

Entrepreneurship can also be understood as a process that can take place in various environments and in various configurations. This is how it introduces changes into the economic system, through the innovations developed by individuals and organisations. These innovations generate economic opportunities, or react to them, and the result of this process is the creation of social and economic wealth for both the individual and the society.

This vision of entrepreneurship highlights the notion of wealth or value creation. Value creation is one of two dimensions proposed by Christian Bruyat (1993) to define the field of entrepreneurship. According to him, an entrepreneurial situation may be evaluated on two axes. The first one indicates the degree of change for the individual and so the degree of personal risk inherent in the entrepreneurial function, and the second measures the intensity of value creation through the potential of the project or innovation. The advantage of this approach is that entrepreneurial situations can be qualified according to these two criteria. This approach also makes it possible to distinguish areas of strong consensus and areas in which using the word 'entrepreneurial' may be debatable.

By way of example, for Christian Bruyat, the creation of a technological and innovative enterprise is considered a highly consensual situation, as opposed to situations of intrapreneurship (acting entrepreneurially in existing organisations) which correspond to more questionable contexts of action and are, in fact, often challenged.

The idea of associating the entrepreneur with the creation of value is very interesting and brings us back to the origins of the understanding of what an entrepreneur is. It is indeed very present in Cantillon's (1755) and Say's (1803) works, and even in Karl Marx's; they all contributed greatly to distinguishing between capitalistic profits and entrepreneurial profits. Their assumption was that the entrepreneur's profits were superior to capitalistic profits, given the novelty created (Say and Marx) and the risk taken by the entrepreneur (Cantillon).[6] In

---

[6] This aspect is also illustrated in the following quotation used as an illustration to the definition of 'entrepreneur' in *The Century Dictionary* (rev. edn 1911):

all these definition attempts, we find more or less explicitly the notions of individual, action, innovation, opportunity, risk, and organisation and value creation. These factors constitute necessary and perhaps even sufficient conditions for the existence of entrepreneurs and entrepreneurship.

Chronology and issues of entrepreneurship as a research field

Entrepreneurship as an academic discipline started to develop in the post-war years with an economic and historical perspective at the Research Center in Entrepreneurial History. This was created in 1948 in Harvard, and experienced intensive activity for about ten years, under the leadership of Arthur Cole. Prestigious authors, like Cochran, and Chandler (in management), came out of it. However, historical research progressively dwindled, owing to a lack of consensus on the concept of entrepreneur and a failure to produce satisfactory theories. In the late 1960s and early 1970s, it prospered again, with the research in management of small and medium size enterprises (SMEs) and in psychology. The 1970s crisis was a formidable boost because of the increase in unemployment and the rehabilitation of SMEs as sources of employment, as well as the loss of momentum of Marxist and structuralist theories. It was not until recently that the field could gain its independence from SME-related research, through the elaboration of its own specific tools. The creation of reviews, specialised conferences and scientific departments all testify to this evolution.[7] The critical mass seems to have been attained in the United States, while the movement is still being structured throughout Europe. As an illustration, we may note here the article by Chandler Gaylen and Lyon Douglas (2001), which lists over a decade the publication of 416 articles concerning entrepreneurship in nine American reviews, two of which alone account for 347 articles (*Entrepreneurship Theory and Practice* and *Journal of Business Venturing*). This does not include

'The most difficult part of Mr Walker's teaching is perhaps his view that profits – i.e. the employer's or entrepreneur's, as distinguished from the capitalist's share of the product of industry – cannot be reduced to the same category as interest or wages [Westminster Review (CXXV, 553)].'

[7] The year 1986 for the Academy of Management in the United States, and more recently in France (1997), with the creation of the Académie de l'Entrepreneuriat (Academy for Entrepreneurship).

all the conferences, communication papers, theses and articles published in French journals or elsewhere. France appears not to be lagging behind in terms of support for company creation, thanks to the Agence pour la Création d'Entreprises (Business Start-up Agency), which has played an important role in this matter, but the situation is quite different when it comes to research and education in the field.

Since Schumpeter, the creation of technological enterprises or innovative activities[8] has represented the archetype of entrepreneurship. In the 1960s and 1970s, Roberts and Wainer (1968) as well as Cooper (1973) took a particular interest in business start-ups initiated by university laboratories and the emergence of technological enterprises in the Route 128 region (around Boston, United States) and in Silicon Valley. These studies,[9] which have since been developed, are essentially exploratory and descriptive. They have made it possible to draw the portraits of founders, to understand better what led to the success or growth of the businesses created, and to identify the environmental conditions that favoured their emergence as well as their stimulating influence on the local economic fabric. This type of research, which was very active in the 1980s and 1990s, has fallen out of favour, because of its failure to produce useful theories and tools for action.

In the 1990s, research developed with the aim of achieving a better understanding of the process aspects of the phenomenon, and to produce theories 'explaining' the growth or performance of these companies. The works of Kazanjian and Drazin (1990) and Naman and Selvin (1993) are good illustrations of this trend. Sandberg and Hofer (1987) attempted, to little avail in our opinion, to test a multifactorial explanatory model. Eisenhardt and Schoonhoven (1990) also used a multifactorial explanatory model including factors related to the environment of the business start-up, its founder's characteristics and the strategies involved. They insisted on the important impact of time on the performance of the companies created. Research highlighting the importance of networks or relying on the resource-based approach has also been developed (Venkataraman and Van de Ven 1998). The types of research previously mentioned which are in line

---

[8] We will not enter the debate about the semantic assimilation of innovation and technology here.

[9] Concerning France, Philippe Mustar's inputs since the mid-1990s should be noted (see particularly Mustar 1997). We may also mention the works by Julien and Marchesnay (1996).

with the classic American paradigm of management run up against two main difficulties which both limit and weaken their results. The first difficulty is linked to the validity and accuracy of the measurement. How do you measure the performance of the companies created? Can the entrepreneur's goals be put aside? The second one relates to the notion of process and temporal non-homogeneity. When should performance be measured, for instance?

Presentation and positioning of this book

The objective of this work is to explore and engage with these important questions. It also aims at providing undergraduate and postgraduate students, teachers, researchers and practitioners with conceptual and theoretical bases, firmly grounded in management science, in this relatively new discipline.

Rather than attempting to represent the diversity and richness of all the research conducted in this field, we have chosen to focus on a particular concept of entrepreneurship and to propose a coherent vision of a complex 'object'. We consider entrepreneurship as a **process** (of company creation, company takeover, etc.), and as synonymous with **movement** and **change** for individuals and organisations. Entrepreneurship is an **individual/new value creation dialogic**, which means that it corresponds to specific situations in which both the individual's and the project's (potentially the bearer of new value creation) perspectives will be combined and confronted to generate a logic of 'duality' or 'couple'. This concept, where entrepreneurship is seen as a process, is in line with the main streams of research in the field. The individual/new value creation dialogic also enables a more scientific approach in conceptualising the individual/project pair which is systematically referred to by the professionals and practitioners concerned.

The book is composed of twelve chapters organised into four parts.[10] We develop the main concepts of entrepreneurship in the first part, as well as the various perspectives and social fields with which it interacts. Entrepreneurship can be addressed as an economic and social phenomenon, a research object and a teaching subject. In the second part,

---

[10] The general introduction does not present the chapters' contents in detail. Readers who wish to have an overview of each chapter should refer to the introductions of each part.

we define the characteristics and components of the entrepreneurial system, based on the works of Bruyat and Julien (2001), then develop the two dimensions of the individual/new value creation dialogic. In the third part we develop the foundations and implications of the process-based approach we have chosen. We propose in particular a model of the entrepreneurial process in its synchronic and diachronic aspects. Finally, the fourth part of the book is devoted to developing entrepreneurial process dynamics. Each phase in the model is explored, and theoretical frameworks aimed at better understanding the phases are proposed and justified. In our conclusion, we show how the study of entrepreneurial processes can be done through research-action approaches in order to overcome the difficulties usually encountered in this type of research.

We hope that this book will provide everyone who is interested in the subject of entrepreneurship with a means of understanding a very complex field, whatever the final objective: be it learning to be entrepreneurial or learning in order better to understand.

Finally, before closing this introduction, I would like to extend my warmest thanks to my colleague and friend Christian Bruyat. The ideas and perspectives developed in this book owe much to his own works in this field, which, together with our regular exchanges, have been a real source of inspiration.

PART I

Perceptions of entrepreneurship

The third millennium seems marked by a renewal of the entrepreneurial spirit, which affects all countries and all sectors of economic and social life: business start-ups or takeovers, associations and even public services. Let us refer to the words of Claude Allègre, French Minister of National Education and Research at the time, in an interview published in *Les Echos*, on 3 February 1998: 'I want to instil an entrepreneurial spirit in the education system' in an attempt to raise awareness of entrepreneurship within this institution. He also added, to clarify his vision: 'The objective, which concerns higher education at large, is to get people used to creating companies while they're young, and to invent new techniques. I would like more innovators, and fewer scholars.'

So entrepreneurship has become a 'burning issue': teachers, managers, executives, consultants, politicians, everybody, or almost everybody, feels concerned. Entrepreneurship teaching is developing; classes for students and specific training courses for entrepreneurs have been available for quite a few years now. Incubators and structures for the support of creation and/or development of new venture projects are springing up everywhere in the world, to meet an ever growing demand. Large corporations are particularly interested in this phenomenon and seek the best programmes and institutions in an attempt to increase the awareness of their executives, and bring them to emulate the behaviours and attitudes of entrepreneurs who create economic and social value. The rapid changes affecting the societies of many countries are clearly linked to this renewed interest. Numerous works have underlined the cause–effect relationship between some environmental changes (globalisation of markets, acceleration of scientific and technological progress, demographic and geopolitical fractures, etc.) and their consequences on societies, companies and individuals (Fayolle 2003a; Fayolle and Filion 2006). It seems to us that these fundamental changes are likely to give entrepreneurship, as a phenomenon and as a sum of individual and collective behaviours, a more important place. However, the more entrepreneurship develops, the more crucial it becomes to define the outlines and clarify the multiple definitions of this concept.

Entrepreneurship is a polysemous and complex notion, and therefore must be approached with a twofold objective of clarification and definition. Can we speak about entrepreneurship without first of all defining our terms of reference, without specifying the adopted perspective (paradigmatic, disciplinary, theoretical, etc.) and the level of analysis (individual, company, organisation or society)? Can we speak about entrepreneurship without defining the field as well as the current of thought we refer to? Entrepreneurship overlaps with at least three spheres of reference (Fayolle 2004a): politics, first of all, because decisions, actions and therefore actors are necessary to design support facilities and define the policies in matters of creation and development of business ventures; practice, secondly, because project bearers act too, and express needs while raising new issues; and finally, the academic world, because teachers and researchers are concerned with and must satisfy an ever growing demand coming from the other two spheres as well as from society at large.

Since the origin of the concept, people have wanted to define the entrepreneur. Should entrepreneurs be defined according to who they are, what they do, their origins, their needs, or their activities and their results? The disciplinary approaches and definitions proposed are numerous, to the extent that there is no consensus and this situation induces great confusion.

It seems to us that one major obstacle derives from trying to reach an agreement on one unique definition. This is why we claim that it is necessary to develop a contingent approach to this question. After all, is there a unique definition of management? Or of the manager?

In this first part, our objective is to clarify and define our own perspective, which serves as a basis for all our research work in this controversial and heterogeneous field. We believe that entrepreneurship can be studied from the perspectives of three main interrelated fields. Each one of these generic fields (in the sense of Bourdieu[1]) offers interesting approaches to entrepreneurship and will be the subject of a distinct chapter.

---

[1] Pierre Bourdieu is a French sociologist.

Entrepreneurship as an economic and social phenomenon refers to social and economic realities at various levels: individual, organisational and societal; and addresses preoccupations and expectations emanating from politicians, practitioners and managers.

Entrepreneurship as a research object refers to the academic world. We will not attempt to account for all the views, definitions and perspectives on this subject, but we will focus on three principal currents of thought around which today's research communities have developed.

Entrepreneurship as a teaching subject relates to education and training issues in various social contexts. A better understanding of the impacts of the pedagogical processes on the intentions and behaviours of the people trained, or of the entrepreneurial spirit development mechanisms, are key social stakes.

These three domains clearly overlap, as knowledge produced by research can be taught and/or used to clarify the questions raised at the societal level. Moreover, at the level of society, the perception of a phenomenon is likely to have an impact on the emergence (or not) of a specialised teaching body. These three domains also relate to politics, practice and the academic context as mentioned above.

Finally, these first chapters will be an opportunity to show the importance of the notion of 'process' in these various perspectives on entrepreneurship.

1 | Entrepreneurship as a social and economic phenomenon

The entrepreneur has a particular and indispensable role to play in the evolution of liberal economic systems. Whether entrepreneurs are self-employed or working for organisations (as employees), they are often at the origin of radical innovations. Entrepreneurs create companies and jobs, they participate in the renewal of the economic fabric. Entrepreneurs are innovators who bring 'creative destruction' (Schumpeter 1934). An economic dynamic of change is only possible if there is a revolution, that is to say a complete upheaval of the established order. Schumpeter highlights and glorifies the disturbing role of the entrepreneur; he even argues that only individuals with a capacity to innovate deserve to be called entrepreneurs. This vision is also put forward by Octave Gélinier, renowned French consultant who insisted, as early as the late 1970s, on the importance of what the entrepreneur could bring to the economy: 'Countries, professions, firms that develop and innovate are those which practise entrepreneurship. Statistics of economic growth, international exchanges, patenting, licensing and innovations for the past 30 years clearly establish this point: it is very costly to do without entrepreneurs' (Gélinier 1978).

In this perspective, entrepreneurship represents a real engine of economic development. The role of entrepreneurship, however, is not limited to economic development; it also disrupts traditional organisation and functioning patterns. We even believe it can give rise to new organisational configurations. Finally, entrepreneurship places the notion of skills at the heart of the relations between individuals and the organisations in which they are employed, or with which they do business: individuals are increasingly becoming entrepreneurs who negotiate and promote their skills.

Entrepreneurship: an engine of economic development

My aim here is not to demonstrate scientifically the link between entrepreneurship and economic development as some research works have attempted with little success (Wennekers *et al.* 2005). I simply aim to show how entrepreneurship contributes to the economy through the creation of new businesses and jobs, economic growth, innovation, etc. I will also consider how entrepreneurship fuels, exploits and accelerates structural change.

New venture creation as a source of renewal of the economic fabric

Venture creation is a multifaceted notion, and new ventures constitute a heterogeneous object (Bruyat 1993; Fayolle 2004b). However, by using the situation in France as an example, we can at least specify the importance of the phenomenon.

For the last few years, the number of companies created every year in France has varied between 250,000 and 320,000.[1] These statistics are provided by the Agence pour la Création d'Entreprise (APCE – business start-up agency) instituted in the 1970s by the French state. The Agence pour la Création d'Entreprise includes in these figures four types of venture creation:

ex nihilo creation: considers business start-ups initiated by individuals or groups of individuals, in which case we can really talk about new venture creation

company takeover: business start-up that retains partially or totally the activities and assets of a formerly existing company

company 'reactivation': reopening of a company that was temporarily inactive.

In this light, it clearly appears that actual new ventures represent only a fraction of the total number of companies established every year in France.

The majority of companies are created in the commercial and service sectors. Industrial activities only make up a small proportion of the total. Although statistics do not give an accurate account of this type of event, business start-ups in innovative technological sectors only account for 4 per cent of the total.

[1] In the USA, during the 1990s and early 2000s, 600,000 companies were registered, on average, every year. In 1995, the figure hit a peak of 807,000 new companies (Kuratko 2005); 16 per cent of all American companies are less than a year old (Reynolds, Hay and Camp 1999).

The regeneration rate of the national pool of companies (ratio of the number of business start-ups to the total number of registered companies) is about 10 per cent, which means that the venture creation phenomenon globally reinjects 10 per cent of new businesses into the total pool of companies. These figures are relatively stable over time and are comparable to the renewal rate of most member countries of the OECD (Organisation for Economic Cooperation and Development). In these conditions, business start-ups compensate for suspensions of activities and company closures.

Recent works by the French Institut National de la Statistique et des Etudes Economiques (National Institute for Economic Statistics – INSEE) show that, in 1992, in France, 40,000 out of 190,000 listed SMEs[2] had been created or taken over in the previous five years (Bonneau 1994). The number of SMEs has increased by 25 per cent since 1987, which clearly shows that the situation is far from stagnant. Nevertheless, what most contributes to the renewal of the economy is not the number of new business start-ups, but the number of initially smaller companies expanding over the ten-employee threshold. Concerning economic sectors, the most dynamic in terms of SME start-ups is the sector of services to businesses. These results also concur with those of other OECD member countries in which the growth of newly created companies and the dynamism of SMEs largely account for the GDP (source: European Observatory for SMEs/OECD website).

Job creation dynamics

For a number of years, and more particularly since the beginning of the 1970s, new venture creation, self-employment and the dynamism of SMEs have appeared as significant sources of job creations, and as many potential answers to the problem of unemployment. Figures are carefully put forward as to the quantity of jobs generated by new business start-ups. One of the main difficulties of this quantification relies in its definition. Are we talking about direct job creation? Indirect job creation? Created or maintained jobs? Part-time or full-time jobs? These elements should be taken into consideration and the data should be analysed accordingly.

---

[2] SMEs are defined as companies employing between 10 and 499 employees.

Based on figures regularly released by the Agence pour la Création d'Entreprise, business start-ups account for the creation of 400,000 to 500,000 jobs every year, while company takeovers make it possible to save around 300,000 jobs on a yearly basis (these figures correspond to the number of jobs created or saved at the time of the company's establishment or takeover). Here again, the role of SMEs seems predominant. SMEs experience a regular growth of their workforce whereas large companies[3] constantly downsize (Berthier and Parent 1994; OECD/European Observatory for SMEs).

These observations concur with Birch's pioneering works on job generation processes in the United States. According to Birch, 70 to 80 per cent of jobs are generated by SMEs. However, not all medium-sized companies play an identical role in the generation of jobs: Birch identified a particular type of firm that contributes significantly to job generation: fast-growing companies, also called 'gazelles'. Some studies seem to indicate that gazelles could account for up to 94 per cent of the jobs created (Kuratko 2005).

Since the beginning of the 1980s, the top 500 large American firms have cut over 5 million jobs, whereas over the same period of time more than 34 million jobs were created by entrepreneurs through venture creation or company development (Kuratko 2005). In the United States companies employing fewer than 500 employees account for 53 per cent of the private workforce.

In a talk delivered during the 2003 IntEnt conference in Grenoble, Bert W. M. Twaalfhoven, a European entrepreneur, presented his career in the following terms: fifty-one businesses created over forty years, in eleven different countries, which generated 3500 jobs.

Economic growth

The idea according to which entrepreneurship and economic growth are closely linked has come a long way since Schumpeter's works. An international research programme (Global Entrepreneurship Monitor) launched in 1997 by two international institutions, London Business School and Babson College, has focused on demonstrating the strength of these links. The results have so far shown that entrepreneurs in phases of creation and development of new activities have significant

---

[3] In France and the rest of Europe, a large company is generally defined as employing over 500 people.

impact on economic activity. Effects are nevertheless variable and depend on the global level of economic development in the countries concerned (Van Stel, Carree and Thurik 2005).

Entrepreneurs play various roles and the impact of their action on economic growth may be assessed from at least three different perspectives (Carree and Thurik 2003; Landström 2005). We have mentioned the first one, the role of innovator as put forward by Schumpeter (1934: 74): 'He or she carries out new combinations we call enterprise; the individuals whose function is to carry them out we call entrepreneurs.' Their second role was notably highlighted by the Austrian economist Kirzner: according to him, the entrepreneur has a particular capacity to perceive profit opportunities. The third role consists in assuming the risks linked to the uncertainty of the entrepreneurial act: for example, the introduction of a new product, or the launch of a new company. This final role is particularly present in Knight's works.

The impact of the entrepreneurial phenomenon on economic growth may also be evaluated through other roles or mechanisms, such as the production and diffusion of new knowledge, the contribution to increasing the number of companies and competition, or even the role played in increasing the diversity of companies at various geographic scales (Audretsch and Thurik 2004).

Innovation and 'creative destruction'

Innovation and entrepreneurship have been closely linked since the Austrian economist Joseph Schumpeter put forward the force of the 'creative destruction' process that characterises innovation. The idea contained in this seemingly paradoxical expression is that the emergence of new innovative activities often puts existing companies and activities (which, comfortably established in their sector, have not managed to adapt their products, services or technologies) in a difficult position, or may even lead them to disappear. According to Schumpeter (1934), entrepreneurs constitute the main engine of this 'creative destruction' process, by identifying opportunities that the actors in place cannot see, and by developing technologies and concepts that give birth to new economic activities.

The notion of innovation is therefore very important and makes the entrepreneur a vector of economic development. Entrepreneurs must look for change, potential sources of innovation and relevant information about business start-up opportunities. They must know and apply the principles that can enable them to implement innovations with the best chances of success. Change therefore constitutes a norm for the entrepreneur who knows how to find it, to act upon it and to exploit it as an opportunity.

Examples of new innovative companies and entrepreneurs who introduced significant innovations over the last few decades are numerous. In the field of IT technologies, Apple, Lotus and Digital are references in the field with their founders Steve Jobs, Steve Wozniak, Mitch Capor and Ken Olsen. More recently, companies such as Amazon, Google, eBay or Yahoo have revolutionised the Internet. In more traditional sectors, one cannot help but notice that the development of the Ford company, at the beginning of the last century, was mainly due to the genius of its founder, Henry Ford, who innovated by successfully applying Taylor's principles of the scientific organisation of work to the automobile industry. In a slightly different area, Akio Morita, Sony's founder, innovated with the Walkman, by combining existing elements into a new configuration. In France, the company Technomed, created by an engineer, invented a new process to eliminate kidney stones based on ultrasound technology.

Of course, innovation is not only the work of entrepreneurs, but, along with Schumpeter, we are convinced that entrepreneurs are more often the instigators of radical innovations than other actors. Large companies use their resources to improve products and processes by introducing incremental innovations.

Structural, political, economic and social mutations

Beside its impact on economic growth, which we have previously mentioned, venture creation often constitutes a powerful vector of structural change (fuelling, exploiting and accelerating it), and political, technological, social or organisational change. These deep changes generate uncertainty and instability, which in turn generate opportunities of creation of new economic activities.

The development of service activities, which compensates for the collapse of industrial sectors in particular, owes a lot to venture creation. The introduction of the Internet and other new computer and

communication technologies has enabled numerous potential entrepreneurs to exploit opportunities. Finally, the radical transformation
of east/west relationships and also the opening of eastern countries
to the market economy have produced numerous business start-up
opportunities.

These changes, and the combination of geographical, political, economic and technological factors, may lead to the emergence of specific
contexts, like industrial districts, for instance. In a totally different
context, company takeover by individuals is an interesting means for
confronting the current problem of developed societies: that of the
retirement of baby boom entrepreneurs. Moreover, these individual
initiatives, which should be further encouraged and supported, also
help resolve succession and transmission problems that could otherwise lead to the closure of some businesses.

Finally, new venture creation is also a powerful means of social reinsertion. Indeed, it enables more or less long-term job seekers to find,
under certain conditions, a job created thanks to their own sense
of initiative, tenacity and enterprising spirit. In France, for instance,
50 per cent of business start-ups are motivated by 'survival motivated:
survival attempts' in which the main objective is to get (out of necessity)
a job.

Entrepreneurship: a new framework for enterprises and organisations

Companies and institutions seek to develop, rekindle or maintain some
entrepreneurial characteristics such as initiative-taking, risk-taking,
opportunity orientation, reactivity and/or flexibility. To achieve this
goal, they do not hesitate to engage in heavy procedures of change and
transformation that prove difficult and resource-consuming. Drucker
(1985) was one of the first authors to observe this trend: 'Today's businesses, especially the large ones, simply will not survive in this period of
rapid change and innovation unless they acquire entrepreneurial competence.' To develop this entrepreneurial competence, organisations
need to use two levers.

First of all, they need to reconsider their structure and operating
mode, as it is impossible to act like a 'gazelle' in an 'elephant' configuration. As early as 1976, Norman Macrae, American journalist for
The Economist, humorously wrote:

The world is probably drawing to the end of the era dominated by very big business corporations, except those big corporations that manage to turn themselves into confederations of entrepreneurs . . . The right size for a profit centre or entrepreneurial group . . . is going to be very small, generally not more than 10 or 11 people, however dynamic your own top management. Jesus Christ tried 12, and he found that one too many.

For a long time, there was a saying that went 'small is beautiful', to underline the informal and convivial aspect of small structures; nowadays, we are more likely to hear 'small is powerful', to indicate that performance can also be associated with small size.

The second lever activated by companies and institutions is more spiritual and cultural. They are highly interested in the entrepreneurial spirit for its capacities to foster imagination, adaptability and the will to accept risks. The entrepreneurial spirit also translates as a strong orientation to seek opportunities and value-generating initiatives. It can also take the shape of a stronger commitment of individuals and greater aptitudes to assume and exercise responsibilities.

Reproducing entrepreneurial attitudes and behaviours within existing companies and institutions therefore appears, theoretically, as a good means to adapt and fight off inertia and lack of innovation in organisations. However, in practice, the difficulties experienced by the organisations that have tried to develop these behaviours and attitudes reveal another aspect of this phenomenon: the existence of contradictions and paradoxes linked to the combination of opposing and conflicting perspectives. In the following section, we will present the foundations of this emerging framework, and then highlight the difficulties related to its implementation in order to overcome them.

Foundations of intrapreneurship

Pinchot (1985) was probably the first to introduce the word 'intrapreneurship' in a management review. For Pinchot, intrapreneurship (or 'intrapreneuring') amounts to developing entrepreneurial practices and behaviours within large corporations, and intrapreneurs are: 'The dreamers who do . . . Those who take hands on responsibility for creating innovation of any kind within an organisation. Entrepreneurs may be the founders or the inventors but they are always the dreamers who figure out how to turn an idea into a profitable reality' (p. 12).

The term 'intrapreneurship' was invented ten years earlier in 1975 by Swedish consultants, pioneers in the field, Delin, Boskjo and Atterheed, who created the Foresight group to encourage the development of the entrepreneurial spirit in large firms. They also developed the first school of intrapreneurship in Sweden.

The notion of intrapreneurship is often associated with fields such as strategic management, change, innovation and resource management. Burgelman (1986) proposes a theoretical framework that bridges the gap between intrapreneurship and strategic management. His model describes the importance of the strategic context in the development of intrapreneurship. Burgelman suggests that two different and active processes co-exist simultaneously in large companies: a planned process and an autonomous process. According to him, entrepreneurial activities (intrapreneurship) can only result from the actors' strategic autonomous behaviours. A firm wishing to develop intrapreneurship must therefore direct its efforts towards creating a favourable strategic context.

In Burgelman's mind, intrapreneurship translates as the existence of a process that concerns various actors in the firm as well as the firm as a whole.[4] This type of entrepreneurial activity is not the work of a few isolated, atypical individuals, be they innovation champions. The diffusion of entrepreneurial practices and behaviours generates energy within the organisation and contributes to the redefinition of its global strategy. It then becomes possible, thanks to specific tools and approaches, to formalise the strategy and rethink the management of innovation within the firm (Burgelman and Sayles 1986; 1987). It is proposed, for instance, to direct innovative projects towards alternative organisational forms depending on their strategic importance and operational convergence with the activities of the firm.

Christensen, Madsen and Peterson (1989) show that entrepreneurial practices and behaviours in large companies facilitate the identification and exploitation of business opportunities that enable the company to create new wealth, whereas planned processes and behaviours are more concerned with the control and allocation of existing resources. Opportunity, in this configuration, is seen more like a future situation perceived as both desirable and feasible, and intrapreneurship is thought of as a process whereby individuals identify and pursue

---

[4] Bartlett and Ghoshal (1993) have a rather similar conception.

opportunities, for themselves or the organisation, without consideration of the resources they directly control (Stevenson and Gumpert 1985).

Innovation is a fundamental notion that cannot be separated from entrepreneurship. However, innovation can take various shapes: the development of a new product, service or technology that will introduce radical change, or a process change adopted by a firm to improve its operational efficiency, meet new market demands or conquer new markets.

Innovation is often only possible through new resource combinations and organisational and strategic change (Guth and Ginsberg 1990). This is what leads firms to engage in complex procedures to modify existing systems and rules in an attempt to answer the question: 'what should we change in our strategy and organisation to encourage innovation and improve its development?'

As we have just seen, the concept of intrapreneurship is linked to notions of change, innovation, organisation, strategy and management. This has consequences on the diversity of perspectives, concepts and situations. To increase even further the diverse nature of the phenomenon, we could, as Carrier suggests (1992), argue that intrapreneurship does not only concern large firms, but can also be applied to small and medium-sized organisations.

The richness of the concept and the variety of applications of the model lead to ambiguity, confusion and general lack of clarity (Covin and Miles 1999). However, in this diversity of shapes, common traits emerge. They relate to business issues that revolve around the search for greater creativity, innovation development and initiative-taking. These common points also concern the creation of new activities, products or services, or processes of acquisition or reallocation of resources, and, finally, learning processes linked to situations, approaches and unusual business practices (Thornberry 2001). Emphasis is sometimes put on the individual (the champion, the intrapreneur), on activities or business units, or the firm as a whole.

The entrepreneur and the organisation: opposing perspectives

The organisation's and the entrepreneur's perspectives do not mix well. We even think they form a complex dialogic. This implies that a company that is engaged in an intrapreneurial logic must integrate and combine two contradictory and sometimes conflicting perspectives: the actor's logic that implies a high degree of autonomy, and that of the organisation that tries to maintain its control over situations, projects and individuals. From this dialogic may arise tensions that can jeopardise the good running of the company and the outcomes of existing practices.

In order better to understand the differences in behaviour induced by these two perspectives, we propose to use Howard Stevenson and David Gumpert's approach (1985). The authors show that the entrepreneur's behaviour is opposed to the behaviour of the administrator, another managerial figure whose main preoccupation is to control the resources and reduce the risks.

Acting entrepreneurially corresponds, according to these authors, to a particular approach of management, defined by the creation or recognition of an opportunity and its transformation, independently from the directly controlled resources. The entrepreneur and the administrator display significantly different behaviours, and it is important to take these behavioural differences into account. Although these figures of the entrepreneur and the administrator are ideal archetypes and should be used with care, they nevertheless point us in the right direction in order to acquire or develop an entrepreneurial spirit, at the individual or collective level. For companies and institutions, possibilities of entrepreneurial development are clearly the way to go, as well as the reflection that would enable them to evolve from a bureaucratic organisation towards a more entrepreneurial one. It is also important for companies harmoniously to combine and balance out both profiles.

In large firms, most managers are recruited, rewarded and promoted for their capacity to apply the rules, fulfil the roles they have been assigned and minimise risks related to acquired positions and managed resources (Thornberry 2001). Given this vision of their role, they are more likely to manage what they have been entrusted with to the best of their abilities rather than look for new perspectives of development. Innovation is not part of their action plan. They are fundamentally in an 'exploitation' rather than 'exploration' mode (March 1991); and again, it is important to find a balance between these two dimensions.

Other sources of tension are worth taking into account: the entrepreneur is involved in unusual and unstable situations of change. The degree of uncertainty is high and the entrepreneur uses experimental approaches, based on trial and error. The entrepreneur's experimental approach is opposed to the large firm's planning approach designed to anticipate and predict, and characterised by aversion to risk and failure.

The experimentation at the heart of innovation and new activity creation processes evolves in a different time horizon to the one that traditionally exists in companies. Innovation processes require time, individuals need time to learn to create and master management tools, and projects need time to mature in good conditions.

This relation to time is opposed to the firm's acting and reacting in the ever decreasing short term. Experimentation, finally, may run up against another obstacle, that of the problematic availability and accessibility of necessary resources (the amount and nature of which is difficult to anticipate at times when they are the most critically needed). This is mainly due to the inertia of structures and the weight of bureaucracy that both characterise large firms to a greater or lesser extent.

One may easily understand, following this list of antagonisms, that the individual who acts entrepreneurially in an existing company is like a bumblebee: 'all aerodynamic tests prove it: the bumblebee cannot fly. Its size, weight and shape mean that it cannot fly. But the bumblebee does not know that, and so it flies.'[5]

Entrepreneurship: a new set of skills for individuals

According to their personal situation and their motivation, individuals (students, employees, job seekers) see, in the creation of a business, a means of professional and social insertion or reinsertion, a way to control their destiny, to find fulfilment or satisfy a need for independence and autonomy. They all want to maximise their chances of success before engaging in a process reputed to be time-, energy- and money-consuming.

However, beyond venture creation and its various motivations depending on the country, it seems to us that all individuals, today, feel concerned about entrepreneurship, to a higher or lesser degree. In our

[5] This metaphor is regularly used by a French entrepreneur who often speaks in intrapreneurship courses organised for undergraduate and graduate students of the EM Lyon School of Management.

changing world, the entrepreneurial perspective may be developed at the individual level, in a broad sense (Kuratko 2005). The new generation seems to have understood this. Kuratko (2005) puts forward a few figures concerning the United States. More than 5 million Americans under the age of 34 are trying to create a company today; one third of them are not even 30 yet, and more than 60 per cent of young people between 18 and 29 declare that they would like, one day, to create their own company. Even though the situation in the United States is slightly different from that in the rest of the world, entrepreneurial intentions have never been so high in France and the rest of Europe (Fayolle and Filion 2006).

'Skills sellers'

Relations between companies and individuals evolve and make individuals' attitudes and behaviours evolve too. In the previous section, we examined how companies and institutions strive to create the best conditions for new, more entrepreneurial organisational configurations. They encourage autonomy, creativity and initiative. Their adaptability to a changing world also leads them to offer less stable jobs to their employees, more seasonal jobs according to cyclical needs, and therefore more precarious jobs. The generalisation of the customer/supplier-type relationship within organisations contributes to the emergence of the notion of skills that replaces progressively that of 'position' and 'qualification'. The social statuses of managerial staff in several European countries are becoming increasingly vague and challenged. Competitive pressure, notably from Asian and eastern European countries, is on the increase. All these evolutions raise questions related to the post-salaried society that is emerging, where the individual at work, whether self-employed or employed by an organisation, is perceived above all as a portfolio of skills.

At the individual level, indeed, every individual is more and more considered as a 'skills seller', somebody who sells his or her own skills, and this vision of the individual reminds us of yesterday's entrepreneurs. The new basis for exchanges between companies and individuals seems to be recognised and useful skills. Everybody can act as an entrepreneur in this new context, without having to sell his or her soul to the devil or work like a slave, despite the image promoted by contemporary Asian entrepreneurs.

New ways of being and learning

We must be aware of the fact that our work organisation systems are currently undergoing dramatic changes and that no economy will survive without implementing change processes that will lead to new, more entrepreneurial organisational cultures and configurations. These evolutions and deep changes manifest themselves at various levels and are starting to challenge education, training and learning, by raising new issues.

In this context, strong demands appear and are imposed upon organisations and individuals. They must adapt, react, innovate, and face change, uncertainty and complexity. All of this raises the question of how new aptitudes and skills, better adapted to the evolutions and characteristics of our societies, can be taught and learnt in order to be applied in new contexts. Education systems, schools and training centres will have to tackle these issues.

How to develop creative capacities? 'Companies have been over-managed, at the expense of creativity . . . The lack of both imagination and entrepreneurs means the fall of our societies. Today we have but administrators.'[6]

How to develop the capacity to change? 'Instead of being offensive, we behave defensively, we try to adapt to the situation when we should change it. Most of our resources, energy, grey matter are devoted to a permanent effort to adjust costs and structures.'[7]

'How to develop anticipation capacities? How to stimulate and develop rigour, team work, imagination, the culture of risk?'[8]

Traditional responses show that managers' behaviours and attitudes revolve around technical or professional knowledge and skills that correspond to classic training. However, these are far from sufficient today. They do not really integrate the capacity for permanent diagnosis or the intelligence of social situations – in firms, organisations, interpersonal relations – or decisional capacity and entrepreneurial behaviour.

In this context, entrepreneurs embody flexibility, reactivity, risk-taking, innovation and value creation, it is because they appear as 'the

[6] Jean-René Fourtou, Rhône-Poulenc CEO, in *Le Monde*, September 1993.
[7] Henri Lachmann, Strafor CEO, in *Le Monde*, September 1993.
[8] Jean-René Fourtou, during a conference organised in Lyons, in September 1998, by the Institut de l'Entreprise This conference was about the entrepreneurial spirit in schools and universities.

right person(s) for the job' that we try to transpose their behaviours and aptitudes in contexts of action other than venture creation.

This situation and the elements of response we have put forward show how fundamental it is to favour new ways of being and evolving in a rapidly changing world. They also emphasise the necessity to imagine new ways of learning, which may be articulated around:

> the multiplication of pedagogical situation simulations, either computer-based or real-life situations, in relation to school, professional or other activities: they must include confrontations with reality, responsibilities, team work on projects, initiative, and calculated and assumed risk-taking;
> life-long learning: learning how to cultivate one's 'skills', like a gardener cultivates his or her vegetable patch, in order not to risk experiencing situations of exclusion.

In other words, learning how to be entrepreneurial, by being, as often as possible, proactive in one's education, in a system where the way to learn is as important as what is learnt.

2 | Entrepreneurship as a field of research

Entrepreneurship is a fragmented field of research and its multiple components are observed and analysed by economists, sociologists, historians, psychologists, and specialists of behavioural science, education or management sciences (Filion 1997). This emerging field is also subject to numerous controversies. While everywhere in the world entrepreneurs and entrepreneurship are increasingly debated topics, a lot remains to be done as to what these notions entail exactly, both theoretically and practically. In this chapter, we present the three main streams of research within which three visions of entrepreneurship seem to emerge. We will first review the genesis and foundations of this academic field.

Genesis and foundations of entrepreneurship

Three fundamental questions synthesise most of the research[1] in entrepreneurship. Inspired from a formulation by Stevenson and Jarillo (1990), this triple question can be put as follows: 'What on earth is s/he doing...?', 'Why on earth is s/he doing...?' and 'How on earth is s/he doing...?' (Tornikoski 1999). We recognise here the functional approaches (What) of economists, the individual-based approaches (Why and Who) of behavioural specialists, and the process-based approaches (How) of management specialists. First, we will examine the points of view of economists interested in the influence of entrepreneurship and entrepreneurs on the development of the economic system. Following this first overview, we will successively present the approaches based on individuals and processes.

---

[1] In a recent review of the existing literature, Danjou (2002) has distinguished three distinct perspectives for researchers in entrepreneurship, based on the entrepreneur, the action and the entrepreneurial context. These three approaches mostly concur with our triple question.

Economists' objects and perspectives

The historical foundations of entrepreneurship belong to economics. The concept of entrepreneurship appeared for the first time in the economic literature in the writings of Richard Cantillon (Landström 1998, 2005; Filion 1997). Cantillon was the first to present the role of the entrepreneur and its importance for economic development. He particularly underlined the role of uncertainty and risk in his analysis of the entrepreneurial phenomenon. Cantillon's entrepreneur 'takes risks insofar as he or she firmly commits himself or herself towards a third party, without being certain of what he or she can expect' (Boutillier and Uzunidis 1999). Jean-Baptiste Say was the second economist who took a great interest in entrepreneurial activities (Filion 1997: 3). According to him, entrepreneurs are above all risk-takers who invest their own money and coordinate resources in order to produce goods. They create and develop economic activities for their own profit. With the publication of Schumpeter's *Theory of Economic Development* (1934), the entrepreneur became a central figure of economic development. Filion (1997) considers Schumpeter as the father of entrepreneurship as a research field. Schumpeter's entrepreneur is above all an innovator and an actor of change: 'the essence of entrepreneurship lies in the perception and exploitation of new opportunities in the corporate world . . . it always has to do with putting national resources to a different use in that they are withdrawn from their usual application and subjected to new combinations'.[2] The entrepreneur thus takes risks in order to innovate, particularly by elaborating new productive combinations. The Schumpeterian definition of innovation is not restrictive, in so far as the five types of recombination he identifies correspond to the five opportunities of profit present in capitalist societies (Boutillier and Uzunidis 1999: 30).

Schumpeter's contribution is essential because it has provided foundations for the field of entrepreneurship. Nevertheless, other economic perspectives have shed a different light on the subject. We would like to mention, among others, the contributions of Knight (1971) about the relation of the entrepreneur with uncertainty, Kirzner (1983) with the opportunities emerging from the gaps or imperfections of the market, Leibenstein (1979) and his model of inefficacy measurement in the

---

[2] Schumpeter 1928, quoted by Filion (1997).

utilisation of resources, and finally Casson (1982) and the importance of decision-making and coordinating rare resources.

In short, the economists' perspective is important because it provides a historical basis to the field of entrepreneurship. It takes into account multiple components and brings to the fore at least two major entrepreneurial figures that encompass four fundamental roles. The figures are those of the entrepreneur as an organiser of economic activities and the entrepreneur as an innovator (Baumol 1993). The four fundamental roles the entrepreneur can play in the economic system (Landström 1998) are that of 'risk-taker/risk-manager' (Cantillon, Say, Knight), 'innovator' (Schumpeter), 'alert seeker of opportunities' (Hayek, Mises, Kirzner) or, finally, that of 'coordinator of limited resources' (Casson).

Individual-based approaches

These approaches aim at better understanding the entrepreneur's psychological and social background, personality traits, motivations and behaviours. They perhaps also aim at finding a typical entrepreneur's profile that could be identified through one principal personality trait, or a given set of personality traits. One of the early questions about individuals was related (and still is?) to the innate nature of the entrepreneur. Are entrepreneurs born with a sixth sense, a kind of entrepreneurial instinct? Some researchers tend to think so.[3] However, many researchers and practitioners refute this assumption.

Specialists in human behavioural sciences have carried out extensive research to try to analyse and understand entrepreneurs' behaviours. Weber was probably one of the first specialists of this discipline to take an interest in entrepreneurs. He highlighted the importance of the value system (Filion 1997: 5). McClelland (1961) proposed a 'desire for achievement' theory, based on solid empirical research. According to him, entrepreneurs are individuals with a strong desire for achievement, a lot of self-confidence, a capacity to solve problems by themselves, and oriented towards situations characterised by moderate risk and quick feedback (on the outcomes of their actions). Based on McClelland's work, numerous researchers have tried to explain new

---

[3] See also the authors cited by Cunningham and Lischeron (1991), in the paragraph entitled 'The great person school of entrepreneurship'.

venture creation, or its success, through the desire for achievement of their founders. Brockhaus (1982) temporarily closed the subject by questioning the relevance of this single link. As they could not demonstrate the existence of one unique variable that could explain this phenomenon, psychologists, sociologists and other behavioural specialists have conducted hundreds of studies on entrepreneurs and identified a set of characteristics that describe them. Louis-Jacques Filion proposed a table representing the most common ones (Filion 1997: 7), drawing on the contributions of Hornaday (1982), Meredith, Nelson *et al.* (1982) and Timmons (1978). Kets de Vries also provided an original point of view (1977), in line with the psychoanalytic approach. He declared that entrepreneurial behaviour resulted from childhood experiences, characterised notably by a hostile family environment and numerous affective problems. These situations would thus lead individuals to develop deviant types of personalities unlikely to fit into structured social environments, in the sense that they would have difficulties accepting authority and working with others as a team.

Typological approaches complete the trait-based approaches. Smith defined a classic typology (1967), which distinguishes two types of entrepreneurs: 'craftsmen' and 'opportunistic entrepreneurs'. Various typologies of the entrepreneur have been proposed in entrepreneurial literature, but their multiplicity does not help distinguish an ideal or scientific profile of the entrepreneur.[4] Individuals are the products of their milieus. Entrepreneurs are influenced by their close environment and reflect, in many ways, the characteristics of the time and place in which they evolve (or have evolved). Research concerned with the factors favouring the emergence of entrepreneurial intention, entrepreneurial careers and the influence of families or role-models highlights the influence of the environment and tends to demonstrate its role in entrepreneurial behaviour (Shaver and Scott 1991; Filion 1997).

Approaches concerned primarily with individuals are regularly subject to criticism, and a memorable debate shook the community of entrepreneurial researchers at the end of the 1980s. It opposed Gartner (1988) and his approach of entrepreneurship focused on organisation

---

[4] For reviews of the literature on entrepreneur typologies, refer to Risker (1998) and Landström (1998) in English, or Hernandez (1999: 77–85) in French.

creation (How) and Carland *et al.* (1988) and their trait-based approach (Who). Stevenson and Jarillo (1990) suggest that it is difficult to model and explain a complex behaviour (entrepreneurship) by relying on a few psychological or sociological traits. This realisation is gradually gaining currency and leading researchers to refocus on entrepreneurship processes.

Process-based approaches

After the 'What', 'Who' and 'Why' questions, researchers have shifted to the 'How' – 'How are new firms established?' and 'How does the entrepreneur proceed?' – two questions, among others, based on the assumption that entrepreneurship is a complex and multidimensional phenomenon (Gartner 1985; Bruyat and Julien 2001). The emergence of this research perspective is linked to the increasingly widespread recognition that there is a great variety of entrepreneurial situations and new venture creations: entrepreneurs and their projects are different from one another (Gartner 1985).

Gartner was one of the first researchers to question the validity of the trait-based approach, dominant in the 1980s, in an article published in 1988, entitled: '"Who is an entrepreneur?" is the wrong question'. He underlined in this article the need for entrepreneurship research to change both its perspective and its level of analysis. He demonstrated the limitations of the trait-based approach and suggested researchers focus on what entrepreneurs do rather than who they are. A sentence that is often attributed to him well summarises his thought at the time: 'Look at the dance, not at the dancer.' As early as the mid-1980s, Gartner integrates the notion of process into the entrepreneurial field when he proposes a conceptual framework to describe new venture creation (Gartner 1985). His model includes four dimensions: 'environment', 'individuals', 'process' and 'organisation'. It is interesting to note that he considers the process as a variable instead of a dimension that would encompass the three others. Gartner considers the process as an activity or a function, and adopts Danhoff's definition: 'Entrepreneurship is an activity or function and not a specific individual or occupation . . . the specific personal entrepreneur is an unrealistic abstraction.' Building on a review of the economic literature, Gartner identifies six types of behaviour that broadly apply to entrepreneurial activities. These behaviours could correspond to as many processes: 'the entrepreneur locates a business opportunity', 'the entrepreneur accumulates resources', 'the entrepreneur markets products and services', 'the entrepreneur produces the product', 'the entrepreneur builds an organisation', 'the entrepreneur responds to government and society' (Gartner 1985: 699–700).

This theory of a process-based perception of the activities has been adopted by other researchers, and the definition of the entrepreneurial process proposed by Bygrave and Hofer (1991: 14) shows great similarities with Gartner's vision: 'The entrepreneurial process involves all the functions, activities and actions associated with the perceiving of opportunities and the creation of organizations to pursue them.' At the beginning of the 1990s Bygrave and Hofer, among others, sought to open new research paths in the field of entrepreneurship and showed interest in the entrepreneurial process in particular. They endeavoured to describe a few of its characteristics, and particularly insisted on its dynamic and holistic dimensions. The entrepreneurial process is dynamic because creation projects and new ventures evolve through time; it is holistic because it evolves within a system of interacting variables.

Entrepreneurship researchers chose to focus on the process initially because it enabled them to free themselves from the previous visions, which were narrow and limited, centred on one single aspect, one human trait or economic function, whereas this complex phenomenon should be considered as a whole. The work of Cunningham and Lischeron (1991) summarises well this feeling. They go beyond the various typological presentations which structured the research activities in the field of entrepreneurship at the beginning of the 1990s. We are of the opinion that their major contribution resides in the affirmation of an original approach/concept of the entrepreneurial process.

Cunningham and Lischeron see entrepreneurship as a multifaceted phenomenon that cuts across several discipline boundaries and consider that each school of thought sheds a particular and unique light on one or the other of these facets. According to them, a first facet of the phenomenon ('assessing personal qualities') lies in the personal qualities and values of the entrepreneur; the second facet ('recognising opportunities') considers anticipation of the future, and recognition and discovery of opportunities as key elements. The third facet ('acting and managing') suggests that the success of the entrepreneur can be improved thanks to technical and non-technical (leadership) managerial tools. A fourth facet ('reassessing and adapting') acknowledges the need to change directions when necessary. We can thus link the various schools of thought to the four facets of the entrepreneurial phenomenon, and regroup these facets inside one model of the entrepreneurial process.

Cunningham and Lischeron's vision of entrepreneurship is not an attempt at combining all the hypotheses and philosophies of the various schools of thought. Above all, they consider entrepreneurship as an iterative process of personal assessment, anticipation, action, a process that calls into question both the individual and the organisation: 'This process involves creating the idea, assessing one's personal abilities, and taking action now and in the future. It assumes that entrepreneurs have the responsibility for the venture, or share some of the risks and rewards of it' (Cunningham and Lischeron 1991: 57).

A synthetic overview of the field of entrepreneurship

The table below presents a synthetic overview of the field inspired by the works of Filion and Landström. It includes the principal disciplines involved in the study of entrepreneurship and their links with the research objects and questions. It also puts forward the various evolutions and shifts of interest in research topics. It is non-exhaustive, and must therefore be used with caution. In some cases, information has been omitted. For example, some sociologists (Aldrich 1999) have shown interest in the 'How', and occasionally quantitative studies have been carried out on the entrepreneurial process. Our approach does not present all the variety and abundance of theoretical and ideological paths that may be found in this field.

Table 2.1 may be compared with another synthesis that we proposed in which we adopted a more historical perspective (Fayolle, Kyrö and Ulijn 2005).

What seems to characterise the evolution of research in entrepreneurship in the last few years is, on the one hand, the reorientation of the focus, which shifted from the individual to the process (Bygrave and Hofer 1991), and, on the other hand, the transition from a clearly positivist epistemology to a more nuanced epistemology, sometimes grounded (perhaps increasingly) in constructivist perspectives.

Table 2.1. Organised and synthetic overview of the research in entrepreneurship

Main question	What (functional approach)	Who/Why (individual-based approach)	How (process-based approach)
Time scale	Last 200 years	Since the beginning of the 1950s	Since the beginning of the 1990s
Main scientific domain	Economics	Psychology, sociology, cognitive psychology, social anthropology	Management sciences, action sciences, organisation theories
Object of study	Entrepreneur's functions	Personal characteristics, individual traits, entrepreneurs and potential entrepreneurs	Creation process of a new activity, a new organisation
Dominant paradigm	Positivism	Positivism, comprehensive sociology	Constructivism, positivism
Methodology	Quantitative	Quantitative, qualitative	Qualitative, quantitative
Basic hypothesis	The entrepreneur plays/does not play an important role in the economic growth	Entrepreneurs are different from non-entrepreneurs	Entrepreneurial processes are different from one another
Link with social demand (who is interested in . . .)	State, local governments/ administrations, economic players	Entrepreneurs, potential entrepreneurs, education system, training staff	Businesses, entrepreneurs, potential entrepreneurs, training staff, entrepreneurship support structures

Table elaborated on the basis of elements proposed by Landström (1998), Filion (1997) and Tornikoski (1999).

Entrepreneurship is about opportunity[5]

The concept of opportunity has existed for a long time in the literature on entrepreneurship,[6] but it has recently taken a more prominent place. Timmons (1994: 7), for instance, considers that the transformation of an opportunity is performed independently of the directly controllable resources: 'Entrepreneurship is the process of creating or seizing an opportunity and pursuing it regardless of the resources currently controlled.' Timmons also talks about the opportunity being created and shaped by the entrepreneur.

Bygrave and Hofer (1991) combine the opportunity paradigm with that of the creation of an entity, and focus more on the entrepreneur than on entrepreneurship.[7] Shane and Venkataraman's vision has fostered a dominant stream of research in this field (2000: 218):

The scholarly examination of how, by whom and with what effects opportunities to create future goods and services are discovered, evaluated and exploited (Venkataraman 1997). Consequently, the field involves the study of sources of opportunities; the process of discovery, evaluation, and exploitation of opportunities; and the set of individuals who discover, evaluate, and exploit them.

These authors are in line with the paradigm of opportunity, and have sought to integrate a process approach (discovery, evaluation and exploitation of the opportunity) and an individual-based approach (discoverer, evaluator and exploiter).[8] This perspective on opportunity leads to a triple question: '(1) why, when, and how opportunities for the creation of goods and services come into existence; (2) why, when, and how some people and not others discover and exploit these opportunities; and (3) why, when, and how different modes of action are used to exploit entrepreneurial opportunities' (Shane and Venkataraman 2000: 218). Shane and Venkataraman add that entrepreneurship does not require, but may induce, the creation of a new organisation. They build upon the works of Amit, Glosten and Mueller (1993) and Casson (1982), postulating that entrepreneurship can emerge within an existing company (or for the entrepreneur's own

---

[5] Part of this section is based on Verstraete and Fayolle (2005).
[6] In this respect, the contribution of the school of Austrian economists is essential.
[7] 'An entrepreneur is someone who perceives an opportunity and creates an organization to pursue it' (Bygrave and Hofer 1991: 14).
[8] See on this subject the article by Bhave (1994).

profit). We will see in a subsequent section that not all authors use the term 'organisation' in the same way.

Another important aspect that goes hand in hand with opportunity is collecting information (information as a means to reduce uncertainty, and therefore to reduce risk), and this for two reasons. First of all, opportunities do not fall into the lap of the entrepreneur. Most of the time, their detection results from a more or less explicit search for information. Secondly, the collected information may allow the development of an opportunity, or rather, the more or less advanced conception of an idea that may develop into a business opportunity, provided that third parties get involved in the project.

There are two main perspectives of research on the question of information. The first one focuses on the cognitive processes used by some individuals to identify opportunities. The works of Gaglio and Taub (1992), Kaisch and Gilad (1991) and Hills (1995) are representative of this approach. Cooper, Folta and Woo (1995) show that entrepreneurs who lack experience and practice receive more information than experienced entrepreneurs. Experienced entrepreneurs, building from their cognitive dispositions and their networks, know better how to recognise the information relevant for their business.[9]

The second orientation adopts a market-based point of view, which, without excluding the entrepreneur's capacities or personal intervention, considers the environment (a territory, network, market, etc.) as bearer of information to be collected, analysed and interpreted. Kirzner is also in line with this perspective when he stresses the impact of price determined by supply and demand on unbalanced and therefore dynamic markets. Yet, this is not a reason to give in to determinism. According to Kirzner (1973), the opportunity stems from a dysfunction in the market, an imperfection or economic unbalance, which can be exploited by the entrepreneur who will thus restore the market balance. Opportunity here is considered as a source of profit made possible by the existence of a solvable demand and the availability of necessary resources. The novelty that the entrepreneur capable of vigilance will put on the market can become a source of income. Casson (1982) considers opportunities to be 'occasions when new goods, new services, raw materials and organisation methods can be presented and sold at

---

[9] See also the text by Ucbasaran *et al.* (2003).

a higher price than their cost of production'. This brings us closer to the paradigm of innovation.

Two visions seem to co-exist in the opportunity paradigm. The first one is concerned with an objective reality, recognisable as such. Opportunities exist, and all one has to do is to be able to recognise them, appropriate them and transform them into economic realities. The second postulates that an opportunity is a social construction born from the interactions and confrontations between an individual and the environment. The opportunity takes shape during a creation process (business creation for example, but not necessarily). In this case, the opportunity is not the starting point, the 'objective element' that has to be recognised to initiate the process (Fayolle 2004).

In this perspective, opportunity refers to the concept of 'idea', or an elaborated version of the idea, partly tested through the existence of prospects (Timmons 1994), the development of a prototype, or a marketing study – particularly difficult to conduct in the case of new ventures (Gumpert 1996). From working on the concept of idea with new venture creators and studying the literature, we have come to realise that opportunity can be constructed as well as detected. The idea may originate in many different ways: trips, employment (present or past), technological innovation, identification of a need, new patents, etc. The constructed nature of the opportunity is revealed even further in works on creativity. In this respect, there is no entrepreneurship without creativity (Brazeal and Herbert 1999). Creativity initiates change (Ford 1996) and entrepreneurs use all the imagination they can muster (theirs and that of their employees) for the benefit of their business (Nystrom 1995). According to Nystrom, entrepreneurship is the projection and realisation of new ideas by individuals who are capable of using the information and gathering the necessary resources in order to implement their visions. Besides the entrepreneur, every member of the organisation has a creative potential. This potential is present everywhere, from the top of the hierarchy to the bottom (Osborn 1988; Nilsson 1994). It is the role of firms to preserve or revitalise this entrepreneurial spirit; hence we go from creativity to entrepreneurship (see the work of Carrier (1997), devoted to these issues).

Of course, the opposition between objectivity/subjectivity raises many debates. One good example is that of Shane and Venkataraman, who initially agreed: 'Although recognition of entrepreneurial opportunities is a subjective process, the opportunities themselves are objective phenomena that are not known to all parties at all times' (Shane and Venkataraman 2000: 220); but they no longer seem to be on the same wavelength (see Shane 2003).

If we consider opportunity as a junction between a more or less structured context and individuals acting in an entrepreneurial way, we can recognise the conventions that govern the confrontation of the uncertainties of the market and the uncertainties of the strategic actor. This approach focuses on the constructed nature of ideas, progressively transformed into economic and social realities. When applied to a process-based approach, this implies that opportunity is not necessarily a precondition to venture creation, as the venture creation process itself may reveal opportunities through interactions between the players. The market may therefore generate opportunities resulting from interactions between individuals or economic players acting upon ideas that their vigilance (cf. Kirzner) enabled them to notice.[10]

This leads us to the second paradigm we are going to present in this chapter, that of the creation of an organisation. Beforehand, we wish to conclude this section by insisting on two essential points.

First of all, as regards the opportunity paradigm, the discovery, evaluation and exploitation processes represent essential research objects. Recent works (notably Wicklund, Dahlqvist and Havnes 2001; or Van der Veen and Wakkee 2002) explore, conceptually or empirically, particular aspects of this domain.[11] However, this approach may entail the omission of failure situations, even relative failure, by focusing too much on opportunity exploitation processes resulting in the creation of products or services. And yet, research in entrepreneurship can benefit from the study of processes that have failed, in particular for a better understanding of entrepreneurial situations. In line with this paradigm, some researchers of the Swedish school (for instance Davidsson 2005) are developing research projects that strive to reduce

---

[10] Our idea resides in acknowledging that interactions between individuals and interactions between companies are both incomplete. Some interactions may be accessible to individuals only once they have created the organisation providing them with a new position from which to explore the surrounding context (social, market, etc.).

[11] The proceedings of the Babson conferences (Frontiers of Entrepreneurship Research) include an 'opportunity recognition' section; see especially the proceedings of the last two editions.

its weaknesses while bringing it together with the paradigm of organisation creation around the concept of the emergence of a new economic
activity. In a different area, and it will be our second point, concerning the issue of opportunity we have mentioned the intersection of the
field of entrepreneurship with the field of strategy, and therefore it is
important not to forget research in the field of marketing which also
focuses on this pivotal concept. The article by Hills and Laforge (1992)
particularly illustrates this interface.

Entrepreneurship is about organisational emergence[12]

The term 'organisation', used over and again, is polysemous, as it can
mean both the 'action of organising' and its result. The process piloted
by the entrepreneur leads to the appearance of a new organisation
(entity or group).

It is no simple task to identify the works and researchers at the
origin of this concept, but we consider this stream of research to be
strongly linked to Gartner's work: 'I think that those who are familiar
with some of my previous writings on entrepreneurship (Gartner, 1985,
1988, 1989, 1990) are aware that the domain of entrepreneurship that
interests me is focused on the phenomenon of organization creation'
(Gartner 1995: 69).

The association of the terms 'organisation' and 'creation' in one
single expression suggests the prior inexistence of the organisation.
Bygrave and Hofer (1991: 14), in the second part of their definition of
entrepreneurship, see the creation of an organisation as necessary in
order to exploit the opportunity: 'An entrepreneur is someone who perceives an opportunity and creates an organization to pursue it' (Bygrave
and Hofer 1991: 14). This 'organisation', or entity, may take the shape
of a firm, but not necessarily.

Gartner (1985) has a different vision which is explained in one of
his works on the concept of organisational emergence (1995, see also
1993). Emergence may be defined, in general, as the more or less sudden appearance of an idea or of a social, political or economic fact.
The concept of organisational emergence applies to a phenomenon that
derives from various stimuli, such as experience, images or ideas, which
make sense in a new combination. Gartner's main interest thus lies in

---

[12] Part of this section is based on Verstraete and Fayolle (2005).

the emergence of new organisations: how do organisations come into existence? He uses Weick's theory of organising in considering the inter-action between the individual and the environment (1979). In his text of 1995, he admits his interpretation of the organisation has changed since his first contribution. He distinguishes the phenomenon of organisation creation from other organisational phenomena. The use of the term 'creation' implies the intervention of a 'creator', willingly involved in the process. To illustrate the act of creation, Gartner quotes Collins and Moore (1964), who acknowledge the capacity of entrepreneurs to translate their dreams (visions) into action, through the creation of a business:

Between the idea and the act falls the shadow. This shadow, which these men had to explore, and out of which they had to hammer a reality, lay immediately ahead. They had now to organize the universe around them in such a way that they could progress in establishing their new business. The first act in this direction is what we will call the act of creation. (Cited in Gartner 1995: 70)

Referring to Weick enabled Gartner to explicate how the 'creator' or the founder organises the world that surrounds him or her.[13] When he speaks about 'emergence', Gartner refers to the appearance of some-thing, something that was previously not visible and then becomes manifest, and that may take place before the existence of an entity such as a firm:

I hope that organizational emergence will convey the image of organizations becoming manifest, that is, organizational emergence is the process of how organizations make themselves known (how they come out into view; how they come into existence) . . . the phenomenon of organizational emergence occurs before the organizations exist. (p. 71)

In other words, the organisation as a process prevails over the organ-isation as an entity. This is relatively remote from the new venture creation concept to which the entrepreneurial process is often reduced.

Verstraete (1999; 2003) uses the polysemy and ambivalence of the term 'organisation' to build a model of the entrepreneurial phe-nomenon based on the 'initiation' of an organisation: 'In our thesis, entrepreneurship is seen as a phenomenon leading to the creation of

---

[13] We will not present here the process modelled by Weick, but instead refer the reader to his work of 1979.

an organisation, initiated by one or several individuals associated for the occasion' (Verstraete 2003: 13).[14] For this author, the study of entrepreneurship must not focus on an analytical disjunction of the organisation (favoured by Jacot 1994) but requires a systemic reflection that integrates both the action and its outcome. In line with Gartner's writings, Verstraete nevertheless clearly distinguishes the process from the phenomenon he is more particularly interested in.[15] He proposes a generic model for the entrepreneurial phenomenon, adding that modelling a process must depend on the context in which the process takes place. In other words, each creation process corresponds to a unique model.[16]

Verstraete also notes that various organisational forms may result from the entrepreneurial phenomenon (they may not systematically be a business or a firm, as can be shown, for example, by social and solidarity-based economy) and that an entity may be only a step in the initiation of a larger phenomenon (for details, see Verstraete 2003). The concept of 'initiation', instead of the word 'creation', is one of the characteristics of the work of this author. To the actual 'birth' of the company can therefore be added its development, and this 'initiation' can rely on a pre-existing entity (which is the case, for example, of some companies taken over by individuals).

One of the flaws of the paradigm of organisation creation is its capacity to integrate other perspectives, sometimes too easily. Where some may consider it a strength, others will, just as legitimately, see a sign of weakness. For example, meeting the actors in the field (here, entrepreneurs seen as founders) in order to identify the discoverers (or builders), evaluators and exploiters of opportunities as mentioned in the previous section is not enough to discard the importance of studying the opportunity itself. By focusing excessively on the act of creation, the tendency to forget other elements of the phenomenon may be perceived as a weakness. Most of the time, the act of creation corresponds to a phase in the life cycle of an entity or an organisational process

[14] Also translated into English in Watkins (2003: 10–65).
[15] The meaning of the term 'process' is not the same for all the authors. Gartner considers it tantamount to the action of organising, whereas Verstraete considers it as more instrumental, as a chain of non-linear actions in the course of time.
[16] A new venture creation process in the USA is probably different from a new venture creation process in Sub-Saharan Africa, a company takeover process is different from a company creation process, etc.

(see on this subject the remarks of Shane and Venkataraman 2000; Davidsson, Low and Wright 2001; Wicklund, Dahlqvist and Havnes 2001). Hamid Bouchikhi (2003) goes so far as provocatively to compare the researcher in entrepreneurship to an obstetrician, an opinion that may not be shared by everyone. The researcher in entrepreneurship often crosses paths with the researcher in organisational theory, which shows the interdisciplinary nature of entrepreneurship (see Thornton 1999, in sociology; Aldrich 1999 or Schoonhoven and Romanelli 2001, for an evolutionist perspective; Giddens' theory of social structuration in Bouchikhi 1990 and 1994a; etc.). The remaining problem is that the sense of what the 'organisation' is (or is not) has not yet reached a consensus: process or entity, action or its outcome, or both if we consider the polysemy of the term and, hence, that one implies the other.

I would like to make one final remark about this paradigm: depending on the exploitation mode selected to make the most of an opportunity or an invention (creation of a business or utilisation of an existing organisation), the process may or may not be entrepreneurial. Moreover, as Bruyat pointed out (1993), not all organisation creations systematically lead to situations where the intensity of change for the individual and the importance of the value creation are really significant. Companies may be created by imitation or reproduction, or with the aim of transferring existing activities.

Entrepreneurship is about new value creation[17]

Ronstad (1984: 28) introduced and summarised this stream of research as follows:

Entrepreneurship is the dynamic process of creating incremental wealth. This wealth is created by individuals who assume the major risks in terms of equity, time, and/or career commitment of providing value for some product or service. The product or service itself may or may not be new or unique but value must somehow be infused by the entrepreneur by securing and allocating the necessary skills and resources.

Entrepreneurship is often considered as a source of wealth and employment, and therefore, globally, as a source of value. Its economic and

---

[17] Part of this section is based on Verstraete and Fayolle (2005).

social impacts have been acknowledged for a long time (see Fayolle 2003), and for several years the international research programme GEM (Global Entrepreneurship Monitor), initiated by Paul Reynolds, has endeavoured to demonstrate the existence of strong links between entrepreneurial activities and economic growth in numerous countries.

As for the academic dimension of entrepreneurship, journals, through their editorial policies, sometimes explicitly put forward entrepreneurship as a process or phenomenon that is a source of value creation. Concerning the definitions proposed in the literature, the one by Ronstadt, quoted above, is perhaps the most significant.

Gartner empirically identified the concept of value creation as a core issue of entrepreneurship (1990). In the francophone world, Bruyat (1993; 1994) used this concept in his thesis that made way for future research. For this author, 'the scientific object studied in the field of entrepreneurship is the individual/value creation dialogic' (Bruyat 1993: 57). The field of entrepreneurship is therefore envisaged through the relation between the individual and the value he or she contributes to create. The dialogic principle, as proposed by the French sociologist Morin (1989), means that two or several perspectives are bound into a unity, in a complex way (complementary, concurrent and opposing) without the duality being lost in the unity. This dialogic is in line with the dynamic of change and can be defined as follows (Bruyat 1993: 58):

Individuals are necessary conditions to the creation of value, they determine its production modalities, its amplitude . . . Individuals are the main actors of value creation. The shape that value creation takes, a company for instance, is the individual's 'thing', so we have:

INDIVIDUAL → VALUE CREATION

Value creation, through the shape it takes, becomes part of the individuals who define themselves in relation to it. It plays a predominant role in the life of the individual (activity, objectives, means, social status, etc.) and is likely to modify his or her characteristics (know-how, values, attitudes, etc.), so we have:

VALUE CREATION → INDIVIDUAL

The entrepreneurial system (value creation ↔ individual) interacts with its environment and is part of a process in which time is an essential dimension (Bruyat and Julien 2001). This representation concurs, to a certain extent, with Gartner's (1985), for whom the important dimensions are: the individual(s), the environment, the organisation and the process.[18]

In this paradigm of value creation, a definition of the concept of 'value' must be agreed upon. Value is a key concept in classic economics (Bruyat and Julien 2001). It relates to exchanges between market players at prices determined by the market. In this perspective, entrepreneurship concerns the trade sector (the private sector, non-profit organisations and active cooperatives in this sector) and the public sector involved in transactions such as the sale of goods and services. Thanks to the research currently led in the sector of solidarity economy, value takes on a social connotation, without discarding the financial guarantees the stakeholders of this type of economy will not fail to require (Boncler and Hlady-Rispal 2003).

If entrepreneurship constitutes a pivotal mechanism in value creation processes (Kirchhoff 1994; 1997), it remains that value creation relates to various practices that do not always fall within the scope of entrepreneurship (as can be shown in the 1998 proceedings of the Congrès des Instituts d'Administration des Entreprises (French academic conference, held in Nantes); see also Bréchet and Desreumaux 1998). The other important aspect of this paradigm lies in the character of novelty of the value thus created. This point is highlighted by Bruyat (1993) in his matrix of the various research perspectives on entrepreneurship.[19] In other words, the value resulting from an entrepreneurial process is new, to the extent that there is, or there will be, a more or less significant change in the environment directly concerned by the process.

As with the other paradigms, the value creation paradigm presents a number of difficulties and limitations. One of them is that processes that have nothing to do with entrepreneurship may also generate new

[18] We may note, however, that 'process' does not have the same meaning for both authors. In Gartner's earlier works, a process was considered tantamount to a way of doing things, a strategy.
[19] The abscissa of his matrix corresponds to the more or less significant novelty of the value created, and the ordinate represents the change produced for the one who promotes it. The more a studied phenomenon or research object brings both novelty and change, the higher the consensus among the academic community about admitting that this phenomenon or object belongs to the field of entrepreneurship.

value creation. For example, a stock exchange operation may bring new value to a listed share, and, in some cases, restructuring a business (change) may also have the same effect. The many definitions of 'value' in the field of management only (finance, marketing, human resources management, etc.) show its polysemy, just like the concepts of opportunity and organisation, and it would be delusory to believe in one unitary framework.

Some authors see compatibilities and possible connections between different streams of research. Verstraete, for example, sees the value creation paradigm as complementary to that of organisation creation (1999; 2002). He clarifies his point of view by referring to the research on stakeholders. Stakeholder theory provides an analysis framework for the management of the multiple relations between individuals and groups involved in strategic activities. The key idea is that every management structure must implement processes that ensure the satisfaction of the various players involved in the business, especially those involved in its success in the long term. In this perspective, a stakeholder corresponds to any individual, group, entity or institution, supposedly interested in the business and with some influence on its future.

At the praxeological level, Verstraete shows that the organisation creation paradigm and the value creation paradigm are complementary (one encompassing the other). For Verstraete, value is relative to the stakeholder to whom the entrepreneur and his organisation must bring satisfaction, hence provide value (which is incidentally an evaluation criterion for the aforementioned stakeholder). We will note that, to become a stakeholder, the player must be converted into one. At the beginning, potential stakeholders are only bearers of resources who must be convinced to commit themselves to the business project proposed by the entrepreneur. The entrepreneur and the organisation he or she has initiated are not positioned in one unique environment, but in as many environments as there are categories of stakeholders. For each category of stakeholders, effective policies must be elaborated and implemented in order to optimise the value of the exchange[20] (Verstraete 2003: 86). A link is thus created between the functional

---

[20] The nature of the value is linked to the expectations of the stakeholders for whom the policy is implemented and to the company itself.

policies dear to strategic management[21] (wage policy for the employees through the human resources department, procurement policy for the suppliers through a purchasing department, etc.).

While the value creation paradigm is partly based on the paradigm of organisation creation, it is also related to the paradigm of innovation. Indeed, to a certain extent, new value creation is corollary to innovation, and, in this respect, it brings us back to one of the first contemporary definitions of entrepreneurship (Schumpeter 1934). Innovation is a specific case of value creation, as it is difficult to imagine there may be innovation without value creation (Bruyat 1993). Innovation that does not create value remains a non-exploited invention (i.e. not generating value for lack of a social and commercial exploitation) or a 'technical object' (Millier 1997), although this last example is debatable.

---

[21] We can refer here to the division adopted by Desreumaux (1993) where three levels characterise strategic activity: primary or corporate (delimitation of the strategic activity domains, etc.), secondary or activity-related (objectives and behaviour within one domain of strategic activity) and functional (strategy deployment in the whole organisation through its major functions).

3 | *Entrepreneurship as an academic subject*

Entrepreneurship is an economic and social phenomenon, a research object, and, more and more, an academic and teaching subject. It becomes particularly obvious when one looks at the fast-increasing number of universities all over the world that propose entrepreneurship programmes and courses. Two recent articles (Katz 2003; Kuratko 2005) published in leading reviews in the field propose, each in its own way, a comprehensive literary review of the subject aimed at defining the characteristics of this development as well as its limitations and challenges. Entrepreneurship education has come a long way since the first ever entrepreneurship course proposed by Myles Mace at Harvard University (Katz 2003). Today, figures show a real boom in this type of training in the United States (Kuratko 2005): 2200 courses in more than 1600 institutions, 277 endowed positions, 44 academic reviews and more than 100 established and funded entrepreneurship centres. In view of these data, we could think that the field is well established; however nothing could be further from the truth, and numerous epistemological, theoretical, pedagogical and practical challenges remain. As we have previously noted, there is no consensus on what entrepreneurship is. In these conditions, how could there be a consensus on what entrepreneurship as a teaching subject is? Some people, especially from the old school, still ask the question: can entrepreneurship be taught? The objective of this chapter is not to answer questions that appeared with the origin of the discipline, but to show that, with method and rigour, it is possible to turn these conceptual weaknesses into strengths towards a renewed and more mature teaching of entrepreneurship. The main condition for this is to accept the diversity of contexts, points of view, definitions and approaches in order to turn them into resources for everyone who participates in these training courses. It seems essential to offer a coherent framework, in terms of perspectives, objectives, contents and pedagogical methods. To a certain extent, it is a comeback to the key questions every educator must ask: What? For whom? Why? How?

This chapter is articulated around the following points. I will first clarify the question of entrepreneurship education, and in the second section will discuss the objectives, contents and methods used in entrepreneurship courses and programmes. I will develop in the third section two educational processes in particular, with two distinct objectives: training entrepreneurs (or professionals in the field) and preparing entrepreneurial individuals. The first perspective clearly has a professional dimension (how to) whereas the second is concerned with a more spiritual dimension.

Entrepreneurship education: a question of definition

The definition of entrepreneurship teaching should be contingent on the concept of entrepreneurship. However, it is not always the case given the variety of points of view (some definitions, for instance, are based on political or economic objectives, etc.). Moreover, defining what entrepreneurship teaching is obliges one to refine the definition of 'teaching'. I will clarify this point, and then show that the question 'can entrepreneurship be taught?' is no longer relevant today. I will conclude this section by discussing the various possible definitions of entrepreneurship teaching.

Teaching and educating

For the vast majority of people, the concept of entrepreneurship is not clear. The word 'entrepreneurship' is polysemous: it may designate skills and aptitudes such as autonomy, creativity, innovation and risk-taking, or the act of venture creation. In this light, training can open people's minds and extend their knowledge. However, is the word 'teaching' appropriate in all cases? Before clarifying the scope of what entrepreneurship teaching covers, we propose to look thoroughly into the meanings of 'teaching' and 'educating'.

We are not sure that the words 'entrepreneurship' and 'teaching', which are often associated, go well together. To check this, we have looked into a few definitions.

Teach – To impart knowledge or skill to; to provide knowledge of; instruct in; to condition to a certain action or frame of mind; to cause to learn by example or experience . . .[1]

Given that entrepreneurship refers to individual initiative, creativity and sometimes innovation, is it possible to favour the emergence of entrepreneurs or make a society more entrepreneurial by giving lessons or 'imparting knowledge'? In the definition proposed above, teaching implies a certain passivity of the learner; maybe the word 'educate' would be more appropriate?

Educate – To develop the innate capacities of, especially by schooling or instruction; to stimulate or develop the mental or moral growth of; to develop or refine (one's taste or appreciation, for example) . . .[2]

The word 'educate' seems more appropriate, at least for some of the actions in entrepreneurship training. Moreover, this type of education relates to the evolution of learning processes and methods from a didactical mode towards an entrepreneurial mode, as demonstrated by Allan Gibb (1996). Table 3.1 presents the main differences between both learning modes.

Teaching and educating have different meanings and do not meet the same objectives. The notion of education seems more appropriate to situations intended for developing learners' minds, raising people's awareness of the entrepreneurial phenomenon, giving them keys to their personal development and professional orientation, and giving them the incentive to act entrepreneurially. The notion of 'teaching' is more appropriate to contexts of knowledge transfer of entrepreneurial themes and dimensions. Notions of both 'teaching' and 'educating' must therefore be combined in entrepreneurship courses and programmes. Opposing these two notions, separating them or favouring one at the expense of the other would no doubt be detrimental to the field.

'Can entrepreneurship be taught?' is no longer a relevant question

Surprisingly, some people still argue that it is not possible to teach entrepreneurship. For them, entrepreneurship is a matter of personality,

---

[1] *The American Heritage Dictionary of the English Language*, 4th edn, Boston: Houghton Mifflin, 2000.
[2] Ibid.

Table 3.1. *Didactical and entrepreneurial models of learning*

Pedagogical methods	
Didactical model	Entrepreneurial model
Teaching by the teacher exclusively	Mutual learning
Passive student, listener	Learning by doing
Learning by reading	Learning through interpersonal exchanges, debates, discussions
Learning through teacher's feedback	Learning through feedback from different and numerous people
Learning in a scheduled and organised environment	Learning in a flexible, informal environment
Learning without pressure of immediate objectives	Learning under pressure: objectives must be reached
Others' input is not encouraged	Learning by borrowing from others
Fear of mistakes and failure	Learning through trial and error
Learning by taking notes	Learning by solving problems
Learning through a network of expert teachers	Learning through guided discovery

Source: Gibb 1996.

and psychological characteristics. One of the arguments that have been put forward is that talent and temperament cannot be taught (Thomson 2004). This is true of all professions and professional situations. Nobody will dispute the fact that medicine, law or engineering can be taught, and yet there are doctors, lawyers and engineers who are talented and others who are not (Hindle 2007). A similar reflection can be applied to entrepreneurship and entrepreneurs. There is no doubt that it is possible to educate people in entrepreneurship; however, as in any discipline, it is impossible to tell whether these professionals will be talented or not, just as it is impossible to guarantee a priori the success of a given course of action. The approach that consists in giving entrepreneurs the knowledge better to manage their process and overcome difficulties during the preparation and start-up phases of the project comes very close to teaching, while the approach that leads entrepreneurs to evolve in their aptitudes, behaviours and personality is more problematic (Fayolle 1997). This analysis is confirmed in Peter Drucker's words quoted by Kuratko (2005: 580): 'It is becoming clear that entrepreneurship, or certain facets of it, can be taught. Business educators and professionals have evolved beyond the myth that entrepreneurs are born not made.'

Defining entrepreneurship teaching

Some recent works we have coordinated (Fayolle and Klandt 2006b; Fayolle 2007a; 2007b), with contributions by some leading international specialists on the questions and issues raised by entrepreneurship teaching, propose several definitions and new perspectives to approach the topic. Fayolle and Klandt (2006b) distinguishes three areas of learning related to mindsets (or culture), behaviours and situations. Hindle (2007) proposes to articulate the definition of entrepreneurship teaching around that of the research object. In this light, if we define the field of entrepreneurship as the 'examination of how, by whom, and with what effects, opportunities to create future goods and services are discovered, evaluated and exploited' (Shane and Venkataraman 2000), then entrepreneurship teaching should be defined as 'knowledge transfer on how, by whom, and with what effects, opportunities to create future goods and services are discovered, evaluated and exploited' (Hindle 2007). This definition echoes the works of some Austrian economists, notably Schumpeter and Kirzner, and March (1991) about the exploration and exploitation dimensions (respectively entrepreneurial and resource management functions), and finally, those of Stevenson and Gumpert (1985). Existing knowledge may as of now be transferred without major difficulties based on this first 'layer', but research based on this definition of the object should produce complementary transferable knowledge.

In the same way we have just presented, other definitions of entrepreneurship teaching could be derived from the other schools of thought presented in chapter 2.

The definitions from the political and economic worlds put forward other dimensions than the research object or teaching domain. They refer particularly to needs and objectives that can be integrated or addressed through teaching and educating initiatives. A recent work conducted by a European group of experts representing all EC member countries proposed a common definition. A consensus was reached regarding the inclusion of two distinct elements:

a broader definition of entrepreneurship education that should include the development of entrepreneurial attitudes and skills as well as personal qualities and should not be directly focused on the creation of new ventures; and

a more specific concept of new venture creation-oriented training (European Commission 2002).

On the basis of this broad definition, it seems relatively simple to establish the political objectives of entrepreneurship education.

The variety of definitions comes from both the diversity of approaches within one same frame of reference (academic for instance), and the coexistence of various spheres which all have interests in the field (academic, political and practical). It is nevertheless important that these different spheres learn how to communicate and understand each other better (Bouchikhi 2003).

In the current context, the root of the problem is more the absence of a precise definition than the significant number of existing definitions. As in the words of Lewin: 'There is nothing as practical as a good definition.'

Entrepreneurship education: a question of objectives, contents and methods

Entrepreneurship education covers a wide variety of audiences, objectives, contents and pedagogical methods. We will not address the variety of audiences here, although it goes without saying that there are significant differences between courses intended for management students or students with a scientific, technical or literary background.[3] Similarly, teaching entrepreneurship to individuals who are strongly committed to their venture creation project is very different in nature from teaching students who have no intention or no concrete project.

In what follows, we will expose and discuss all the diversity of objectives, contents and pedagogical methods that exist in entrepreneurship teaching. We will not present a typology, but recommend readers who are interested in this type of approach to refer to the works of Jean-Pierre Béchard, a Canadian researcher who specialises in both education sciences and entrepreneurship (see Béchard and Grégoire 2005 and 2007).

---

[3] See for instance Brand *et al.* (2007).

Benefits and objectives

To examine in more detail the benefits and objectives of entrepreneurship training, we will first look at the various sources behind the increasing demand for this type of education.

Sources of the demand

The increasing demand for entrepreneurship education and training courses has multiple sources. We will deal with the three main sources here. The first one is governmental: economic growth, job creation(s), renewal of the economic fabric, technological and political change, and innovation, in the post-industrial paradigm, depend largely on company and activity founders. Hence an increasing interest for entrepreneurs and such questions as 'How and where can we foster entrepreneurial vocations? How should we educate and train future entrepreneurs?'

Students represent the second source of demand. Some students wish to create their own company, in the more or less long term, while others wish to acquire professional skills that are indispensable to their careers in companies of any size. Indeed companies are more and more interested in entrepreneurship and increasingly recruit their young executives among individuals with knowledge, attributes and possibly experience that can be useful to the entrepreneurial act.

Small, medium-sized or large companies therefore constitute the third main source. Nowadays their executives seem to favour other managerial skills and behaviours than those which prevailed in earlier years.

Benefits and objectives

Benefits and objectives are two facets of one single phenomenon. We will first see what the main benefits are before presenting the key objectives.

Benefits

Benefits are linked to the fulfilment of individuals, the improvement of entrepreneurial culture and increasing success rate of entrepreneurial actions and initiatives.

Contribution to personal development   Entrepreneurship enables individuals to develop their talents and creativity, to realise their dreams, to acquire more independence and a certain feeling of freedom. Even if acting entrepreneurially is often difficult (many are called but few are chosen), the venture creation attempt in itself implies a learning process which is useful for the individual's personal development. In this light, entrepreneurship education should aim to develop a taste for entrepreneurship (in its broadest sense) and to stimulate a spirit of enterprise (entrepreneurship in a commercial sense, in order to generate profits).

Development of countries' entrepreneurial culture   Entrepreneurship is linked to societal and economic dimensions. While entrepreneurship participates in one's personal development, it is also an engine of economic growth in a market economy. The entrepreneur, as the central element of the entrepreneurial process, is always in search of opportunities to organise and use appropriate resources in order to turn these opportunities into economic or social activities. In so doing, the entrepreneur activates the 'creative destruction' process, to borrow Schumpeter's imagery, and creates an enterprise that produces innovations, which, in turn, will force existing companies either to adapt or to disappear. The varying levels of development and economic growth between countries, or within one country over different periods of time, show that these levels are directly linked to the intensity of the countries' entrepreneurial activity at the time.

Entrepreneurship education therefore constitutes an essential tool in developing a country's entrepreneurial culture. Beyond the development of an entrepreneurial spirit and taste for entrepreneurship, this form of education can also contribute to improving the image and highlighting the role of the entrepreneur in society. This is all the more important since some countries, as is the case in France for instance, are not particularly aware of this culture.

Increasing the chances of new venture survival and success   Entrepreneurship education can be seen as a means to increase the survival and success rate of newly created companies. It constitutes an excellent way to help people discover what enterprise is and the way it works, to develop a systemic approach, to learn how to think of the company in a more global and less compartmentalised perspective and, finally, to go beyond the common binary point of view of civil servant versus employee. Entrepreneurship education also entails proposing new career perspectives for part or all of one's professional life.

Objectives
As I have shown, expectations and benefits are varied, implying a broad variety of objectives too. I group them into three categories.

Raising awareness   Here the objectives are to make students aware of the possibilities, to help them see in new venture creation a possible career option, and to develop in them positive and favourable attitudes towards entrepreneurial situations. Raising students' awareness may be done in different ways, by emphasising what entrepreneurs bring to our economies and societies for example. Entrepreneurs' motivations, values and attitudes should also be presented and discussed, through testimonies or case studies.

Teaching techniques, tools and how to handle situations   Objectives may also be articulated around the transfer and development of knowledge and specific techniques and skills to increase the learners' entrepreneurial potential. In this case the objective is to prepare them better to think, analyse and act as entrepreneurs in specific situations and in various contexts (small and medium-sized businesses). This concerns creation, takeover or intrapreneurship situations. Some of the themes that could be developed cover entry strategies, innovation, creativity or intellectual property.

Supporting project bearers   Here the objective is to work with students or participants who are concretely engaged in venture creation projects. Emphasis is more on facilitating individual learning processes, putting individuals in touch with potential partners, gaining access to and acquiring key resources, and finally coaching.

Contents and structuring dimensions

Drawing on Hindle's findings (2007) and Johannisson's levels of learning (1991), we distinguish three main dimensions that orient and structure the contents of entrepreneurship education.

The professional dimension

The professional dimension of entrepreneurship teaching focuses more specifically on practical knowledge, which can be divided as follows:

Know-what: what one has to do to make decisions and act in any given situation. For example, what one must do to create a technological company, to validate an opportunity, to conduct a market study, etc.

Know-how: how to deal with any given situation. For example, how to check the adequacy between a given project and one's personal profile, taking into account accumulated experience, how to identify the risks, how to deal with them, etc.

Know-who: who are the useful people and which are the useful networks according to the situation. For example, being able to identify the generic players of new venture creation in the sector of biotechnologies, locating those who may be interested in the project, identifying venture capital agencies and business angels who could be interested in a given project, etc.

The theoretical dimension

This dimension deals with knowledge in its broad sense. The contents taught concern the effects and impacts of entrepreneurship, or any other question related to the entrepreneurial phenomenon and process.

The spiritual dimension

Contents in this dimension focus mainly on two aspects:

Know-why: what determines human behaviour and actions, and entrepreneurs' attitudes, values and motivation. What makes entrepreneurs who are ordinary human beings do what they do. Testimonies of entrepreneurs in various situations with varying degrees of performance may, along with debates with teachers and feedback, constitute appropriate and interesting modes of learning for this type of content.

Know-when: when is the right time to go ahead? What is the best situation according to my profile? Is it a good project for me? These are some of the key questions students are confronted with.

Case studies, interviews with experts and professionals generally constitute good ways to address these points.

To conclude on this final dimension, we would like to underline the fact that successful teaching in entrepreneurship should enable individuals to position themselves in space and time as regards the entrepreneurial phenomenon. Positioning oneself in space consists in identifying the entrepreneurial situation(s) consistent with one's profile. Positioning oneself in time implies recognising the moments in one's life when it is both possible and desirable to commit to an entrepreneurial project.

Pedagogical methods

These make up the 'how' of pedagogical issues, which follows the 'why' (objectives) and 'what' (contents). Although some teachers tend to overemphasise pedagogy, it is not an end in itself, but is meant to serve the objectives. As soon as objectives have been set and specific constraints have been identified, methods can be selected.

In the field of entrepreneurship teaching, there is a wide range of pedagogical methods, approaches and modalities (Carrier 2007; Hindle 2007), a selection of which is included below, as an illustration:

elaboration or evaluation of business plans by students
development of a new venture creation project
guidance of young entrepreneurs through support missions to help them in their project
interviews with entrepreneurs
computer simulations
videos and films
behavioural simulations
traditional lectures.

There is no universal pedagogical recipe to teach entrepreneurship. The choice of techniques and modalities depends mainly on the objectives, contents and constraints imposed by the institutional context. 'Learning by doing', which is often praised by teachers in the field, is well suited to some pedagogical situations, while it may be particularly inappropriate in others. The watchword here is to be cautious, and all the more so as little research has been conducted on the assessment of entrepreneurship teaching (Fayolle 2005). It remains to be proved that one pedagogical approach is better than another, which provides interesting challenges for the next few years.

Entrepreneurship education: a question of learning processes

Learning to be entrepreneurial is a matter of learning processes. We have presented the objectives, contents and dimensions of these processes; we will now develop two processes in particular which we deem essential for our field of interest. The first process focuses on how to become an entrepreneur. It is intended for people engaged in an entrepreneurial project who wish to benefit from some support and training. There are numerous programmes of this kind throughout the world. They emphasise the professional dimension, and the core pedagogy is 'learning by doing'. The objective is to train entrepreneurs by guiding them throughout their project's development. The second process is aimed at helping individuals position themselves as regards entrepreneurship and become more enterprising. In this case, the spiritual dimension is put forward and a wider range of pedagogical methods is used. Using entrepreneurs' testimonies can also be key in reaching the objectives, thanks mainly to the role models they can represent.

The learning process to becoming an entrepreneur

This learning process must take into account contexts or situations in which entrepreneurs operate. In this process, learning is accomplished in an emergency mode and constrained by the situation and previous experience. This type of learning produces very personal conceptions of the future management style and the role of manager. The characteristics of this approach must be fully understood and training programmes must be adapted and tailored according to these specific needs.

The idea that, in venture creation training, real-life situations and learning in the field should be preferred is not new. 'Learning by doing' and other inputs by Gibb (1993; 1996) constitute an interesting conceptual basis in this regard. However, the type of learning in question here is real-time learning, in a real situation, with high economic and personal stakes.

Learning is made necessary by the number of incidents, events and problems that occur in the first few years of the company's life.

It happens at an individual level and concerns the key actors (the entrepreneur and members of the team), but it also happens at a collective or organisational level.[4] The actors' learning is an indispensable reaction to the new venture's dynamic of change and is a central element of success (or failure) in start-up situations, as Bruyat underlines it (1993: 352):

Considering learning as one of the key factors of success of a new venture creation is seldom taken into account by researchers. There seem to be two reasons for this. The first one relates to the ideological and paradigmatic foundations of entrepreneurship: considering that entrepreneurs need to learn challenges the assumption that acting entrepreneurially and succeeding are entirely determined by the initial conditions, hence that entrepreneurs possess, right from the start, particular characteristics. The second one relates to the fact that, most of the time, researchers study entrepreneurs who created their company several years before, and so the learning has already been done.

The entrepreneur's learning could therefore consist in finding, increasingly quickly and appropriately, satisfactory answers to the diversity of problems encountered. Insisting on the individual dimension of learning while including the complementary and structuring collective dimension concurs with Bouchikhi's vision (1991). While working on managers' biographies, he identified several common characteristics in company management learning processes that can be adapted to the entrepreneur's learning process. They are presented below.

The learning process is emergent

The intention of entrepreneurs is not to learn how to manage a firm or become a manager, but to learn how to face problems and find the most appropriate solutions, not optimal ones.

An entrepreneur with no previous experience of the role will therefore learn the job of manager by analysing and dealing with a number of issues of a varied nature (human, financial, commercial, technical, legal or competition-related problems, etc.). The diversity of these problems and their recurrence will enable the entrepreneur to develop specific routines and skills, linked to the role of company manager.

---

[4] See for instance the works on collective learning in the sector of innovative technology venture creation by V. de la Ville (1996; 2001).

In this context of emergence, undoubtedly, the entrepreneur's ability to act quickly and to solve permanently the numerous problems encountered is the essential, even critical, quality.

An emergency learning process

During the development of a project, in an entrepreneurial process, it is necessary to move fast, very fast, especially during the start-up phase. In these particular conditions, it is simply impossible for the entrepreneur to identify all the potential solutions, analyse them and select the optimal one. First, there is no time to do this, and second, there are too many problems to solve at once, so the entrepreneur will turn to a cost/benefit or cost/stakes approach to find the most appropriate solution. This way of proceeding is far from the traditional approaches and methods applied, for instance, in large firms or administrations, which rely mostly on procedural rationality.

A trial/error learning process

Learning processes of new entrepreneurs are based on experimentations, therefore trials and errors succeed one another at a fast pace. In this context, failure is an important element of the learning process. Entrepreneurs learn as much from their failures – provided they are not prohibitive – as from their successful attempts.

Learning processes depend on the entrepreneur's mental patterns

The entrepreneur's mental patterns, which are linked to previous experience, condition the learning process and limit its influence. Entrepreneurs engage in a company creation process with their background and cognitive core (Bouchikhi 1991: 59). That is to say that they have a set of mental representations shaped by their professional and personal history. This cognitive core will influence the approaches implemented to face the problems encountered during the start-up phase. By acknowledging this, we also acknowledge the limits of learning. First, large discrepancies between the entrepreneur's cognitive core and the characteristics of situations encountered may generate incompatibilities between the nature of the problems and the nature of the answers proposed. Second, as Bouchikhi highlighted (1991: 61), there is a great risk that 'entrepreneurs will cease to learn when their cognitive system has reached such a degree of closure that it becomes impossible to change the tiniest element, whatever data that may come out of the experience'.

The learning process to becoming an enterprising individual

While the learning process we developed above is highly contextualised (and specific to the context of the entrepreneurial project in development), the process below is its direct opposite (non-specific to a given project).

This learning process is meant to develop individuals' entrepreneurial spirit, to make them more entrepreneurial, first in their minds, then through their actions. Education and training can influence students' perceptions of entrepreneurship, as it enables them to understand better the roles and actions of entrepreneurs, their values, attitudes and motivations.

Numerous authors have attempted to describe this learning process and to assess it in terms of results. As far as I am concerned, I consider that the process that turns an individual who is indifferent to entrepreneurship into an enterprising individual is characterised by two interconnected notions, desirability and feasibility, which are, in Shapero's model, considered as two antecedents of the intention (Shapero 1975; Shapero and Sokol 1982). Self-efficacy and intention models can therefore be used as guides as well as evaluation tools of educative actions.

Developing the intention to go entrepreneurial

Intention is a social psychology construct. A great variety of intention models have been developed and tested by entrepreneurship researchers (Bird 1988; Boyd and Vozikis 1994; Shapero and Sokol 1982; Davidsson 1995; Autio *et al.* 1997; Tkachev and Kolvereid 1999). Most models integrate contributions from the theories of planned behaviour (Ajzen 1991), perceived self-efficacy and social learning (Bandura 1986). The emergence and development of the intention to go entrepreneurial may result from education and/or training programmes. Moreover, Krueger and Carsrud (1993) underline the importance of increasing the use of intention models in the field of education.

I will take intention model as an example and show its usefulness for teachers and educators. I have elaborated an evaluation method based on this model (Fayolle 2005) that draws mainly on the theory of planned behaviour. The central element of this theory is the individual's intention to perform a given behaviour.[5] Intention is the cognitive representation of a person's will to perform a particular behaviour, and is considered to be a good predictor of planned and controllable human behaviour. According to the author of this theory, intention is, above all, the result of three conceptual antecedents that I will now present and apply to business start-up processes.

1 *Attitude towards behaviour*: Intention to create a company is related to the degree of favourable or unfavourable assessment of this behaviour. For the creation intention to emerge, favourable attitudes towards the behaviour must have been formed. Various environments (family, territory, profession, etc.) may impact on these attitudes. Schools, universities and awareness programmes also play an important role.

2 *Perceived social norms*: Intention to create a company depends on how individuals perceive the opinions of the people or social groups who count for them, regarding the envisaged behaviour. What will my family, my friends, my teachers think of my idea of creating a company? Will they think it is a good idea for me, a good career move? These perceived social norms come mainly from the environments mentioned above and are also influenced by societal and cultural variables.

3 *Perceived behavioural control*: Intention to perform the behaviour – here starting up a business – depends on the hindrance or facilitation factors perceived. In an intentional behaviour, individuals reason and ask such questions as: 'Do I have the required skills?', 'Do I master the indispensable management techniques and tools?', 'Have I identified the right networks and will I be able to use them?', etc.

We could summarise the above by saying that for there to be an intention to start up a business, the behaviour must be perceived as both **desirable** (antecedents 1 and 2), and **feasible** (antecedent 3). Training

[5] See Ajzen (1991).

programmes undoubtedly influence both variables and therefore can be designed and evaluated according to their impact on the students' (or other learners') attitudes, perceptions and intentions towards the entrepreneurial behaviour.

Developing self-efficacy

The idea is to develop the self-efficacy of the students and participants engaged in training programmes. The concept of self-efficacy developed by Bandura (1986) and that of perceived behavioural control (Ajzen 1991) are two closely related notions which impact on both the intention and the behaviour.

Perceived behavioural control plays a significant part in the theory of Ajzen. Behavioural achievement depends jointly on motivation (intention) and ability (behavioural control). Perceived behavioural control refers to the perception of control the individual has about how easily or not he can perform the behaviour. It calls upon a specific behavioural context and not upon general predispositions to act. Therefore, people may exhibit a low or a high degree of perceived behavioural control, which can originate from either internal or external factors.

Bandura's perceived self-efficacy (1977; 1982; 1986) is a similar theory that refers to 'people's beliefs about their capabilities to exercise control over their own level of functioning and over events that affect their lives' (Bandura 1991).

From our point of view the distinction between both approaches is that perceived behavioural control is more focused on the ability to perform one particular behaviour. We would like to underline that, according to this definition, self-efficacy is about control over the behaviour itself, not about control over outcomes or events. Incidentally, owing to some mistakes in interpretation, Ajzen (2002) clarified the concept of 'perceived behavioural control', which was redefined as 'perceived control over performance of behaviour'.

Empirical research provides considerable evidence of the distinction between measures of self-efficacy and measures of controllability. Measures of self-efficacy deal with the perceived ease or difficulty in performing the behaviour or confidence in one's ability to perform it. On the other hand, measures of controllability concern the belief of having control over the behaviour, that is to say, to what extent performing the behaviour is up to the actor (Ajzen 2002). Perceived self-efficacy and perceived controllability are conceptually independent from internal or external locus. Each one may reflect beliefs about the presence of both internal and external factors (Ajzen 2002).

Drawing on the review of five studies that examine the factorial structure of perceived behavioural control (Ajzen 2002), it appears that perceived self-efficacy is a key factor in predicting intention (and sometimes behaviour) whereas controllability is not always significant in predicting behaviour. The combination of both factors significantly improves the emergence of intentions but not of behaviour.

The concepts developed above show that, despite a few differences, there are strong similarities between Ajzen's and Bandura's concepts. In all cases, the development of positive perceptions linked to self-efficacy or (perceived) behavioural control impacts both the intention level and the performance of the behaviour itself. The acquisition of operational skills, specific techniques and tools also strongly influences these perceptions, which underlines all the potential of education and training.

PART II

Entrepreneurship and the entrepreneurial system

In the first part of this book, we looked at various perspectives of entrepreneurship, articulated around three broad approaches. Regarding entrepreneurship as a field of research, we examined three currents of thought[1] that we also called 'paradigms' (acknowledging the fact that this term may give rise to discussion and controversy). The first paradigm, within which Shane and Venkataraman's vision (2000) emerged, focuses on the notion of opportunity. The second concerns the creation of an organisation and generated another important vision of entrepreneurship, initiated by and largely based on Gartner's work. Finally, the paradigm value creation is at the heart of our perspective on entrepreneurship. However, in our definition of entrepreneurship we do not discard the concepts of opportunity and organisation creation, as they are essential in supporting our thesis. Beyond the simple presentation of the various threads and theories we refer to, we will also endeavour to give a precise definition and semantic clarification of the concepts mentioned.

In order to introduce this part, we will rely on Gartner's research (1990), in which he attempts to answer the following question: 'What are we talking about when we talk about entrepreneurship?' With this objective in mind, he used a DELPHI method consisting of three rounds. The objective of the study was to gather experts' opinions about the definition of entrepreneurship. The findings, unsurprisingly, showed that there was no consensus on one definition; everybody seemed to have their own. However, some themes stand out, and venture creation is spontaneously recognised as being at the heart of the matter. With a factorial analysis, Gartner brings out eight themes, which account for 67.3 per cent of the variance:

1 entrepreneurship concerns the entrepreneur as an individual with particular characteristics

---

[1] We could also use the term 'dominant research perspectives'.

2 entrepreneurship is linked with innovation in general
3 entrepreneurship implies the creation of an organisation
4 entrepreneurship implies the creation of value
5 some limit the scope of entrepreneurship to the private sector, some
   include the public sector
6 entrepreneurship is of interest to high-growth organisations
7 entrepreneurship implies something unique
8 entrepreneurship concerns owner-managers.

Gartner simply exposes the results of his factorial analysis, which we would like to comment upon. This factorial analysis relies largely on his judgement and interpretation. Gartner proceeded with an analysis of the contents in order to bring out ninety attributes associated with the definition of entrepreneurship. These attributes were evaluated according to Lickert's scale (from 'very important' to 'not important') by forty-one experts, which led to the identification of eight factors or themes. This method, if common for researchers in this field, is not without its flaws, inasmuch as it does not take into account relations of inclusion. We would like to take this analysis a step further.

Concerning the first theme, we think it results from either a tautology ('entrepreneurship is the study of the entrepreneur'), an inaccurate interpretation of the question or a lack of logical thinking.

Themes 2, 4 and 6 seem to overlap: value can be created through an innovation, but innovation must always be a source of value creation, otherwise it is merely an invention. Innovation is a particular case of value creation. Rapid growth can be considered as a degree of value creation. Then theme 5 specifies whether this value creation should only be associated with the private sector.

Theme 7 covers several qualities and behaviours that innovative entrepreneurs or entrepreneurs initiating high-growth-potential businesses must exhibit (creating a competitive advantage, bringing a new way of thinking, identifying a market, etc.), and therefore can be linked to themes 2 and 6.

Theme 8 emphasises the classic definition of the entrepreneur as the individual who assumes all the responsibilities and the risks. Gartner highlights two groups among the experts: those who stress the importance of the entrepreneur's characteristics, and those who focus on the results of the entrepreneur's actions. The creation of an organisation seems to be a point of convergence, although, for some of the experts, all processes of organisation creation belong to the field, while for others, only those based on innovation or with high growth potential should be included.

Entrepreneurship can only be defined by referring first to the entrepreneur, and this is, to a certain extent, what the first theme reveals. In this respect, the entrepreneurial individual represents an essential dimension of our perspective that we develop in chapter 5.

The entrepreneur is someone who starts, initiates and organises something: the creation of value (an innovation, an activity, a business, etc.). Hence value creation is the second essential dimension of our vision of entrepreneurship, and we will present its constituents in detail in chapter 6.

For us, the core of the field is that the entrepreneur can only be defined in relation to an object (value creation), of which he or she is part and parcel, the source or the 'creator', and also the result. We are therefore faced with a subject/object dialogic, which resists all attempts of disjunction, in so far as one cannot exist without the other, at least in the field of entrepreneurship. This dialogic, which we explain in chapter 4, constitutes the foundation and probably the originality of our approach to the field of entrepreneurship.

4 | A *new perspective to understand entrepreneurship*

The perspective presented here largely draws on the works of Bruyat (1993). As already mentioned in the section on new value creation, for this author, 'the scientific object studied in the field of entrepreneurship is the individual/value creation dialogic' (Bruyat 1993: 57). As presented in chapter 2, the dialogic principle proposed by Morin (1989) implies that two or several perspectives are bound into a unity, in a complex manner (complementary, concurrent and opposing) without the duality being lost in the unity. This brings us back to the original postulate and ideology of our field where legitimacy depends on the acceptance or rejection of the idea that the individual is a necessary condition to the creation of value. Far from being a truism or a sophism, I will show that this perspective brings about theoretical and practical consequences. In the first section I develop the individual/new value creation dialogic, and I then discuss the related notion of change, which will bring us to another essential element, that of time. We will conclude this chapter by developing one significant consequence of our definition: the systemic vision of the dialogic pair.

The individual ↔ new value creation (I↔NVC) dialogic

A brief review of Gartner's research, which was presented in the introduction of this second part, shows that among the experts questioned, the author highlighted two groups: one focused on the characteristics of entrepreneurship, while the second put forward the outcome, with new venture creation as a common theme. The subject/object dialogic tends to show that despite a few differences in perspective, there are no real divergences. However, the typological analysis distinguishes two groups.[1] Gartner asked his experts (thirty-four questionnaires

---

[1] Gartner's method inevitably led to a dead-end for the author's topic, as factorial and typological analyses naturally lead to disjunction, whereas it seemed to me

completed) to rate from 1 (not important) to 4 (very important), the eight themes derived from the factorial analysis. The typological study thus performed revealed two groups, the second group focusing on the outcome. Does it mean that the members in this group reject the subject, the entrepreneur, as not relevant to the domain? Results show that this is not the case, as the average for the second group is 2.43, whereas the average for the first group (focused on the individual) is 3.15.

In our approach, the outcome (a new venture creation, for instance) and the subject (the entrepreneur) are inseparable. This has brought us to define the object studied in the field of entrepreneurship as an individual/value creation dialogic.

The dialogic thus defined is not hermetic. In the field of entrepreneurship, it is assumed that the entrepreneur is a necessary condition for the emergence of the outcome. The entrepreneur is not the only necessary condition, however, as the environment, for example, must also tolerate the entrepreneur's activity. Similarly, the outcome is a necessary condition for the entrepreneur to exist and be recognised as such, but it is not sufficient either. New companies (in the legal sense of the word) are sometimes created as subsidiaries of existing organisations, without it being possible to credit a specific individual for the creation of such structures. Differences in point of view may bring researchers to favour one of these two aspects in their approach to entrepreneurship. Nevertheless all the research issues relating to the field should include both dimensions.

Definition of the dialogic

To take our demonstration one step further, we must now make it more operational. The individual/value creation dialogic may be defined as follows (Bruyat 1993: 58):

Individuals are necessary conditions to the creation of value, they determine its production modalities, its amplitude . . . Individuals are the main actors of value creation. The shape that value creation takes, a company for instance, is the individual's 'thing', so we have:

INDIVIDUAL → VALUE CREATION

that Gartner's aim was to determine a definition of the domain on which specialists could agree. Using the DELPHI method, on the other hand, could have led to a conjunctive logic.

Value creation, through the shape it takes, becomes part of the individuals who define themselves in relation to it. It plays a predominant role in the life of the individual (activity, objectives, means, social status, etc.) and is likely to modify his or her characteristics (know-how, values, attitudes, etc.), so we have:

VALUE CREATION → INDIVIDUAL

I wish to make two observations here. First of all, I would like to clarify what I mean by: 'The shape that value creation takes, a company for instance, is the individual's "thing".' For Mintzberg (1991) entrepreneurial strategy implies that individuals impose their vision on a whole organisation. Crozier and Friedberg (1977) distinguish four different sources of power, originating in various sources of uncertainty within the organisation: a specific competence; the control of the relations with the environment; control of communication and information; and authority and rules. Founders of new ventures *ex nihilo*, generally possess these four sources of power. They have, at least at the beginning of the creation process, total control over the project they are trying to set up: their project is their 'thing'. However, in the dialogic, individuals go on to create a new venture (an open system) that will be modified by its environment, and individuals likewise will be transformed by their project. Secondly, I would like to comment upon the changes in individuals resulting from their value creation project. For Martinet (1990), the political and strategic dimensions interact in a conflicting context in which the actors' productions are indissolubly linked to the 'production' of their own identity. However, what also characterises these dimensions is calculation, reason, or at least the rationalisation of the struggles.

A graded approach to the field

This dialogic we have just explained is essential to a real understanding of the situation of a new innovative company manager/founder/owner during the start-up phase. This dialogic can be graded according to the situation. The individual responsible for the creation and development of a new innovative activity within an existing company, who coordinates rather than manages a team, under the watchful supervision of the manager/head of the company, is on the extreme fringe of the field. However, the intrapreneur who, in comparable conditions, initiated the project, managed to convince his superiors and some of his colleagues, and managed to gather the necessary resources, should naturally be considered as an entrepreneur.

The same goes for the ageing company founder and manager who has entrusted a successor with the operational management tasks in order to enjoy semi-retirement and limit his or her role to monitoring and advice. What we suggest here is that the notion of ownership does not seem to be a necessary and sufficient condition to define the entrepreneur. Those who put forward the notion of ownership generally refer to the notion of 'owner-manager'.

The dialogic can only take place if it involves the individual's strategic will and a certain freedom of action. To illustrate this remark, we propose the following case:

A was, until he started his own business, a lorry driver, employed by a food-processing company, located in a rural zone, isolated from urban centres. Of rural origin, married and father of three, he worked for the firm in the morning, while he also kept, with his wife, a farming activity of breeding. His employer, having met serious economic difficulties, decided to sub-contract his transport activity (collection and distribution) and gave his drivers the choice of either starting their own businesses or being made redundant. A accepted, for lack of a better option, the first proposal. He bought the lorry off his former employer, and signed a contract binding him to his only client. In practice, one single thing had changed for him: his income as a lorry driver had become uncertain. (Bruyat 1993)

Is A an entrepreneur with regard to his transport business? He has not taken the initiative, nor defined the modalities of his activity. Besides, if he sees himself as self-employed for his farming activity, he considers himself as an employee (without the benefits any longer) as regards his activity as a driver. Still, he is considered as a business founder, and sometimes, as such, as an entrepreneur. However, from our perspective, he is not an entrepreneur as there is no dialogic individual/value creation, because A is not indispensable to the creation of value.

In the graded forms of the dialogic individual/object, the boundaries of the field are blurred. However, cases in which no identifiable individual can be considered as necessary to the new value creation do not belong to the field we have defined. This vision is consistent with Bird's

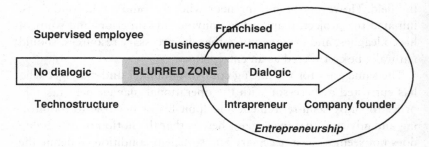

Figure 4.1. Defining the scope of entrepreneurship (source: Bruyat 1993)

affirmation (1988): 'Entrepreneurship is the intentional creation of value through organization, by an individual contributor or a small group of partners'.

Based on these criteria, Figure 4.1 presents a definition of the field of entrepreneurship.

Clarifying the notions of 'individual' and 'value creation'

This representation comes up against two main difficulties: one related to the individual, the other to the creation of value.

First, in some cases, value creation does not originate from one individual, but from a team. When this team is led by an identified leader (without whom nothing would have been possible), then the entrepreneur is, without a doubt, the leader of the team. But should we include a business start-up initiated and managed by a small team (often just two or three) if no leader can be identified? We would tend to say yes. If we assume that nothing would have been possible if one of them had failed to participate, or that any defection could bring the disappearance, or at least a significant modification of the individual/value creation dialogic, then the entrepreneur is the team. The creation of value by a team poses specific problems, and constitutes an interesting research path for the future.

Secondly, another difficulty appears with the notion of value creation. The concept of value is a key concept of economic science. What is value, how does it emerge? For some, like Condillac or the first Austrian marginalists (Menger, for instance), value is generated through exchanges at prices determined by the market. In this light, the field of entrepreneurship concerns only the private sector, non-profit organisations and areas of the public sector that sell products or services on a market. Others, mostly classic economists (John Stuart Mill, Say, Ricardo, Smith) and Marxists, have taken the field of entrepreneurship beyond the trade sector by considering value in relation to production and its costs. The following example should help understand the debate. Should we consider as an entrepreneur the university scholar who, thanks to his or her charisma, personal commitment and energy, has initiated the founding and development of a public research laboratory recognised internationally as a beacon of excellence; even though the resources come exclusively from public funds and not from the sale of services on a market? This situation involves an individual/activity creation dialogic (activity that, in this case, is supposedly new). We can probably speak, at least, of entrepreneurial behaviour, or an entrepreneurial-type phenomenon. As is shown by Gartner's work (1990), the scientific community does not seem opposed to a broader definition of the field in order to include the non-commercial sector. Besides, this position is coherent with the foundations of the field. Considering the entrepreneur as a necessary element of the creation of value implies a vision focused on the supply rather than the demand.

The case of A also illustrates another issue linked to the definition of value. A's business has a turnover, in the respect that it produces value on the transport market. However, nothing seems to have changed with regard to his former situation. We take this opportunity to state that our preoccupation is not to claim that value creation always represents a progress for the community,[2] especially so as value creation can bring about, by a perverse effect, the immediate or subsequent disappearance of an even greater value (external diseconomy).

Change and time: two essential interrelated notions

While the individual/value creation dialogic is pivotal in our definition of entrepreneurship, it is the notion of time which completes it and makes its diversity. Entrepreneurship refers to movement, change, something in the making, creative time.

---

[2] The notion of progress would deserve clarification, but this would take us beyond the scope of this work.

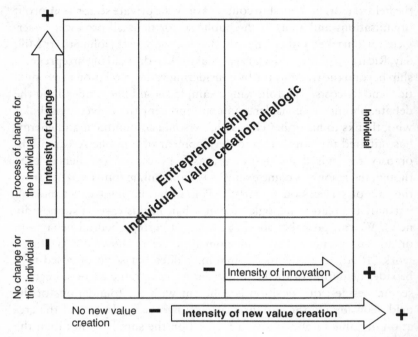

Figure 4.2. The field of entrepreneurship in its broad sense (Bruyat 1993: 63)

The importance of change

According to Bruyat (1993: 62): 'the subject/object dialogic evolves in a creative dynamic of change'. This concurs with Ansoff's contribution (1965) in line with Schumpeter's work, which describes any strategic behaviour entailing significant change, risks and uncertainty as entrepreneurial.

Change concerns both dimensions of the individual/new value creation dialogic. The assessment of change in a given situation must therefore take into account the creation of value from both the individual (or team) perspective and the environment perspective. This implies that, in order to define the entrepreneur, or to assess the entrepreneurial nature of a situation, it is indispensable to consider both notions in a dialogic. Figure 4.2 is a representation of the dialogic. The directions of the arrows correspond respectively to the intensity of change for the individual and the intensity of the value created in a given environment.

For individuals, change concerns aspects of their personal and professional life, and the initial as well as the resulting situation (even though this is an arbitrary definition, as it is really about a continuum). The individual who abandons a top executive career within a large corporation to set up a business will experience a change in social status, and will find himself or herself in a totally different professional situation. Individuals in this case leave a situation in which they are assisted and supported by a whole organisation, to face a new context in which they will need to do numerous things on their own. Entrepreneurs must learn how to perform tasks they are not used to. Individuals who start up businesses in new sectors of activity are also confronted with significant change at a professional level, owing to their social status, new responsibilities, the work itself and the know-how they must master. Yet, there are cases when new value creation does not foster any change for the individual.

The second dimension, that of new value creation, can also vary in intensity. Innovation (product innovation or technological innovation) is a good example of new value creation. Innovation is a particular instance of value creation that fosters a great deal of interest from numerous actors in the field of entrepreneurship. We will come back to the subject of innovation in the final section of this chapter. In this individual/value creation dialogic, rare are the cases when significant value is created without innovation. Yet, while innovation generally involves development and growth potential for the company that exploits it, it does not always generate significant value. To simplify, we can consider that an innovation, whatever its nature, creates (more or less) value (Barreyre and Lentrein 1987). Technological and innovative business start-ups are good examples of new value creation.

There are also cases of value creation where the value created is not really new. It is the case, for instance, of existing activities, which are pursued under different legal and/or organisational forms, without inducing changes in the market or the supply. Additional value can be created through a new organisation or within an existing organisation. This value is more or less significant: there is little in common between the development of a new activity with strong potential and the creation of a seasonal activity for instance.

Lastly, new value creation is compatible with an individual approach (e.g. new venture creation by an individual) or a collective approach (e.g. creation of an activity or a company by an existing organisation).

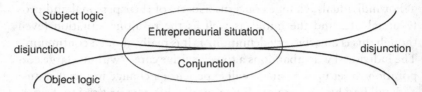

Figure 4.3. A representation of the concept of entrepreneurial situation

Time as an essential dimension of the phenomenon

The individual/value creation dialogic evolves in a dynamic of change, and change requires time. Including change in our definition therefore implies considering the time necessary for the change process to produce lasting results and therefore requires considering the dynamic of change. In other words, an individual cannot be a born entrepreneur. Given our definition, to assert that individuals can be born entrepreneurs one would have to prove that some traits, present in early childhood, are necessary and sufficient conditions to become an entrepreneur. Yet, if being born into a family of entrepreneurs increases the chances of becoming one, not all entrepreneurs were born into such families. Individuals therefore do not start life with entrepreneurial qualities, but some of them will become entrepreneurs, for a more or less significant period of time. Schumpeter, at the time of writing (1934: 54), defended this point of view:

Because being an entrepreneur is not a profession and as a rule not a lasting condition, entrepreneurs do not form a social class in the technical sense, as, for example, landowners or capitalists or workmen do. Of course the entrepreneurial function will lead to certain class positions for successful entrepreneurs and their families.

Including time in our definition leads us to explore another notion: the entrepreneurial situation (Fayolle 2003b), which is shown in Figure 4.3.

An entrepreneurial situation characterises a subject/object dialogic in a dynamic of change. The dialogic exists and is stable: we are in a zone of conjunction. It does not exist, or disappears: we are in a zone of disjunction. This vision translates the strong conviction that the entrepreneurial phenomenon is both temporal and temporary. As we have previously demonstrated, there is no such thing as a born entrepreneur, one becomes an entrepreneur in a specific situation, and one does not remain an entrepreneur for one's whole life. This type of situation may last for three days, three months or three years, but it has a beginning and an end. The concept of entrepreneurial situation helps define and date the phenomenon.

In an entrepreneurial situation, the individual's main behaviours are related to taking initiatives, the changes faced, desired or initiated, the evaluation and acceptance of the risks and their implications. The entrepreneurial situation will also call upon the individual's capacity to identify, appropriate and implement the resources necessary for the realisation of the project, the emergence of the organisation and its day-to-day running.

In an entrepreneurial situation, value creation may take the shape of a company or activity start-up project, the development of a product or innovation, or a company or activity takeover. Another important aspect of the entrepreneurial situation is the project's organisational, social, cultural and economic environment, which is more or less favourable. Two key characteristics of the entrepreneurial situation are, on the one hand, the uncertainty (linked to the intensity of change for the individual and the environment) and on the other hand, the importance of individual and/or collective stakes, which generally raise the awareness of the risks incurred.

Time plays a key role in the entrepreneurial situation, as a factor of evolution and transformation of the project and/or the organisation. A situation can be entrepreneurial at a point in time and may not remain so for very long. Some individual behaviours may weaken, lose intensity and even disappear to leave room for other behaviours, less compatible with the value creation process. It is difficult for individuals and organisations to be constantly subjected to change. Contexts evolve as well as people's perceptions of them. In the perspective we have chosen, for instance, not every business start-up project corresponds to an entrepreneurial situation. For a situation to qualify as entrepreneurial, several conditions must be met: the decision to act must have been made, and a certain degree of irreversibility in the process must be reached, notably at the level of personal commitment, with all the implications in terms of time and money consumption. Similarly, not all organisations resulting from a business start-up project can be considered as entrepreneurial situations. The 'settled' organisation (resulting from a constantly adapting construction) may well, at the end of a given period, fall into routines which are incompatible with the identification and exploitation of new opportunities of value creation.

In the general representation we proposed above, a specific case of individual/value creation dialogic and its evolution over time would be represented by a curve in the figure.

The ideas and concepts developed above are not new. We can mention for example the stages of business growth theory as developed in our field by Churchill (1983), following the works of Steinmetz (1969) and Greiner (1972).

This perspective also relies on two semantic approaches.

The first one concerns the definition Stevenson gives of the entrepreneur, a definition that largely draws on Kirzner's economist argumentation. Entrepreneurs are defined as individuals who are always on the lookout for new opportunities to capture: professional entrepreneurs can express themselves through the creation of a new organisation, or in other contexts (see in particular Stevenson and Jarillo 1990).

The second one is that proposed by Davidsson (1989), who tries to understand and explain the fact that some individuals can be entrepreneurs for life (which he calls 'continued entrepreneurship'). He proposes to distinguish entrepreneurs from SME owners or managers along the following lines (Davidsson 1989: 6):

1 The entrepreneur may or may not be the creator of a new product or process (inventor). The essential thing is that s/he recognizes the value of an idea and actively exploits it.
2 The entrepreneur exploits ideas through forming and/or expanding (a) business firm(s). Thus, s/he is (for some time) a (small) firm manager.
3 The entrepreneur may or may not bear the (full) financial risk. A passive investor is not an entrepreneur, however radical and risky the idea is. Active involvement is required. All small business managers are not entrepreneurs. To qualify as an entrepreneur s/he has to be oriented towards and actively pursue change.

This definition shows again that the ideas we express are not new, neither in the field of entrepreneurship nor in the field of economics. Our work is simply an attempt of articulation and representation in line with an active stream of research.

The key characteristics of the entrepreneurial system

The entrepreneur is the individual (or the small team) who creates new value (an innovation and/or new organisation), and without whom the value would not be created. This new value creation results from a process. At first, we have an individual's project or an entrepreneur in the making (Carter, Gartner and Reynolds 1996). Indeed, can we talk about an entrepreneur when there is only intention, before any value has actually been generated? I do not think so. An individual would not be called a sportsman before achieving some significant results, a writer before writing a book, or a painter before producing a painting. It is therefore preferable to speak about a potential entrepreneur, or an entrepreneur in 'gestation' (Reynolds and Miller 1992). At the beginning of the process, we thus have:

Individual (I) → *new value creation (NVC)*

During the set-up phase, the project gradually puts constraints on its initiator. It becomes part of the individual. Individuals then define themselves, to a great extent, in relation to the project. It takes an important part in their life (activities, objectives, means, social status, etc.); it enables or compels them to learn, to modify their social networks, etc. Individuals build and manage 'something' (company, innovation, etc.) but they are also constrained and shaped by this object they are building. We thus have:

Individual (I) ↔ *new value creation (NVC)*

As seen previously, this subject/object dialogic resists any attempt of disjunctive logic.

The scientific object considered here is therefore the individual (I) ↔ new value creation (NVC) dialogic. By convention, the symbol '↔' implies a dialogic between two entities, and the fact that they form a system (Bruyat 1993). This system cannot be split if it is to be understood, even if, for greater convenience, it may be useful to isolate the components in order to analyse it.

The system interacts with its environment and is embarked on a change process in which time is an essential dimension (Bruyat and

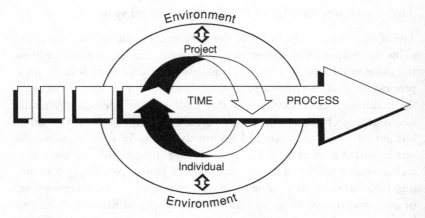

Figure 4.4. The dialogic individual/value creation as an open system

Julien 2001). Moreover, this system is a complex type 9 (or 'transcendental') system in the sense given by Boulding (1956) and Le Moigne (1990). This system is capable of learning and creating; it is also capable of intention and may transform itself. Numerous works (Vesper, 1989; Woo *et al.* 1990) have shown how the strategies, or the projects themselves, may change in a significant manner even in the early stages of the process. As we have previously mentioned, this system is an open system. It interacts with its environment. It is also subjected to it and can be stimulated by the networks and milieus with which it interacts (Johansson, Karlsson and Westin 1994; Conti, Malecki and Oinas 1995). The system also draws resources and opportunities from its environment. To a certain extent, it can choose its environment and adjust it (Marchesnay and Julien 1989). The object studied in the field of entrepreneurship can thus be represented by Figure 4.4, with the individual/new value creation dialogic in its centre.

This representation includes the main dimensions of the phenomenon, such as they have been highlighted by numerous researchers, and particularly Gartner (1985): the individual, the object created (creation and/or innovation), the environment and the process. The main difference lies in considering the individual and the object created as a dialogic, and placing this dialogic at the centre of our representation. In the following chapters, we explore both elements of the dialogic in more detail: the individual and new value creation. This will give us the opportunity to examine more closely the aspects linked to the distant or close environments interacting with the dialogic pair. The notion of process will be the object of our third part. All these elements, like the pieces of a jigsaw puzzle, will be assembled in the modelling project introduced in chapter 9 then developed in the final part of this book.

5 | Individual dimension in the I↔NVC dialogic

The main thesis I wish to develop in this chapter is that there are no born entrepreneurs, but that individuals become entrepreneurs in situations they have desired or are subjected to. They become entrepreneurs through a learning process thanks to which they acquire know-how and personal skills at various levels. Drucker (1985) clearly emphasised this point: 'The entrepreneurial mystique? It's not magic, it's not mysterious, and it has nothing to do with the genes. It's a discipline. And, like any discipline, it can be learned.' Admittedly, not all the aspects of entrepreneurship can be taught and acquired, but, for a number of years now, teachers and professionals have given up the idea of a born entrepreneur (Kuratko 2005). Shapero (1984: 28) confirmed this in one of his contributions:

I have said nothing of the psychology of entrepreneurs. It is not by over-sight. The more I study entrepreneurs, the more I am impressed by the great variety of kinds of people who are entrepreneurs, and the more I find it difficult to be satisfied with simple psychological profiles. Entrepreneurs are not born, they are developed. The great majority of people are capable of being made more entrepreneurial.

Individuals first acknowledge the possibility of the entrepreneurial act (and process) owing to changes in perception and behaviour that in turn lead to the emergence of the entrepreneurial intention. The process evolves through changes in perception that modify what we call the perceived instantaneous strategic configuration of the actor. The individual who undertakes to do something is influenced and guided by cognitive processes that contribute to the emergence of the intention, its development or even the identification of the new value creation opportunity. In our perspective, entrepreneurial individuals are strategic actors with 'bounded rationality' (Simon 1983) and whose behaviours are influenced by their psychological environment.

84

Below I start by presenting briefly the various schools of thought concerned with the entrepreneur, before moving onto our vision of the entrepreneurial individual and of the cognitive processes that influence his or her actions. In the second part of this chapter, I will clarify the concept of perceived instantaneous strategic configuration, real driving force of the entrepreneurial process.

Entrepreneurs and the traditional schools of thought

Of all the studies that have been conducted on entrepreneurs, not one answers the question: 'Are entrepreneurs different from non-entrepreneurs?' It has not been possible so far to identify discriminating personality traits and psychological characteristics. Many representations of the entrepreneur have emerged from these studies. Drawing on Cunningham and Lischeron's work (1991), I am going to present and comment on various perspectives that synthesise the various perceptions of the entrepreneur. These approaches cover a broad range of perceptions of the entrepreneur, from the idea of an exceptional being, different from common mortals, who accomplishes great things, to the ordinary entrepreneur whose skills are no different from those of the average executive or manager.

The great person school of entrepreneurship

This first school of thought sees the entrepreneur as an extra-ordinary being, in the etymological sense. The entrepreneur is seen as an individual endowed with a sixth sense, an intuitive capacity to undertake and accomplish spectacular deeds. If we consider the accelerated development of entrepreneurship teaching everywhere in the world (Fiet 2001a; 2001b; Fayolle 2003a; 2004b; Katz 2003; Kuratko 2005), and the fact that this development somewhat supports the idea that it is possible to learn how to become an entrepreneur, then a current of thought that supports the idea that being an entrepreneur is an innate quality as well as the theory of a sixth sense indispensable to acting entrepreneurially may seem a little contradictory. Yet, if we take a closer look, most economic papers still regularly feature success stories of great entrepreneurs. They generally paint a picture of energy, power and success. Entrepreneurs' biographies frequently underline the instinctive capacity of these uncommon people to recognise opportunities that would be inaccessible to the majority of people as well as their capacity to make the right decisions. This implies that without this innate intuitive faculty, these individuals would be ordinary people (Cunningham and Lischeron 1991; 46). To show the predominance of this perception, at least in the media and popular representations, I would like to quote the following portrait featured in the French press: 'The legend has it that Li-Ka Shing, the owner of Cheung Kong and Hutchinson Whampoa, two holdings representing about one fifth of Hong-Kong's stock exchange, has a sixth sense for good deals.'[1] The example of Li-Ka Shing may not be a very famous one, but literary and academic works (case studies in particular) abound that are devoted to the likes of Francis Bouygues, Steve Jobs, Richard Branson and Bill Gates, and they contribute to perpetuating the myth of the born entrepreneur.

The psychological characteristics school of entrepreneurship

The second school of thought relies on distinct traits and particular psychological characteristics. These can be values (ethics, sense of responsibility, etc.), behaviours (risk-taking, initiative-taking, autonomy, etc.) or needs (autonomy, achievement, recognition, etc.). Numerous works have endeavoured to demonstrate that entrepreneurs have psychological traits that non-entrepreneurs do not possess (McClelland 1961; Brockhaus 1980; Hisrish and O'Brien 1981; Carland *et al.* 1988). These works have highlighted several characteristics or personality traits such as optimism, idiosyncrasy, flexibility, perseverance, tolerance to ambiguity and uncertainty, self-confidence, long-term implication, internal locus of control (the feeling one individual has of being directly in control) and moderate risk-taking. However, the findings have generally been inconclusive and disappointing, and have not made it possible to link one particular trait to entrepreneurial behaviour.

The classical school of entrepreneurship

This school of thought focuses on innovation and the identification of business opportunities. Its main postulate is that the entrepreneur's

---

[1] 'La bonne fortune de Li-Ka Shing', *Le Figaro économie* 17258, cahier 2, 5–6 February 2000.

main role is to innovate and introduce new combinations of production factors in a given environment (Schumpeter 1934). In this respect, creativity and the discovery of opportunities are key components of the entrepreneurial phenomenon (Cunningham and Lischeron 1991: 51). Economists who have worked on innovation (notably Schumpeter and Drucker) or opportunity (notably Mises, Hayek and Kirzner), and specialists in management science who consider the opportunity recognition process as essential (Stevenson and Gumpert 1985; Stevenson and Jarillo 1990; Bygrave and Hofer 1991; Bygrave 1994; Venkataraman 1997; Shane and Venkataraman 2000) are in line with this perspective. Discrepancies remain, however, and may even oppose those who think that innovation, opportunity identification and creativity rely on skills inherent in individuals' innate personalities, and those who are convinced that these aptitudes can be acquired.

The management school of entrepreneurship

The fourth school of thought focuses on the pursuit and realisation of business opportunities. From this point of view, some of the authors previously cited (Stevenson, Gumpert, Bygrave, Hofer, Shane and Venkataraman) also belong to this current of thought, as they more or less agree on this definition of the entrepreneur: 'An entrepreneur is someone who perceives an opportunity and creates an organization to pursue it' (Bygrave 1994: 2). Here, we can also include process-based approaches as well as some journalists' analyses that see in the entrepreneur a coordinator of resources (Casson 1982). Entrepreneurs' training, preparation and appropriation of specific management tools that can enable them to develop a business plan, to evaluate opportunities and to acquire resources in a business start-up context (Bird 1988) appear to be possible and even desirable stages in the entrepreneurial process.

To illustrate how the entrepreneur is perceived in this perspective of research, I propose a brief summary of Stevenson and Gumpert's work (1985). They describe at length entrepreneurs' modes of thinking, behaviours, the questions they have, and the problem-solving techniques they apply. They also explain how entrepreneurs deal with opportunities and resources, how they transform them, and what managerial and organisational choices they make. Stevenson and Gumpert also show that the entrepreneur's behaviour is opposed to that of another managerial figure: the administrator whose main preoccupation is to ensure control of the managed resources and reduce the risks. According to Stevenson and Gumpert, acting entrepreneurially corresponds to a particular approach to management, defined by the creation or identification of an opportunity and its transformation, independently from the directly controlled resources. The entrepreneur's behaviour is different from that of the administrator. Stevenson and Gumpert show that these behaviours differ on five levels at least:

Strategic orientation: whereas the entrepreneur is stimulated by any new business opportunity, the administrator is mainly motivated by the control of resources.

Reactivity: entrepreneurs are extremely quick to react, because they are action oriented, whereas administrators are slower to act as they are mainly preoccupied with reducing risk.

Investment of resources: entrepreneurs use the resources they have gathered in an optimal way, following a multiple-stage process with minimal risk at each stage. Administrators invest all the resources that are necessary to transform the opportunity at once.

Control of resources: occasionally and with a lot of flexibility, entrepreneurs use resources that do not (in most cases) belong to them, whereas the administrator, for reasons of coordination and efficiency, owns the useful resources (human, material, financial, etc.).

Company structure: the entrepreneur sets up horizontal structures with numerous informal networks whereas the administrator relies on a highly hierarchical and more bureaucratic structure.

The leadership school of entrepreneurship

The fifth school proposed by Cunningham and Lischeron focuses on leadership. Entrepreneurs are people who assign objectives and goals and lead their team towards the achievement of these goals. Entrepreneurs are meant to assist their collaborators in their personal development, and, from this point of view, they are more than 'managers': they are also 'leaders of people' (Carsrud, Gaglio and Olm 1986). Cunningham and Lischeron consider that this school of thought merely constitutes the non-technical aspect of the one developed above, and that the entrepreneur must also be a 'people manager' or a 'leader/mentor' who plays a role in the motivation, the management and the leadership of his or her staff. To support this thesis, they quote Kao: 'Thus, the entrepreneur must be a leader, able to define a vision of what is possible, and attract people to rally around that vision and transform it into reality' (Cunningham and Lisheron 1991: 52). This of course influences the education and training of entrepreneurs (Filion 1991; Harrison and Leitch 1994).

The intrapreneurship school of entrepreneurship

This last school of thought introduces the intrapreneur.[2] The intrapreneur is a particular type of entrepreneur who acts within existing organisations. Companies often lack innovation and reactivity potential in a world where everything goes faster all the time and they see intrapreneurship as an answer to this problem. Entrepreneurial behaviours, collective or individual, such as opportunity recognition, initiative-taking and an increased sense of responsibility, can enable companies to innovate, develop and diversify their activities (Burgelman 1983). If we admit that it is possible as well as profitable to develop entrepreneurial behaviour within existing companies, then we implicitly accept the idea that various entrepreneurial contexts and situations may exist. Gartner (1990) and Bruyat (1993) have demonstrated that entrepreneurship could concern both the public and the private sector, and even non-profit organisations. Accepting this vision of intrapreneurship implies accepting the existence of a persistent form of entrepreneurship that would resist, to a certain extent, the ineluctable bureaucratisation process of companies (Bouchikhi 1994).

Cognitive capacities of the entrepreneurial individual

Describing the entrepreneurial individual is no easy task, so it is understandable that several definitions should co-exist. In the scope of this work, I consider that an individual acts entrepreneurially as soon as he or she is engaged in a process that can lead to the creation of a new venture. In a recent review of the literature, Shook *et al.* (2003) proposed

---

[2] For a review of the scientific literature on this subject, see the special issue of *Entrepreneurship Theory and Practice* (23, no. 3, spring 1999) and more particularly the article by Sharma and Chrisman that attemps to define the concept.

a model of the entrepreneurial individual that includes psychological variables (personality traits, beliefs, values, attitudes and needs), personal variables (age, gender, education, experience and abilities) and cognitive variables (knowledge structures, reasoning modes and heuristics). These variables are as many keys that can help us understand the main steps of the entrepreneurial process as formalised by these authors: the entrepreneurial intention, the search for and recognition of an opportunity, the decision to act upon the opportunity, and the activities necessary to exploit the opportunity and start a business.

The psychological attributes and the demographic and sociological variables have been extensively researched in order to demonstrate what is common to all entrepreneurs and may distinguish them from non-entrepreneurs. Up to now, these works have shown that entrepreneurs cannot be considered as different from the rest of the population; they have also highlighted the diversity and contingency of the phenomenon. These findings lead us to consider that an individual engaged in an entrepreneurial process is above all confronted with strategic problem-solving. Accordingly, in the following section we have chosen to focus on the cognitive capacities of this entrepreneurial individual. As pointed out by Shook *et al.* (2003), while knowledge in the fields of psychology and cognition is greatly improving, we are still a long way from an operational model applicable to complex issues such as business start-up processes; we will therefore simply highlight the most important and well-established characteristics. These elements relate to the actor's bounded rationality, strategic intelligence and learning capacity.

The 'bounded rationality' of the entrepreneurial individual

The rationality of an individual engaged in a business start-up process or any other entrepreneurial process is bounded, which does not imply that he or she is irrational or has surrendered all rationality. Simon's concept of bounded rationality can be summarised as follows: in its simplest form, bounded rationality is a theory of 'how to live' in an infinite world while having at one's disposal only limited computation means. These means are related not to the complexity of the real world, but to the local environment and what one can do with it. Integrating this concept of bounded rationality amounts to integrating uncertainty and randomness, the costs and time involved in collecting and processing the information, and the limited knowledge of the entrepreneur and those who support and advise him or her (Bruyat 1993). We better understand, therefore, the reasons why the business start-up process is considered rational. It should be all the more rational if the various steps in the creation and set-up process of the company are rigorously planned and detailed in a business plan. Rationality is therefore associated with the type of management techniques developed for the benefit of large companies and taught in management schools.

Acknowledging the importance of the individual's bounded rationality does not imply that all individuals in all circumstances will experience the same limitations. The emotional charge of the act of venture creation is also of importance. This is particularly well illustrated by Sfez's response (1986: 701) to Simon: 'No, there is not one "human thinking pattern" but several within each individual. This depends on circumstances, emotions, goals and beliefs, all inseparable from my active intelligence, that is to say ready to be called upon. To me, the "how" is definitely inseparable from the "why".' Entrepreneurs challenge their personal image, as regards both their environment and themselves. Entrepreneurial individuals will sometimes refuse to take advice from a consultant to prove that they are capable of dealing with the most difficult situations without help. Some will simply refuse any form of institutional aid. Others will try to prove that their project is viable despite the negative opinions of advisers and investors. All this goes to show that entrepreneurial projects are not only of an economic nature, and that the actors' behaviours follow a contingent rationality which leads them to choose what is best for them, or more to the point, what they think is best (Bruyat 1993).

The strategic intelligence of the entrepreneurial individual

Looking for and collecting information, deliberating and deciding/acting are processes which do not fit within defined and coherent frames. The factors that influence these sequences can evolve and the objectives of entrepreneurial individuals are often blurred, multiple and contradictory (Bruyat 1993). Hence the decisions that are taken are probably not optimal or ultimately the best, but, more modestly, they at least appear to be satisfactory compromises that suit, temporarily, the actor.

The entrepreneurial individual's strategic intelligence is action-oriented. He or she must demonstrate a number of skills that may be acquired and developed through concrete situations. Morin (1986) attempted to define strategic intelligence, and we have listed some of his ideas below to illustrate our point of view:

> the capacity to prioritise what is essential and what is secondary, to select the significant and eliminate the irrelevant or superfluous
>
> the capacity to carry out circular analysis of the means to an end and the adequacy of these means in reaching these ends, in other terms the ability to conceptualise retroaction in means-to-an-end loops
>
> the capacity to combine the simplification of a problem (breaking it down into a simple exposition of facts) without losing sight of its complexity (taking into account diversities, interferences, uncertainties)
>
> the ability to reconsider one's perception and preconception of a given situation
>
> the ability to take advantage of serendipity to make discoveries, and the ability to show perspicacity in unexpected situations
>
> the capacity to reconstruct a global configuration, event or phenomenon from fragmented traces or clues
>
> the ability to imagine the future and develop possible scenarios integrating various possibilities and integrating uncertainty and unpredictability
>
> the capacity to enrich, develop and modify one's strategy according to information received and experience acquired
>
> the ability to recognise novelty without attempting to reduce it to established representations and the capacity to situate this novelty in relation to that which is already known
>
> the capacity to recognise the possible and acknowledge the impossible, and elaborate scenarios which combine both the unavoidable and the desirable.

The kind of intelligence described here is not easily measurable, but it seems clear that, as is the case with bounded rationality, each entrepreneurial individual has his or her own strategic intelligence necessary to find satisfactory solutions.

Learning capacities of the entrepreneurial individual

The concepts of bounded rationality and strategic intelligence imply that of knowledge acquisition. Engaged in a process that may take several years, entrepreneurial individuals will have to acquire knowledge and develop their ability to learn in the field and through action. They will be changed by this learning experience that can take various shapes, as Graham *et al.* underline it (1985: 500):

Some educators have provided a third definition of the venture development problem. Until recently entrepreneurs were assumed to be a special breed of people with an almost in-built natural ability to develop ventures. The myth of the naturally knowledgeable entrepreneur has now given way to our understanding that entrepreneurs learn like the rest of us. Entrepreneurs can learn not only from their mistakes and from informal mentors but also they are susceptible to learning by reading and through formal education designed for their purposes.

This stresses how important it is to consider entrepreneurship as a teaching field (as developed in our third chapter).

Fits and gaps in the entrepreneurial system

Entrepreneurs act on the instant, according to their own personal characteristics, although they are bearers of memory (history) and projects (projected future); decisions are made and courses of action decided on the instant. At various points in time, entrepreneurial individuals have different perceptions of their environment, capacities, aspirations and goals. They can elaborate more or less definite and formalised projects that, to succeed, must not be too far removed from the coherence zone of their perceived instantaneous strategic configuration. Adapted by Bruyat (1993), the concept of instantaneous strategic configuration relies on the conjunctive and complementary notions of contingence and coherence. This concept draws on the traditional strategic management approach as well as modelling works on decision-making behaviours and is supported by numerous works in multiple streams of research by such authors as Ansoff, Mintzberg, Simon and Weick (for the American authors) or Le Moigne and Morin (for the French).

During the process that sees the realisation (or abortion) of a business start-up project, its success, its development or its relative failure,

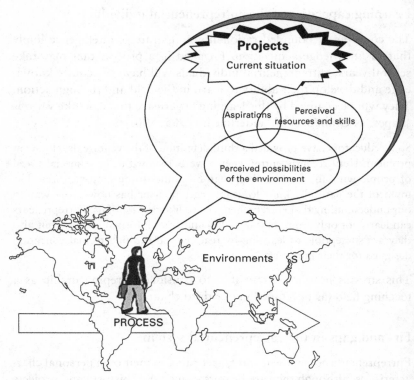

Figure 5.1. A synchronic representation of the system (Bruyat 1993: 197)

the strategic actor (the entrepreneur) will find information/decide/act according to his or her strategic intelligence and cognitive style, and perceptions of his or her instantaneous strategic configuration. The entrepreneurial individual's cognitive style and representations are directly linked to time and an active and evolving environment.

The perceived instantaneous strategic configuration and the project are permanent but evolving structures of the system. Coherences and incoherencies resulting from interrelations and interactions between these structures will develop and disappear. Figure 5.1 shows a representation of this system.

The following section clarifies the concept of perceived instantaneous strategic configuration and addresses some related issues.

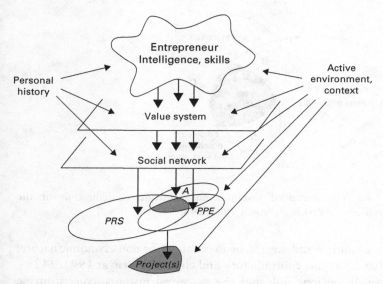

Figure 5.2. The perceived instantaneous strategic configuration and the importance of history and context (Bruyat 1993: 243)

The entrepreneur's perceived instantaneous strategic configuration

The entrepreneurial individual's behaviour depends on his or her perceived instantaneous strategic configuration. Entrepreneurial actors look for coherence and harmony (congruence or fit) between their aspirations, the state of the environment – present and future – and their capacities, skills and internal resources. Their perceived instantaneous strategic configuration is their decision/action matrix. Entrepreneurial individuals deal with every situation with their own strategic intelligence and cognitive style. Their decisions and actions are also influenced by their value system and social networks, developed over time and influenced by their active environment. These aspects (value system, social network) can be seen as information 'filters' and may evolve during the entrepreneurial process. Thus, the perceived instantaneous strategic configuration may be represented as in Figure 5.2.

The behaviour of entrepreneurial individuals is intentional: they have aspirations and are capable of formulating goals and objectives. These

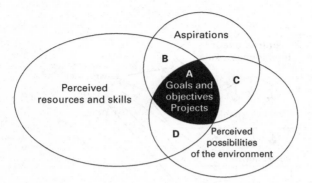

Figure 5.3. The perceived instantaneous strategic configuration of the entrepreneurial individual (Bruyat 1993: 248)

goals are multiple and diverse, of an economic or non-economic nature; they may be vague, contradictory and changing (Bruyat 1993: 248).

Three dimensions influence the perceived instantaneous strategic configuration: the individual's aspirations, his or her perceived resources and skills, and perceived possibilities of the environment. These perceptions apply to both the present and the future. The schematic representation in Figure 5.3 highlights the three dimensions and the way they overlap.

Several zones arise from the intersection of the three areas.

Zone A is the most interesting one. It corresponds to the actions perceived by the individual as both desirable and possible. It is the zone of coherence in which opportunities are recognised and projects developed, then implemented through goals and objectives. In this zone, individuals consider they have the means and skills to develop projects with a good chance of succeeding; they have a positive perception of their efficacy.

Zone B corresponds to actions and projects coherent with individuals' aspirations and their resources and skills, but that do not seem to be compatible with the environment.

Zone C corresponds to desired and possible actions as regards the environment, but for which the individual does not believe he or she has the necessary resources and skills and does not see the means to acquire them at the given time.

Zone D is a zone of possible actions that do not correspond, at least for the time being, to the aspirations of the entrepreneurial individual.

Implications of the perceived instantaneous strategic configuration

Our vision of entrepreneurial individuals, their cognitive capacities, and the importance of their aspirations and personal history leads us to draw the following implications.

The notion of opportunity is contingent

A particular project can be in the coherence zone of an entrepreneurial individual but far removed from the coherence zone of another. An opportunity can be perceived (built) and have value (the project can be attempted and has chances of success) only if it corresponds to the coherence zone of the individual. There is therefore no opportunity in the absolute but opportunity is contingent to the entrepreneurial individual's perceived instantaneous strategic configuration.

Current situation and coherence zone

An individual's current situation may happen to be within the coherence zone of his or her perceived instantaneous strategic configuration: individuals can be employed in positions that correspond to their aspirations and have interesting perspectives open to them. However, there are cases when the current situation may be outside this zone: the position held may be far removed from the individual's aspirations, or even threatened.

Absence or abundance of projects

Perceived instantaneous strategic configurations vary, depending on the individuals, their histories, and the contexts in which they evolve. Some perceived instantaneous strategic configurations are more prolific than others and projects in the coherence zone may be conflicting with a current satisfactory situation. Conversely, individuals may be at a dead end and find it very difficult to formulate projects that are coherent with their perceived instantaneous strategic configuration. Lastly, in the coherence zone of a given individual, there may be only one project corresponding to the continuation or the development of his or her current situation.

Perceptions are not reality

In any change process, the perceptions individuals have of their perceived instantaneous strategic configuration may be different from reality. Setting up a business is a complex process that involves aspects that the first-time entrepreneur, by definition inexperienced, may not grasp. This lack of knowledge is sometimes the motivation for acting: in many cases, individuals would not have committed themselves to the project if they had had all the information to start with. Entrepreneurs discover the various difficulties as they go along, progressively, and try to overcome them, which will sometimes lead them to make significant changes to the project, or even give it up.

Evolution of the perceived instantaneous strategic configuration and the project

During the process, the entrepreneurial individual's perceived instantaneous strategic configuration and his or her project are subjected to significant modifications. These can be intentional: individuals may reflect upon their perceived instantaneous strategic configuration in relation to their project, look for information concerning the market and the competition, acquire new skills, expand their social networks, or modify the project in order to minimise risks and maximise its value. However, modifications can also be unplanned: the individual may be compelled to give up pursuing some of his or her initial goals, partnership opportunities may appear on the way, or a competitor may release a similar product on the market. Entrepreneurial individuals are constrained by their perceived instantaneous strategic configuration, but they have the possibility to act in order to alter it.

6 | *New value creation dimension in the I↔NVC dialogic*

In chapter 2, I gave a definition of 'new value creation', and also suggested that a new original current of thought was emerging around this notion in the field of entrepreneurship.

It is difficult to dissociate the notions of new value creation from innovation. Successful innovation, be it technical, commercial or organisational, is always a source of new value, but innovation is not the only source of new value creation. For example, human skills or specific resources that are applied to operations in association with key factors of success can lead to new value creation (Deeds *et al.* 1998). These skills and resources may, for example, ensure a better control of the key factors, thus entailing a new competitive advantage.

New value creation is therefore linked to innovation and the creation of sustainable competitive advantage. The notion of value is linked to that of opportunity. We cannot speak about opportunities of business creation, recovery or growth without referring to the creation of new value that these opportunities bring about. We use the term 'value', here, as in 'useful value for the final customer', as opposed to financial value for the entrepreneur or the shareholders. In our field of research, new value creation appears to be a pivotal notion that interlinks various other key notions. In this chapter, we will first develop the concept of innovation from this new value creation perspective. We will then show that the concept of value makes it possible to classify entrepreneurial projects, and that being able to understand the differences between the various types of projects improves the relevance of project piloting. Finally, we will come back to the notion of the project itself and its capacity to change throughout the whole process under the influence of the dialogic.

Innovation and new value creation

The concept of innovation extends far beyond the scope of entrepreneurship. Numerous disciplines are interested in innovation. *The New*

Shorter Oxford English Dictionary[1] gives the following definition of innovation: '1. The action of innovating, the introduction of a new thing, the alteration of something established; . . . The introduction of a new product on to the market. 2. A result or product of innovating; a thing newly introduced; a change made in something; a new practice, method, etc.' In our field, Drucker (1985: 35) claimed: 'Innovation is the specific instrument of entrepreneurship' – a vision confirmed by Carland *et al.*, for whom innovation is what distinguishes entrepreneurs from managers. We also find this perspective with francophone authors:

Innovation constitutes the foundation of entrepreneurship, as entrepreneurship implies new ideas in order to propose or produce new goods or services, or even to reorganise firms. Innovation means creating a different company to what was known before, it means discovering or transforming a product, proposing a new way of producing, distributing or selling. (Julien and Marchesnay 1996: 35)

Now that I have defined the concept of innovation in relation with the field of entrepreneurship, I will develop Schumpeter's founding ideas and show that they still influence contemporary authors. We will then examine how different types of innovation affect the intensity of the new value created.

A perspective inherited from Schumpeter

Schumpeter's definition of innovation is rather wide ranging: 'Any attempt at doing things differently in the economic field should be considered as an innovation likely to provide a firm with a temporary advantage, and to generate profits' (Schumpeter 1939: 84). There are five main types of innovation that can generate profits, and these five types cover a wide range of activities. Indeed, in his historical, social and economic vision of the evolution of the capitalist system, Schumpeter (1934) considers that firms are instruments for the execution of new combinations that translate into what he calls 'exploitations'. These new combinations or realisations correspond to five well-known types of innovation: new consumer products (goods, services or exploitation of new sources of raw material), new methods of

---

[1] *The New Shorter Oxford English Dictionary*, ed. Lesley Brown, 1st edn 1933, this edn 1993, Oxford: Oxford University Press.

production or transport, new markets, new sources of supply and new types of industrial organisations. The execution of new combinations is the entrepreneur's deed, an entrepreneur who is not always the manager. The entrepreneur is not necessarily the owner either, fully or partly, of the exploitation or means implemented. The notion of risk depends on whether or not entrepreneurs are using their own money (in which case they combine the roles of entrepreneur and capitalist). If entrepreneurs are the first to carry out the new combination, the profits generated are increased (Schumpeter 1934). According to this theory, being an entrepreneur is a temporary function. Indeed, over time, the exploitation of what has been created may take over at the expense of the execution of new combinations. Another pivotal aspect of Schumpeter's theory is that carrying out new combinations initiates change by destroying the existing structures made obsolete by the contribution of a novelty.

Drucker, atypical author and emblematic figure of management, is one of the main supporters of this perspective.[2] According to him, innovating is the specific role of the entrepreneur (Drucker 1985). He even considers innovation as a necessary condition for new value creation.

Julien and Marchesnay (1996) largely concur with Drucker's position. They claim that technological as well as organisational innovations can be radical, systematic, sporadic or global. In other words, innovation can be radical (breakthrough) or incremental.

The idea that innovation is a source of economic development goes beyond the simple introduction of innovative products and services on the market by an established firm. It highlights the need to be entrepreneurial. We can thus consider entrepreneurship as a stage in a broader process, as Martin (1994: 30) suggests: 'Commercially successful innovations require the synthesis of scientific, engineering, entrepreneurial, and managerial skills, combined with a social need and a supportive socio-political environment, if a sustained chain reaction is to be achieved.' The author considers entrepreneurship as the *sine qua non* condition to exploit innovations, through *ex nihilo* business start-ups (which he emphasises), partnership between established firms, spin-offs, intrapreneurship or takeovers (external growth). Figure 6.1 illustrates his thesis.

---

[2] In 1953, Peter Drucker developed an Entrepreneurship and Innovation course at New York University.

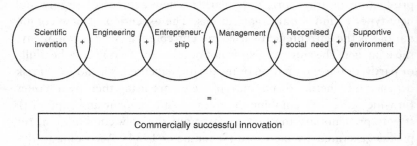

Figure 6.1. The innovation chain equation (Martin 1994)

The globalisation of markets and the role played by technology in hypercompetition (cf. D'Aveni 1994) contribute to making innovation a key factor of companies' competitiveness, and entrepreneurship a crucial lever in the creation of new value.

Multiple forms of innovation

An innovative initiative may draw on something existing and endeavour to explore all the possibilities for its improvement. In this respect, it is always possible to do better, faster, cheaper, stronger, easier to maintain or simply differently.

Innovation can be in the continuity of a product or process: the improvement is incremental and concerns the profit margin; or it may introduce a breakthrough, in which case it is a radical innovation.

From the point of view of the individual or the organisation, innovation can be the result of an initiative or be perceived as a necessity, an obligation. Incidentally, in companies, people may be referred to as 'first movers' or 'leaders' as opposed to 'followers'.

Like strategies, innovations may be predetermined and planned or, on the contrary, emergent and opportune.

Innovation can significantly transform an organisation or a process or only affect them slightly. Global or total innovation is opposed to local or partial innovation. In the same line of thought, the fields and sectors affected by innovation are multiple. If we take the example of the French pantheon of innovation, we will find technological innovations such as Concorde or Ariane as well as social innovations, like paid leave and the 35-hour week. In the corporate world, innovations can concern the organisation (autonomous groups, quality circles,

Table 6.1. *Typology of the various types of innovation*

Innovation type	Characteristics
Breakthrough innovation (radical)	Introduction of a totally new product, process or service on the market, by an entrepreneur or an intrapreneur.
Imitation of a breakthrough innovation	Adoption of a breakthrough innovation by another entrepreneur or intrapreneur who is behaving as a follower.
Modification of a breakthrough innovation	Adoption and more or less significant modification of a breakthrough innovation by another entrepreneur or intrapreneur.
Incremental innovation	Innovation that creates new value, implemented on an existing product, process or service by an entrepreneur or an intrapreneur.
Imitation of an incremental innovation	Adoption of an incremental innovation by another entrepreneur or intrapreneur who is behaving as a follower.
Modification of an incremental innovation	Adoption and more or less significant modification of an incremental innovation by another entrepreneur or intrapreneur.

Source: Risker 1998.

just-in-time systems, total quality systems, etc.), products (computers, automobile electronics, etc.), processes (manufacturing lines, automation, etc.) and finally, the distribution and logistics (mail order, internet and information systems, etc.).

In Table 6.1 I have combined various levels of innovation intensity (breakthrough versus incremental) with types of entrepreneurial behaviour (leader versus follower), to propose a typology of the various types of innovation in which can be found some highly contrasted situations. Breakthrough innovation is relatively rare. It implies that an entrepreneur introduces a product, service or process that did not previously exist on the market. For example, the founder of the French company Technomed developed the lithotripter (a device that relies on shock wave technology used in the treatment of kidney stones), and thus introduced a breakthrough innovation in the health sector. The

American company 3M did something comparable when it introduced Post-it notes.

Entrepreneurs who attempt to copy radical innovations are more common. They may strictly imitate the product, but this does not represent the majority of cases, as breakthrough innovations are protected. Generally, these entrepreneurs will bring some modifications to the initial product in trying to increase its attractiveness (and its value creation potential) while bypassing the protection measures. This is how, for example, some entrepreneurs have followed in the tracks of Technomed and 3M to propose competitive products.

Incremental innovations are, by far, the most common. Small adaptations and modifications made on existing products, services or processes do not involve major difficulties for someone who knows how to observe and analyse behaviours, habits, needs or operating modes. These changes may prove to be extremely positive and improve greatly the adequacy between the supply and the demand that must be met. For example, in the sector of dry-cleaning, a few years ago, a French entrepreneur proposed a new service to a segment of his clientele: it consisted in collecting the laundry at home, cleaning it and delivering it back home, all within twenty-four hours. Compared to the existing service, a reduced lead-time was thus introduced, along with an additional service (home collection and delivery) saving the customer the trouble of having to go anywhere. For some people such as busy executives and managers who are highly committed to their professional activities and have sufficient funds, the offer undeniably generated new value. This service has since been reproduced by several entrepreneurs who have contributed to making it available in several major French cities.

The typology presented above shows that to innovate and create new value, entrepreneurs may adopt various strategies, which call upon various qualities, skills and resources. These strategies may rely on scientific and technological knowledge associated with great curiosity; others may call upon more ordinary qualities, such as a good sense of observation, analogy and analysis, as well as a great capacity for listening to signals emitted by the environment.

New value creation and types of entrepreneurial projects

Not all projects have the same value potential or require the same amount of resources. There is often a correlation between the value creation potential and the amount/nature of the resources required.

These resources are necessary to develop models, prototypes and products, to apply for patents and extend legal protection, and to invest in research and development and production means. The value creation potential is variable as is the level of risk. At the end of this section, four types of entrepreneurial projects are proposed/presented, based on two key variables: new value and risk.

New value and risk potential

The value of a given project depends on its competitive advantages and how they are exploited. Measuring the potential value of a project can be done by analysing its development potential, analysis that should be supported by market and competition studies in order to demonstrate the fit between the product and the market.

Entrepreneurs cannot better their competitors on every link of the value chain (Porter 1985). They must therefore make choices regarding the competitive advantages they intend to (or can) develop. These advantages may be the following:

lower costs
better quality of the product or service
improvement of the distribution system
geographical focus or strategic location
strategic alliance or partnership with a client, opinion leader or
    supplier
introduction of a complementary service.

These competitive advantages must be valuable to the customer and sustainable. Incidentally, the higher the value, the higher the risk of being copied; it is therefore important to consider adequate protection means at an early stage. Competitive advantage may be improved for the whole activity sector or only the segments that are particularly attractive for the entrepreneur, and of course, having a competitive advantage does not dispense the business from competing on other levels.

To develop competitive advantage, the entrepreneur must absolutely:

acquire a good knowledge of the competition in his or her given
    sector; in most cases, competitive forces can be analysed with
    Porter's model (1981)

develop internal abilities based on his or her assets; these capacities can be developed around physical resources (financial resources, equipment, brand, location) and/or around human and organisational capital.

One must never forget that competitive advantages are only temporary sources of income and that, given the dynamic nature of competition, the research and creation of competitive advantages is perpetually ongoing.

We have examined the value creation potential of projects, and we will now turn our attention to the related risks. Risks are often directly linked to the means required for an entrepreneurial project. Of course, uncertainty and the issue of minimal performance (which is hard to achieve quickly for a newcomer) also constitute factors of risk. However, most risks often amount to the financial resources that are required. Elements that must be taken into account are:

the development of the products and services on offer

patenting (if necessary)

the size of the project, in terms of employment, investment, production equipment, R&D and logistics

the time necessary to overcome initial difficulties and reach breakeven point

costs related to experimentation and mistakes

costs related to learning the job of entrepreneur

hidden costs related to recruitment and personnel training, acquisition of new clients and the development of the management system.

Any mistakes or adjustments will have financial repercussions. All these elements must be assessed in relation to the potential entrepreneur and his or her environment. The risks depend on the type of project of course, but also on the way it is elaborated and pursued.

The adequacy individual/project (Fayolle 2004b) and the search for coherence at all levels constitute strategic approaches which will increase the project value and/or reduce the risks involved. Coherence may be improved at the personal level (preferences, know-how, social networks, resources, etc.), at the level of the process (available time, degree of urgency in the implementation, etc.), and at that of the environment (characteristics of the activity sector, availability and

Table 6.2. *A project typology*

High value		
HIGH POTENTIAL	'BIG GAMBLE'	
LOW POTENTIAL	'DEAD-END'	
		High risks

accessibility of the necessary resources, aid and support structures, opportunities and threats, etc.).

Throughout the project development process, individuals will therefore need to work on the global coherence and acquire the necessary knowledge, set up new partnerships, constitute a team, increase organisational slack, convince and get new favourable players involved.

A project typology: from 'big gamble' to 'dead-end'

I have identified four types of projects according to the value and risk variables (presented in Table 6.2).

Low development potential projects imply low risk as well as low value. Entrepreneurs try to create a self-employment structure and/or manage a small team. Their management style is centralised and often informal. It is essential for the entrepreneur to know the job and the activity sector well. Management is simple; it relies on common sense and pragmatism. The entrepreneur must work very hard. The business may start small, and the entrepreneur should be careful with structure expenses and investments. This type of project may also concern technological businesses.

The high development potential project involves low risk and offers a high value potential. Entrepreneurs in this configuration are innovative and ambitious; they do not necessarily have a lot of capital; they know how to delegate and motivate a team. These types of entrepreneurs are rather open-minded, know how to develop social networks, and are willing to open their capital. In this case, it is also possible to start small in a garage, but it is crucial to move fast and close the strategic window to get effective protection. It is essential to sell fast, to get a large share of the market and to build a strong relationship with customers.

Environment may be supportive, notably the venture capital environment, especially if it is used to this type of project.

The 'big gamble' types of projects imply both high risks and high value potential. These are the most delicate projects and the most complex to develop. Entrepreneurs in this configuration are generally talented professionals, recognised as such by relevant environments. They are capable of raising large amounts of capital and benefit from developed social networks. They are likely to recruit and motivate a team of highly skilled collaborators. In the development process, planning is crucial and should leave no room for mistakes. There are often problems in finalising the project, and capitalisation is a critical issue. It is especially important not to start the activity in a sub-capitalisation situation. The environment is generally favourable as soon as the financial system is accustomed to this type of project.

The 'dead-end' types of projects are characterised by high risk and low value potential. In these cases, entrepreneurs have social or political motivations, or no better alternative. They are talented professionals, recognised by the relevant environment, with developed social networks. Any mistakes in this configuration are unforgiving, and rigorous planning is essential. Problems of insufficient capitalisation may also appear, with the risk of important financial losses. The environment may be interventionist; it is very often a condition for the resources provided.

From initial idea to new value creation

In some cases, the wish to create a company or become an entrepreneur appears first; the entrepreneurial individual subsequently looks for an idea, before engaging further into the process if it seems to correspond to his or her aspirations. Conversely, the idea to create may only be secondary, resulting from the development of a project and constraints linked to an unsatisfactory situation. Thus, at the beginning of the process, the entrepreneur may have a rather precise idea of his or her project or a fairly vague idea of it.

The initial idea is personal and may occur in various circumstances. It may be stimulated or impelled, or come naturally. The idea may or may not find its place in a given environment; it may also 'germinate' and create more or less value.

Opportunity is linked to a given environment or a market. To a certain extent, an opportunity amounts to an environmentally acceptable or accepted idea. To translate the initial idea into a business start-up or takeover opportunity can be a bumpy ride, a process that happens progressively as the project is elaborated and developed. We may even make the following hypothesis: the more defined the project is at the beginning of the process, the less uncertainty there is, and conversely, a project originating from a vision involves great uncertainty, which the entrepreneurial process will try to reduce.

Emerging ideas, opportunities and projects, which are evaluated and transformed during the process, are key concepts in our approach, as these elements constitute the raw materials that will produce new value at the end of the process. I develop these notions in the following sections.

Role and origin of ideas in the entrepreneurial process

In this context, the first myth I would like to dispel is that of the 'brilliant idea' or the 'best idea ever'. Observations I have made in the past twenty years on numerous cases of business creation have shown that:

> A good idea is nothing more than a tool in the hands of an individual or a team. The main ingredient is not the idea, but the work that can be done with this idea.
>
> Good ideas do not always make good opportunities, this depends on the individual, available time and resources, and probably chance.

I present two examples to illustrate this thesis. The first example is concerned with a fundamentally brilliant idea, which came at a suitable time when it was developed. It was about designing, producing and distributing an automatic postcard vending machine, intended for postcard retailers in France and meant to greatly reduce postcard theft. However, the product never came out and the company set up to produce it filed for bankruptcy a year after its creation. This is typically what a dead-end type of project is: a lot of risk, and little value created for customers and users. The problems and mistakes that were made in terms of product design and technical development as well as in terms of marketing and positioning swallowed up the initial capital.

Our second example is that of a seemingly trivial idea, considered by many experts as a very bad idea. A young French university graduate had it in mind to set up a project to do with wine and oenology. A significant part of the activity was to trade in a particularly competitive and traditional sector. Undeniably, the project had low development potential with rather unfavourable prospects. Yet, ten years after the creation of this activity, the company is still there, settled in its market, with a turnover of over €2M, and employing several people. This goes to show just how relative the genius of an idea is, and how important is the quality of the work that must be done throughout the process.

Ideas can take various channels to feed a business start-up process. However, two non-mutually exclusive channels can be put forward that are linked to preliminary decisions. Individuals can scan the environment for ideas and/or make sure that they pick up emerging ideas. Systematic scanning can imply being part of the right networks and socialising with the appropriate players. An individual interested in company takeovers, for instance, will try to be in contact with professional organisations, bankers, judicial administrators, corporate raiders associations, etc. A person intending to set up a business may participate in start-up projects, assist entrepreneurs in start-up situations, or choose to work first as an employee in the professional sectors involved in this type of activity. Even while working in a company, it may be possible to look out for expansion opportunities or to look for the companies that do expand. Licence of franchise acquisition may be another way to find ideas.

Capturing opportunities implies the existence, acquisition and development of scanning and observation skills. Ideas come naturally to those who know how to observe and question their surroundings, who pay attention to needs that are not yet satisfied (or only partially so), and who know how to take advantage of chance meetings or discoveries.

Personal and professional environments are good sources of ideas. Personal interests, leisure activities, hobbies, daily life and the family environment may also provide opportunities. Current or past employment, contacts, and exchanges with customers or suppliers are also fertile ground. Internship projects and training periods, research laboratories and institutes for industrial property/patent offices complete and increase the number of possible sources. The most difficult thing therefore is not to have an idea when one wants to become an entrepreneur, but rather to know where ideas can be found, and how they can be captured. And most of all, what one can do with them.

Business opportunities

By business opportunity, we mean either a business (or activity) start-up or takeover opportunity, or the development of an internal start-up within an existing company.

The notion of opportunity has always been, and still is, subject to numerous attempts to define it. For Schumpeter (1934), one derives from the other when he suggests that entrepreneurial opportunity results from 'a new combination of production factors, which manifests itself through the introduction of a new product, a new production process, a new market, a new source of supply, or finally, a new form of industrial organisation'. For the Austrian economist Kirzner (1983), opportunity stems from a dysfunction in the market: 'an imperfection or economic unbalance, which can be exploited by the entrepreneur who will thus restore the market balance'. Opportunity here is considered as a source of profit made possible by the existence of a solvable demand and the availability of necessary resources. For Casson (1982), opportunities are 'occasions when new goods, new services, raw materials and organisation methods can be introduced and sold at a higher price than their cost of production'. In this approach too, opportunity and novelty go hand in hand. Other points of view give more importance to the individual's subjectivity. For instance, Stevenson and Jarillo (1990) define opportunity in reference to 'a future situation deemed both desirable and feasible'.

Regarding the emergence of opportunities, two schools of thought are opposed, one that sees this notion as an objective reality, identifiable as such, and one that postulates that opportunity is a social construction born from the interactions and confrontations between individuals and their environment. From this point of view, opportunities would develop following an emergence process. These two perspectives are not necessarily incompatible. In economic theory, a business is often presented as the meeting point of supply and demand. In this respect, the market may generate gaps conducive to the emergence of new organisations. A business start-up would become the answer to a 'de-adjustment' of supply and demand. The market would thus generate opportunities. But supposing they really exist, these opportunities cannot be identified and exploited by all potential entrepreneurs. To identify and then exploit an opportunity, the individual must first be in a position to do so, and have the required skills, resources and networks. Therefore opportunities depend on the individual and his or her possible room for manoeuvre. To illustrate our theory, a company for sale, for instance, is a real, objective market opportunity, but the individual interested in takeovers must have access to this information in order to identify the opportunity. Furthermore, this opportunity must be compatible with the individual's aspirations and resources in order for him or her to act upon it.

A system is born, is transformed and creates new value

When the process succeeds, the project emerges, fuelled by the initial idea or vision and all the work accomplished. Then the project gives way to a new activity or a new business. The individual is initially the bearer of a project and then becomes a business manager. The entrepreneurial individual/new value creation dialogic emerges and the project or created object progressively puts constraints on the individual.

During the process, individuals will commit themselves more and more to the project (Becker and Sexton 1989), which will lead to irreversibility, if they do not opt out. Irreversibility stems from economic, social, psychological and professional disengagement costs. Irreversibility of commitment means that individuals focus exclusively on their project (Becker and Sexton 1989; Sapienza *et al.* 1991). Entrepreneurs will put all their time, efforts and resources into setting up the project, and later into running the new company, at the expense of their other activities.

The system is progressively transformed, and Figure 6.2 attempts to represent these transformations.

Before commitment takes place, the vision or the project (V-P), at this stage still an internal process, is totally dominated by the individual who is embedded in environments that influence him or her. But as commitment escalates, the project will be partly autonomous while becoming a new business. A project emerges from this process, which can in turn generate a new autonomous organisation. It also transforms the individual who, along the way, will change social identity, experiencing the evolution of his or her social network, value system,

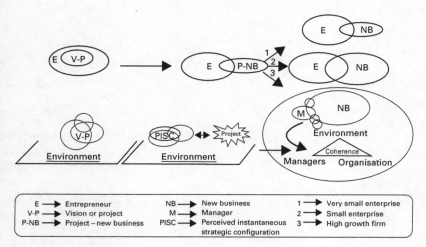

Figure 6.2. From vision to new business (Bruyat 1993: 284)

intelligence and perceived instantaneous strategic configuration. Moreover, as is suggested by Starr and Fonda (1992: 69):

The newcomer's experience is viewed as an ongoing, sense making process, whereby initial expectations and experiences are revised and reinterpreted within the new organizational context. The newcomer's critical tasks include mastering job basics, building role identity, building relationship, updating one's frame of reference (finding out how and why things are done), mapping key people and social networks in the organization, positioning oneself in networks, and learning the organizational vernacular. The objective is to develop coping strategies that reduce cognitive uncertainty, improve perceptions and interpretations, and enable the newcomer to gain control and acceptance in the new environment.

Thus, during the process, the system will change and, in some cases, end up being destroyed and giving birth to a company manager and an autonomous organisation. The intensity of the new value created will depend on these changes and the variety of possible configurations.

PART III

Entrepreneurship and entrepreneurial processes

The notion of process has long been overlooked by researchers in entrepreneurship. Its recognition and use in entrepreneurship research can be traced back to the early 1990s. To a certain extent, the failure of atemporal causality research has contributed to the notion of process being finally acknowledged, and has led to the reorientation of research onto the 'how'. Moreover, the notion of process was initially closely associated to the 'how', one objective being to identify market strategies and penetration modes applied by entrepreneurs. This appeared particularly in Gartner's early works. Later, in the works of Van de Ven and his team (1989; 1992; 1995; 2000),[1] the study of processes focused on the identification of phases and/or actors, the description of operating modes and configurations, and explaining variations through differences in the sequence of events.

The various ways of seeing, thinking, and applying the concept of process have evolved over time. However, one element has remained constant: the methodological and theoretical difficulties linked to the use of this concept in entrepreneurship research (Davidsson 2005). This is all the more unfortunate since our field is a recent one and still in search of its unity, as Aldrich and Baker (1997: 338) put it: 'Judging from normal science standards, entrepreneurship research is still in a very early stage. If no single powerful paradigm exists, then there is even less evidence for multiple coherent points of view.'

Part of the problem lies with the nature of the approaches. Research focusing on processes poses numerous problems related to the breakdown of the process (its representation or modelling), its definition and its chronological sequencing (Thiétart 1999; Davidsson 2005).

Other problems stem from an ambiguous relation between the notion of process and entrepreneurship. This is directly linked to

---

[1] These are only a few references and this should not be considered as an exhaustive list of works on the issue.

the insufficient or imprecise definition of the semantics of process. Ambiguity also originates in the confusion generated by two different visions of the process that partially overlap but should be distinguished. The process may be studied as the main research object, or included in research works as a key dimension. It may be the object or the variable. Some authors, for instance, addressed more particularly the process of organisational emergence (Gartner 1988; Katz and Gartner 1988; Bouchikhi 1993; Aldrich 1999). In this case, the organisational emergence process is considered as an object of study that can be investigated through the scope of various perspectives and research methodologies that are more or less relevant (Van de Ven *et al.* 2000). Conversely, Gartner, in his 1985 contribution, considered the process as a variable in his model of the new venture creation phenomenon. These examples also go to show that authors may change their point of view and perspective and contribute to increasing the degree of polysemy of this notion.

Research works on the notion of process vary greatly in terms of the methodology and theoretical frameworks implemented (Pettigrew 1992; Thiétart 1999; Van de Ven *et al.* 2000; Hlady-Rispal 2002). Although most of the time the objectives consist in describing the evolution over time of the object studied, the number of possible research strategies as well as the variety of visions all contribute to increasing the diversity of situations and perspectives.

To put it simply, in its descriptive approach, process analysis leads to the observation of the elements that make up the process, their order of occurrence and their dynamics. This first type of objective is well illustrated by Van de Ven and Poole (1990: 313), who wish to describe rigorously 'the chronological order and the sequential phases that occur when innovative ideas are transformed and implemented in concrete reality'.

In a more explanatory perspective, process analysis attempts to explain the evolution over time of an object according to the evolution of variables that directly impact on the phenomenon observed.

In the field of entrepreneurship, research works on the notion of process are hindered on at least three levels. First, definitions of key concepts are generally insufficient or, quite simply, missing. Indeed, few research works give a definition of the process, although several perspectives exist (Van de Ven *et al.* 2000). Similarly, few researchers define precisely what they mean by 'entrepreneurial process', although the expression, often used in entrepreneurship research, covers a broad variety of situations. The other two hindrances stem from the insufficient integration of two essential dimensions that seem indispensable to the concept of process itself: process dynamics and time. Although the time dimension has been addressed in some research works, notably under the supervision of Andrew Van de Ven, it has been largely overlooked.

In this third part, I will discuss these issues and propose a contribution. Chapter 7 is aimed at defining and characterising the notion of process, from a general perspective and in the context of entrepreneurship. In chapter 8, I address the dynamics of the process, by presenting first a theoretical framework useful for studying the logic of change. I then demonstrate that time and contextual variables constitute key elements of entrepreneurial process dynamics. The final chapter of this third part presents a generic model of the process. Two visions of this model, synchronic and diachronic, are also presented and commented upon, following a discussion about our perspective and its limitations.

7 | *Introduction to the concept of entrepreneurial process*

As we noted in the introduction to this third part, a lot remains to be done at the theoretical and methodological levels to make better use of the notion of 'entrepreneurial process' in entrepreneurship research works.[1] This chapter will present the semantic and conceptual bases on which the subsequent chapters rely. I will first try to define the notion of process from a general point of view, before considering it from the entrepreneurial perspective and examining its various uses. Finally, I make analogies with other fields of research to help us represent the entrepreneurial process and see how useful these representations can be for both the practitioner and the researcher.

Defining the notion of process

There can be many definitions of 'process'. However, good research should always define its object as precisely as possible in relation to previous theoretical or empirical research works that structure the field. It is therefore important to clarify our definition of the concept in reference to our perspective of research as well as the type of process we are examining. This requires a thorough reflection on the notion of process itself, which we develop below.

An evasive subject

While numerous publications underline the polysemy of 'entrepreneurship', many academic authors do not always define exactly what they

---

[1] While the notion of process is pivotal to a number of entrepreneurship issues, we acknowledge that there are of course other issues and questions that justify other types of research.

mean by 'entrepreneurial process'.[2] In chapter 4 we saw to what extent the situations encountered can vary and whether they may be considered as entrepreneurial depending on the case. In this light, what kind of 'entrepreneurial process' are we talking about? Why not clarify this formulation, as some researchers have attempted to do,[3] or be explicit about which particular perspective on entrepreneurship the research relates to? Why not, for instance, refer to the start-up process of innovative companies, of the opportunity identification process, or of the company takeover process, to mention but a few situations? Yet the last one, 'the company takeover process', is still too general: the company may be healthy or in bad shape and managed by a collective entity; it may be handed down to a family member, or taken over by its employees or external players. In each case, are we really talking about the same process? As we can note here, the lack of definition and/or the lack of clarification of the object studied can induce research problems. In this respect, without further definition or clarification and without a reference framework, is the expression 'entrepreneurial process' still relevant for researchers who wish to carry out their research in a logic of continuity and knowledge accumulation?

There is an added advantage to defining precisely the research object: it ensures easier elaboration or identification of the conceptual research framework. This is how Van de Ven and Poole's 'innovation process' is presented, as 'the invention and implementation of new ideas developed by individuals who are engaged in transactions with others for a certain period of time within an institutional context and who evaluate the results of their efforts and act accordingly' (1990: 314). This definition relies on the core concepts of 'ideas', 'individuals', 'transactions', 'results' and 'context', which will structure the research activities.

This example is representative of what research on processes should be. Within the context of a vast research programme involving several sites, the researchers collected and analysed data in four main stages. The initial question was: 'How do these innovations appear and grow within the organisation?' (Van de Ven *et al.* 1989; Van de Ven and Poole 1990). Van de Ven and his colleagues sought to describe as concretely as

---

[2] A search request on 'entrepreneurial process' through Google generates 9 million results.
[3] Delmar (2002) for instance, when using the expression 'entrepreneurial process', refers to Venkataraman's definition of entrepreneurship (1997).

possible 'the chronological order and the sequential phases that occur when innovative ideas are transformed and implemented in concrete reality' (Van de Ven and Poole 1990: 313). The first stage of the research programme consisted in defining the process variable of the study: the innovation process, or even the emergence, transformation and implementation of new ideas. The period of observation and research sample were determined in the second stage. The third clarified the key concepts of the definition quoted above. These variables all illustrate how the authors define the innovation process in organisations. They are important as they subsequently make it possible to monitor and describe the evolution of the innovation variable over time. Thus, the history of a given innovation is dissected into critical incidents, and each incident is described and analysed through the scope of the five key concepts selected by the researchers. Finally, the fourth step consisted in grouping the critical incidents into phases in order to understand the evolution over time of the innovation processes studied.

This example shows just how important it is to define rigorously the object studied and the concepts that delimit it.

Multiple perceptions of the notion of process

Just as the rigorous definition of a research object determines a conceptual framework, the definition of 'process' that is adopted also has theoretical and methodological repercussions. It impacts on the subsequent choices about the strategy of research and the theoretical model through which the process dynamics will be conceptualised.

Numerous definitions of the concept of 'process' may be found in the general literature: the *Merriam-Webster* focuses on the notion of change: 'a natural phenomenon marked by gradual changes that lead toward a particular result'; whereas the *Shorter Oxford Dictionary* introduces the notion of objective: 'a series of actions or operations directed to some end'.

In the scientific literature, 'process' is the description and analysis of how a variable evolves over time (Van de Ven 1992). In other instances, a 'process' corresponds to sequence of change in an organisational variable (Miller and Friesen 1982: 1014). The process is often considered as a set of activities, as in Lorino's definition (1995): 'set of activities linked together by meaningful information flows (or flows of material bearing information) that combine to provide an important and well-defined material or immaterial product'. Here the activities are grouped and organised according to purpose and product. Regulation is ensured via information or material flows. This notion of regulative 'flows' can also be found in a definition of automation science, introducing the notion of system: 'a process is a dynamic system, that is to say an evolving system in which time plays a key role. In general, the process is a system criss-crossed by information, energy and material flows, while subjected to perturbations in one of the three forms cited' (Borne 1992). This systemic vision has inspired other authors in management science, as can be shown in the following definition given by Jacquet-Lagreze *et al.* (1978: 21): 'the process is a sequence of concomitant and/or successive configurations and interactions under the impact of compensating and amplifying regulations specific to the system concerned'.

Researchers' visions of the process, whether they consider it as a succession of stages, an ordered chain of facts or phenomena, an organised set of activities or a system interacting with its environment, have a major impact on their research works.[4] Lorino (1995) thinks a process is not a causal chain (cause–consequence), but an informational or material flow, and researchers who agree with his point of view will not look for causal links. However, other visions are possible, as suggested by Van de Ven *et al.* (2000) in one of the three definitions they propose to guide the work of researchers. A process may be represented as a 'logic that explains a causal relationship between independent and dependent variables'. Van de Ven *et al.* (2000) also represent the notion of process 'as a category of concepts or variables that refer to actions of individuals or organizations'. Thanks to this last perspective, it is possible to model, for instance, the decision-making, strategy-forming, etc. processes in terms of organisation (of change). Research questions often relate to antecedents or consequences of individual and organisational change and may be approached from the angle of causal relations and/or through longitudinal analysis. Finally, this perspective proposed by Van de Ven *et al.* (2000) is probably the one that most requires original research methodologies. In this approach, the process is described 'as a sequence of events (or activities) that describe how things change

---

[4] Langley *et al.* (1995) present five basic models describing how a process unfolds over time, that is to say how the various periods of time that compose it are articulated: sequential, anarchistic, iterative, by convergence and by inspiration.

over time'. This perspective focuses on the historical development of the process, which requires a systematic collection of considerable data during the process life cycle. The essence of this approach consists in monitoring precisely and faithfully the evolution of the object studied through events, activities and incidents.

Discussing the concept of entrepreneurial process

A chronological reading of the research works published in the field of entrepreneurship in the last two decades shows that the concept of process was used in at least three types of context. First of all, in the early 1990s, it signalled a change in the research works of the time, mostly focused on entrepreneurs' personal traits and characteristics. As a possible alternative to the trait-based approach, the concept of process made it possible to focus more on acts and activities, taking into account the 'how'. This gave rise to numerous conceptualising and modelling works, continuing to this day. Finally, it appears to me that the notion of process has become denser and is nowadays at the heart of the field's definition. The three steps I have identified have appeared chronologically, but I think that they overlap to a large extent.

The notion of process as a new research perspective

As we saw in chapter 2, Gartner was one of the first researchers to question the validity of the trait-based approach, which was the dominant current of research in the 1980s. Gartner (1988) showed the limits of this approach and led the way in focusing on what entrepreneurs 'do' and not on who they 'are'. The conceptual framework he proposed as early as 1985 to describe the phenomenon of new business start-ups used the notion of process and included four dimensions: 'environment, individual(s), process and organization' (Gartner 1985). In this work, Gartner likens the process to an activity or a function and adopts Danhoff's definition: 'entrepreneurship is an activity or function and not a specific individual or occupation . . . the specific personal entrepreneur is an unrealistic abstraction'.[5] Relying on a review of the economic literature, Garner identifies six behaviours that broadly

[5] Quoted by Gartner (1985: 699).

describe entrepreneurial activities. These behaviours could represent as many processes: 'the entrepreneur locates a business opportunity'; 'the entrepreneur accumulates resources'; the entrepreneur markets products and services'; 'the entrepreneur produces the product'; 'the entrepreneur builds an organization'; 'the entrepreneur responds to government and society' (Gartner 1985: 699–700).

In continuity with these early works, other researchers have endorsed this vision of the process as a chain of events, notably Bygrave and Hofer (1991), who opened new perspectives by integrating the dynamic and holistic dimensions of the entrepreneurial process.

Researchers in the field of entrepreneurship decided to give more attention to the question of process mainly because it provided them with an alternative to the previous visions which could only lead to dead-ends by focusing on one single aspect: the human characteristic or the economic function of a complex phenomenon which should be studied as a whole in order to be fully understood.

The notion of process as a theoretical model

The notion of process lends itself to being modelled, thus it is not surprising to find an abundance of literature on the subject in the field of entrepreneurship. Conceptual frameworks and theoretical models are proposed that describe and/or explain all or part of the entrepreneurial process. If we refer to recent decades, modelling attempts started more or less with Shapero's work in the early 1980s. This stream of research remains active today and draws on emerging currents of research.

Shapero (1975; 1984; Shapero and Sokol 1982) proposed a model aimed at explaining what he called the entrepreneurial event, based on psychological, sociological, economic and contextual variables. Watkins (1976) integrates the notion of time in his model and hypothesises that starting a new business venture can be compared with an everyday professional decision. To support his position, he uses the factors that influence the entrepreneurial decision as listed by Cooper (1971). Liles' model (1974) introduces the notion of 'readiness'. This concept suggests that individuals who are interested in starting a business reach a point in their life when they think their capacities are optimal to do so (between the ages of 27 and 37). Martin (1984) considers the identification of a business start-up opportunity as a key factor. As for the other important variables, they are borrowed from the models previously mentioned. Pleitner (1985) distinguishes three levels in his business start-up model: the emergence of a preference for the career of entrepreneur, the development of a motivation to create one's own business and the actual commitment to doing so. Long and McMullan (1984) modelled venture creation as a process of opportunity identification and elaboration in which the opportunity is not 'given' but built by the entrepreneur.

This brief review of the literature only illustrates a fragment of the number of existing models,[6] but I will now comment upon some key aspects of these modelling attempts.

The first comment I will make is that these models have never been put to the test, or confronted to empirical data beyond their initial presentation. This raises the question of the usefulness of these contributions and of the continuity of research projects.

Secondly, these models aim to describe and/or explain processes that are, in most cases, little defined, or not defined at all. This flaw appears even in the contributions considered as founding works by the community of researchers. For example, Gartner's position (1985) as regards the notion of process is rather peculiar. The process, in his model, is considered as an independent variable. Consequently, the process cannot include the other variables of the model, whereas we would be tempted to think that the main interest of the notion of process is precisely its capacity to integrate variables. Bouchikhi (1993) proposes a constructivist model to understand performance as a result of the entrepreneurial process. Yet Bouchikhi does not define the concept of process that he uses throughout his demonstration. What seems to emerge implicitly is the business start-up process; but what type of business start-up and what type of entrepreneur are considered in this work? For this author who relies on the constructivist theory elaborated by Giddens (1984a), the entrepreneurial process is an emergence process: 'structuration theory provides an alternative representation of the entrepreneurial process. The outcome is determined neither by the entrepreneur nor by the context, but emerges in the mere process of their interaction' (Bouchikhi 1993: 557).

---

[6] Numerous reviews of the literature about the entrepreneurial process are available. Here we have drawn mainly on Bruyat (1993), Hernandez (1999) and Tornikoski (1999).

Our third and last comment concerns the diversity of models and representations elaborated by researchers in entrepreneurship. The models all attempt to describe, for instance, processes concerning various situations within the field of entrepreneurship. This is how the focus may be on new venture creation (Gartner 1985; Bruyat 1993), company takeovers (Deschamps 2002), spin-offs (Daval 2002) or intrapreneurial situations (Covin and Slevin 1991). Another factor of diversity stems from the various outlooks on the process. Some researchers have worked on the process as a whole (Martin 1984; Moore 1986; Bruyat 1993; Hernandez 1999), while others have chosen to study only parts of it. Sammut (1998), for instance, focused on the activity start-up process; Van der Veen and Wakkee (2002) modelled the process of opportunity identification and exploitation; Tornikoski (1999) broke down the entrepreneurial process into sub-processes too. Finally, the diversity of models is also increased by the number of contributions focusing on some important aspects of the entrepreneurial process, such as intention (Krueger and Carsrud 1993; Tkachev and Kolvereid 1999), organisational learning (de la Ville 1996), decision (Learned, 1992) or performance (Bouchikhi 1993; Marion 1999).

The process as centre of gravity of entrepreneurship research

Among the most promising works that give a central place to the notion of entrepreneurial process, three perspectives on entrepreneurship have emerged and contributed to forming new research communities.

The first stream of research argues that entrepreneurship is an organisation process that leads to the creation of a new organisation (Gartner 1988; 1990; 1993). There are other researchers whose works are in line with this approach: Bouchikhi (1993), Aldrich (1999), Thornton (1999), Verstraete (1999), Sharma and Chrisman (1999) and Hernandez (2001). We can note that in this research perspective, organisation creation as much as (or even more than) entrepreneurship is at the heart of the researcher's preoccupations (Shane and Venkataraman 2000; Davidsson, Low and Wright 2001; Wicklund, Dahlqvist and Havnes 2001). Depending on the mode of exploitation selected to transform an opportunity or invention, by setting up a new business or by using an existing organisation, the process may or may not be entrepreneurial. Moreover, as Bruyat points out, not all instances of organisation creation lead to situations in which the intensity of change for the individual and the new value created are highly significant. Companies may be created by imitation or reproduction, or even with the aim of transferring an existing activity.

The second perspective, based on Shane and Venkataraman (2000) and grounded in an older stream of research, focuses on the notion of opportunity (Stevenson and Jarillo 1990; Bygrave and Hofer 1991; Venkataraman 1997). In this approach, entrepreneurship is defined as 'the scholarly examination of how, by whom and with what effects opportunities to create future goods and services are discovered, evaluated and exploited'. In this light, discovery, evaluation and exploitation processes constitute essential study and research objects. This perspective, like the one previously mentioned, focuses on emergence, but in this case on the emergence of a new economic activity, not necessarily linked to the emergence of a new organisation. Some of the authors in line with this approach consider that opportunities exist in the environment, and that, as such, they simply have to be identified, appropriated and transformed into economic realities by potential entrepreneurs: 'although recognition of entrepreneurial opportunities is a subjective process, the opportunities themselves are objective phenomena that are not known to all parties at all times' (Shane and Venkataraman 2000: 220). As far as I am concerned, however, I do not believe that opportunity is the starting point of the process, the 'objective' element that must be discovered; I am convinced, on the contrary, that opportunity is built during the activity creation process. The other pitfall of this approach is that researchers might be tempted to focus exclusively on successful processes, whereas in my view the projects that lead to abandonment or failure are just as interesting.

The third approach is Bruyat's (1993; 1994) based on the individual/value creation dialogic. His perspective relies on a dual dynamic of change for both the entrepreneurial individual and the environment concerned. This original approach is the cornerstone of this work and our reference framework. I will not develop it further here as I have introduced it at length in chapters 2 and 4.

Metaphors of the process

The metaphorical approach is often explored in management science. Morgan (1989) uses this method to generate images of the organisation. In the field of entrepreneurship, Hernandez (2001) points out that Anglo-Saxons and French researchers have often resorted to metaphors. They originate in various disciplines: biology, physics, mechanics and politics, and despite their limitations they offer interesting representations of the entrepreneurial process. For instance, some researchers of the field have drawn on chaos and catastrophe theories (Bygrave 1989; Stevenson and Harmeling 1990) or complexity science (Lichtenstein 2002).

In the following section, I present four metaphors applied to the process and its dynamics, which can be useful to researchers looking for representation tools despite the limitations usually associated with this type of representation.

The energy metaphor

The concept of energy, used in numerous scientific disciplines, notably the dynamic study of systems, is still fairly rare in management sciences. It is therefore unsurprising that publications about the entrepreneurial process should not explicitly refer to it. Yet, some works have implicitly drawn on the notion of energy. This is the case, for instance, in Sammut's work (1998), when she writes: 'the legal creation of the company, and the processing of the first orders represent the initial elements of a development spiral which will only stop with the end, forced or deliberate, of the activity' or 'there occurs, as a consequence, a snowball effect, activated when the company begins trading' or even 'the strategic dynamics of the company are regenerated by the availability of new resources, an evolving environment, an organisation in formation, an active production and a manager just as determined'. Some expressions, like 'development spiral', 'snowball effect', 'regenerated by the availability of new resources' all refer to the symbolism of energy.

Energy seems an interesting analogy to understand the evolution of the individual/project system, as it is useful to overcome the resistance linked to the environment, which is indispensable to launch activities and ensure their sustainability during the start-up period. What are the energy sources of the process? The vital energy of the entrepreneur and his or her team and the entrepreneurial potential could represent endogenous sources. Marion (1999) defines the entrepreneurial potential as an individual or collective capacity to act entrepreneurially, which includes a wide range of knowledge, skills and know-how.

Exogenous sources could be linked to flow exchanges and resource acquisition mechanisms (advice, information, financial resources, relations). Using the concept of energy to elaborate and carry out research on processes in the field of entrepreneurship could offer interesting new paths of research.

The mechanical metaphor

The second metaphor is borrowed from the theory of fluid mechanics. The idea proposed is that the process dynamics are subjected to resistance. This principle of resistance applies to both the individual and his or her project. At the individual's level, it mainly stems from resistance to change, a well-known and extensively studied subject in human and social sciences, while at the level of the project, the environment's resistance to penetration seems a relevant concept. We could compare this to the phenomenon of air-resistance observed in the study of moving objects such as vehicles intended for the transport of goods or persons. If one wishes to improve the speed and quality of penetration of a project into a given environment, it is necessary to decrease its 'frictional resistance', by finding the optimal profile for the project that makes it the most attractive for the environment.

The thermodynamic metaphor

The third metaphor comes from thermodynamics. Thermodynamics studies the changes in the states of a system, resulting from energy transfers and modifications of the initial conditions: the phase transitions between the gaseous, liquid and solid states of matter. The knowledge and models used to study the changes of the state of matter could be useful in understanding phase transitions (changing from one system configuration to another).

The biological metaphor

Embryogenesis inspired this final metaphor. The formation and evolution of the entrepreneurial process can be compared with the formation and development of a human embryo. After all, the images of 'bearer of project', 'birth of a company', even '*accoucheurs de start-up*',[7] all rely on the imagery of birth. In this case, the business start-up process could be studied by distinguishing three different phases: one corresponding to the 'embryogenesis' of the organisation, the second corresponding to the legal 'birth' of the company and a third related to its development (growth).

[7] Meaning, literally 'start-up obstetrician(s)'. 'Accoucheurs de start-up' is the title of an article published in *Le Monde Interactif*, on 8 March 2000.

8 | The dynamic dimension of the entrepreneurial process

Process definitions often include more or less explicitly the notion of dynamics. In my opinion it is absolutely essential to integrate (conceptualise and operationalise) this key dimension in order to understand processes. Indeed, without the notion of dynamics, it seems difficult to study evolutions or transitions from one phase or one configuration to another.

Bygrave and Hofer (1991) attempted to describe some characteristics of the entrepreneurial process and put forward, notably, the importance of its dynamic and holistic dimensions. The entrepreneurial process is dynamic because start-up projects and businesses evolve over time; it is holistic because this evolution results from a system of interacting variables (Bygrave and Hofer 1991).

We will open this chapter by presenting useful theories that can illustrate some 'engines' of the process evolution. The subsequent sections will draw on Bygrave and Hofer's assertions as we investigate the role of temporal variables in the entrepreneurial process, before examining the role and influence of contextual variables in the various environments with which the entrepreneurial system interacts.

Some theories for modelling the dynamics of the process

Van de Ven and Poole (1995) propose a typology relying on four theories to explain organisational change and development. These theories can be used alone or combined, virtually all possible combinations having been envisaged by the authors, in order to provide as many engines capable of 'propelling' (and explaining) the evolution of a phenomenon. This framework, originally intended for the study of innovation processes, seems particularly well adapted to the preoccupations of researchers in entrepreneurship. Table 8.1 presents the four generic theoretical engines. I will develop them in the following sub-sections and apply them to the field of entrepreneurship.

Table 8.1. *Process development theories*

Theories	Logic of change	Progression of events
Life cycle	Change is perceived as a continuous phenomenon; change and evolution are customary states of living systems.	Events follow a pattern of phase sequences naturally following one another through time; the sequence of phases is logical, linear.
Teleology	Change is managed according to a vision of the final state to achieve; it is a voluntary process that is made possible because the system is capable of adaptation.	Events follow a pattern of multiple, cumulative sequences, during which alternative means are implemented in order to achieve the desired final state.
Dialectic	Change happens following a dialectic between thesis and antithesis, order/disorder, stability/instability, etc. These opposing forces help explain the evolution of the process.	Numerous contradictory events are confronted (to one another), resist or disappear as a result of this confrontation, and finally converge towards a new state of the system studied.
Evolution	Change is a process of variation, selection and retention by the environment.	The system varies; numerous events are selected then retained in a new configuration of the system.

Source: Van de Ven and Poole 1995.

The life cycle theory

The life cycle theory is recurrent in various scientific disciplines. Indeed, the organic growth metaphor seems well adapted to the question of organisational change and development. In the life cycle theory, development follows a pre-programmed internal logic that eventually leads the phenomenon studied, through well-identified phases, from a starting point to an identified final state. The various development phases of the enterprise, which is conceptualised as an organism, are traditionally: conception, gestation, birth, growth, decline and death (Hernandez 2001). Some researchers in the field of entrepreneurship have worked within this theoretical framework. Burgelman and Sayles (1986), for instance, studied the development of a new activity within the context of an existing organisation. Churchill and Lewis (1983), going beyond the limits of the field, proposed a five-step evolution pattern for the young company: existence, viability, success, development and optimal exploitation of resources.

Dialectic theory

According to dialectic theory, change emerges from the confrontation of viewpoints or conflicts between influential people and/or opposed organisational entities. Power is central to this process and movement is triggered by internal struggles and competition between the actors who seek domination and control. I have not found references of works in our field of interest that rely on this theoretical framework. However, I believe that it could constitute a possible engine of the business start-up process in the specific context of a business created by a team, provided the power is evenly distributed between the associates.

The teleological theory

Teleological theory provides a third possible engine of the process dynamics. This theoretical framework postulates that change is the consequence of the assignation of goals and the expression of the vision of a desired final state. The development of a process follows a pattern of successive sequences of formulation and implementation of goals, and evaluation and modification of objectives according to the learning accomplished, or what is desired by the entity concerned (Van de Ven *et al.* 2000). Bruyat's thesis (1993) and my own work are in line with this theoretical framework. The propelling force of the teleological engine appears particularly in the idea that company creation projects arise from, and develop within, the zone of coherence of the perceived instantaneous strategic configuration. As noted previously, the perceived instantaneous strategic configuration includes goals, objectives and projects that potential entrepreneurs develop by combining their personal aspirations, skills and perceived resources with the environment possibilities they think they have detected.

The evolutionist theory

This last engine used to explain process dynamics is probably the most popular today. It relies on the theoretical framework of evolutionist theory. The concept of evolution originates in biology, and has been used for centuries to designate the sequence of phases that all human beings experience before achieving their definitive form. Evolutionism here seems a very useful theory, and many researchers have drawn on it to explain change in fields such as economics, sociology or management sciences. In the field of entrepreneurship too, its use seems promising (Aldrich and Martinez 2001; Delmar 2001). Just as in the biological evolution process, change in this theoretical framework proceeds through a continuous cycle of variation, selection and retention (Van de Ven *et al.* 2000). These authors consider that this theory is applicable to multiple entities or populations. In other words, as far as business start-up is concerned, the unit of analysis is made up of a number of start-up projects. Aldrich (1999) is of a different opinion. Two units of analysis (and of selection) are possible according to him: routines and skills within an existing or emerging organisation, and the organisations within a given population. In his approach, Aldrich highlights the existence of four generic processes – variation, selection, retention and struggle – which are more or less simultaneous rather than sequential: 'analytically, the processes may be separated into discrete phases, but in practice they are linked in continuous feedback loops and cycles' (Aldrich 1999: 33).

The evolutionist perspective can be used to understand how particular forms of organisation emerge in particular environments. Some evolutionist models have been proposed to theorise the business start-up or organisational emergence processes (Aldrich 1999; Gomez *et al.* 2000; Delmar 2001; 2002). Aldrich and Martinez (2001) highlight two theoretical breakthroughs in this stream of research, which, according to them, may become pivotal in the next few years. The first one is the emergence of the concept of 'nascent' entrepreneur, which embodies, to a certain extent, the idea that the business start-up process may be characterised by its chaotic and disorderly aspects. From the evolutionist perspective, 'nascent entrepreneurs are a major source of organizational variations, beginning with their intentions and continuing through their activities oriented toward a realized founding' (Aldrich and Martinez 2001: 42). The second theoretical breakthrough consists in establishing a clear distinction between entrepreneurial activities in situations of innovation and situations of reproduction, which dissociates the notions of entrepreneurship and innovation and thus contributes to the demystification of entrepreneurs.

Integrating time variables

Although a recent experience has revealed that time does not exist at the quantum level or in the microscopic world (reported in the French magazine *Science et Vie* of January 2003), it is nonetheless true that no scientific discipline can make do without it.

Time is an essential element of daily life, science and almost all human activities. While time is present in all the disciplines of management sciences, each discipline has its own perception and approach of it (Batsch 1997).

The *American Heritage Dictionary* gives the following definition of time: 'a nonspatial continuum in which events occur in apparently irreversible succession from the past through the present to the future'. This definition was also quoted by Ancona *et al.* in an issue of the *Academy of Management Review* entirely devoted to time (2001). This definition suggests the existence of an indefinite milieu in which events proceed in a chronological succession, and in an irreversible manner. As researchers constantly work with the notion of time, it seems important to define it rigorously. First, behind the notion of time, we can find:

> the notions of reversibility or irreversibility, successive or overlapping phases, the rhythm and organisation of these phases
> possible change, time being an essential condition for change
> the notion of duration, phases that take more or less time
> the measurement of time and its subjectivity: time perceived differently depending on the actors.

Time is also closely associated to the notion of process. According to Le Moigne (1984), the process is indeed a concept of change that affects an object in a 'time', 'space' and 'shape' referential. In this light, time should play a central role in process-related research, and yet, to this day, time variables have received little attention in works of management science in general, and entrepreneurship in particular.

Time-related issues are numerous and often complex. We will first show that the notion of time raises problems of understanding as regards processes in the field of entrepreneurship. We will then present an analysis framework including the time variables we consider to be the most important.

Issues raised by the notion time in understanding processes

The various issues fall into three groups. The first group concerns the difficulty of defining the boundaries of the process; the second is linked to the problem of the accuracy of time measurement; and the third group relates to the subjectivity of time.

Boundaries of the process studied

The delimitation of the process in terms of time constitutes a major problem. Research on processes aims at analysing the evolution of a given phenomenon; and evolution is 'the empirical observation of the differences in the shape, quality or state of an organisational entity over time' (Van de Ven and Poole 1995: 51). How can we define the boundaries of a process (beginning and end) by relying on phenomena that generally require long periods of maturation? This is all the more difficult since the actors of the process have difficulties acknowledging and formalising a certain number of things. As far as venture creation is concerned, it is necessary to define the moment when the creation process starts, and the moment when the creation phase is over. When does somebody start to be an entrepreneur? When does somebody stop being an entrepreneur? These questions show how difficult it is to define the beginning and the end of a process. The choice of time boundaries is often varied, and depends on the authors and the perspectives adopted (Bruyat 1993). The limits that are most often used are the most identifiable ones: the legal act of constitution of the company (beginning) and operational breakeven point (end). However, if one is interested in the phases preceding the legal creation of the business, how far back should the boundary be set? If the beginning of the process is when the idea first emerges in the mind of the individual, how can one identify in real time, let alone retrospectively, that particular moment that marks the beginning of the process? What is the option if the process studied relates to something other than a business start-up? All these questions concerning process boundaries are important because they impact on data collection and because, depending on what event is chosen as the starting point, the level of analysis and the interpretation framework may change (Thiétart 1999).

The accuracy of measurement over time

Other time-related issues appear when research focuses on identifying cause–effect relations or statistical regularities in samples. Using non-factual data that have been collected in a non-synchronic way supposes that the aspects studied do not change over time. Yet all those who have studied business start-up processes from their beginning up to the business's growth phase know that there is not much in common between what is told afterwards and what really happened. During the development of the process, the system is transformed. The project and the entrepreneur sometimes undergo significant change (Bruyat 1993). Asking successful entrepreneurs, five years later, what pushed them to set up a business poses problems of measurement accuracy. If one wishes to study the relation between a psychological trait and the propensity to create, the measure should be taken before, and not after, that is, unless it is assumed that traits are stable over time. The same goes for motivations, behaviours and opinions. Considering the difficulties identified here, data should be collected in real-time, a procedure that greatly complicates research operations.

Subjectivity of time

The last problem we will mention here is linked to the perception of time for the various actors. In the same way that the researcher works with objective and measurable time, he or she must also consider a more subjective form of time that corresponds to the perceptions and representations of individuals or human groups. Time is not experienced in the same way by the entrepreneur and his or her partners, and the same goes for the entrepreneur and the researcher. Time does not seem to pass by at the same pace for all the actors involved. This may induce discrepancies, misunderstandings and erroneous interpretations, for instance between the individual who develops a project and those who advise him or her through this process. The same difficulties may appear in the relationship between the entrepreneurial actor and the one studying his or her actions.

Analysis framework of time variables

Although numerous research works have been carried out on the entrepreneurial process, the time dimension has received relatively little attention.

In this respect, it is interesting to note that even some reference works in the field do not mention this time issue, like the one by Shane and Venkataraman (2000). In the introduction to the special issue of *Entrepreneurship Theory and Practice*, which proposed an overview of ten years of entrepreneurship research and its perspectives for the future, Davidsson, Low and Wright (2001) did not explicitly mention the question of time either.

Taking time into account implies focusing on specific variables: it is not only the actors (what they do) and the processes (what happens) that should be studied, but also the chronology of events and actions, their duration, the perception of time by the actors, the synchronisation (or not) of several events or several actions, the rhythm, etc. In the following, I split time variables into two categories: positioning and pace.

Time positioning variables

We can speak of absolute and relative positioning in the time continuum.

- **The date and time:** *a variable to position an event or an action on a time scale*

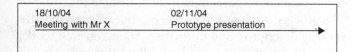

Longitudinal time series analysis generally measures this type of variable. Each event is represented according to its date of occurrence.

The work done by Andrew Van de Ven *et al.*, for instance, is in line with this approach. 'Incidents' are identified and time-coded. The dynamics of the time series are then analysed (random, periodical, chaotic, etc.) and hypotheses are made as to the links between the various factors studied (ideas, transactions, individuals, context, results, processes, etc.).

Date is an absolute positioning variable that requires the definition of a measuring scale in a given referential system. For example, A and B are two events of one process that happen, for A on 12 February 2005 at 10.00 a.m., and for B on 12 February 2005 at 5.00 p.m. If the measuring unit is a 'day', then we can say that A and B happened simultaneously. However, if the time unit is 'an hour', then we will conclude that A happened before B.

With this example, we can introduce our second positioning variable, a relative variable: order.

• *Order: a variable to position various events, actions, incidents in relation to one another*

In a business start-up process, the order in which the different phases and events occur is not pre-established and this has consequences on the success of the various operations. For example, acknowledging the desire to start a business and finding the opportunity are often presented as successive steps. In reality they may be concomitant or in reverse order: an opportunity and/or possibly a threat can trigger a process that was not a pre-existing goal for the entrepreneurial individual. This reverse order may lead potential entrepreneurs to enter a process for which they are not sufficiently prepared. Things will also be different depending on whether the entrepreneurial individual is a first-time entrepreneur or not (nascent, parallel or serial entrepreneur). As this last remark shows, the notion of order can apply to phases, events, or processes.

The notion of chronological order has so far been the subject of theoretical research aiming to develop models describing the order of the phases in the process, often in a linear perspective. The perspective adopted is generally descriptive and normative. Some research works have attempted to show that there is a relationship between order and performance. For example, Delmar *et al.* (2001) examined the order of three activities in the process (quest for legitimacy, development of social networks and recombination of resources) and the consequences for the survival of the company.

It is both possible and desirable to multiply research perspectives that integrate the chronological order variable. This may be done, for instance, by varying the levels of analysis (process, phase, event) or by elaborating typologies which link the chronological order of the various phases or events with their consequences (in terms of duration and performance for example).

Pace variables

The duration of an event or of all or part of the process as well as rhythm and timing are all, in our view, pace variables.

• **Duration:** *a variable used to measure the amount of time taken in the continuum by an event or an activity*

This time variable is rarely taken into account in entrepreneurship research, although it seems very important to us.

The majority of company or activity creation processes are dissipative. Until the moment when the activity starts generating resources that will ensure its survival and development, it consumes resources that will need to be regularly supplied. During this particular phase, and this is even more significant if the activity is innovative and different, any supply of new resources will give more time to the project or the new activity. The notion of duration is crucial in the context of innovation, as there is always great uncertainty as regards the time required to implement an innovation or differentiated product successfully.

The duration of the whole process and of the different phases can vary greatly. This depends on the characteristics of the project, of the entrepreneur and of the environments (of both the project and entrepreneur), and on how these elements are interrelated. In an innovation project, some phases, such as the technological development and the introduction on the market can be carried out simultaneously (Moreau 2003). Entrepreneurs may have plenty of time, be free of pressure, or may require more time to better master one or several components of their new career and project; they can be experienced (or not), they may know to a greater or lesser extent the activity sector in which they intend to create the company, etc. The incidence of these various parameters could be analysed in terms of the duration and order of events, phases and processes. This could generate knowledge likely to improve the quality of business or activity start-up support systems.

• **Rhythm:** *a dynamic variable to evaluate the pace at which events succeed one another in time*

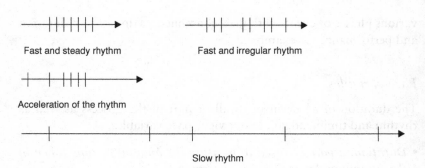

Rhythm can be defined as a variable that makes it possible to measure the pace at which events and activities follow one another during a process. Business start-up processes with a similar duration or a similar order of events and phases may present different rhythms.

When events closely follow one another, we can talk of a fast rhythm, and in the opposite case, of a slow rhythm. Rhythm may be steady or not, it may accelerate or slow down. The following illustrations give a more concrete idea of what we have in mind here. To a certain extent, rhythm is a notion similar to that of frequency.

Rhythm can be one of the characteristics of a project, an individual's profile or an entrepreneurial system configuration. This leads us to wonder whether we could go as far as considering the possibility, by analogy with physiology, of studying the process's 'pulse'?

• **Timing:** *a variable of synchronisation and adequacy between the actor's perceptions of the environment and the possibilities of the environment*

The notion of timing implies that certain events must appear at the right time: this or that activity must be accomplished at a certain point in time.

The notions of opportunity or threat are linked to time. An idea developed too early will not coincide with its demand, whereas a threat perceived too late may ruin the chances of the project or the new company.

Entrepreneurs have different needs in terms of support and training at different times in the process. Information and training must take place at the right time. The same goes for partnership possibilities. An interesting piece of information received too late is useless.

The final idea linked to the issue of timing is the notion of strategic window. It may apply to the individual, and is then called 'commitment window' (or 'readiness' as proposed in Liles' model, which was presented in chapter 7). During an individual's life, there are times when the individual is able start a business, and others when it is impossible. There may be several such windows, just one, or indeed none at all. We may refer here to Shapero's model (1984). The same thing goes for the projects themselves. Some projects have no strategic window – it does not exist, or is not yet open – and for other projects the opening time may vary in duration. Another important parameter is the concomitance of the individual's window and the project window: one may be available, the other not, and reciprocally. From this we may deduce that randomness or chance (Bouchikhi 1993) can play a great role as regards the synchronism between both windows.

The environments and contextual variables of the system

The environment of the system, open in an entrepreneurial individual/new value creation dialogic, can play an important role in the initiation and the development of an entrepreneurial process. The entrepreneur's cultural, professional and family environment influence his or her perceived instantaneous strategic configuration. Numerous research works have attempted to identify the environmental factors liable to explain the entrepreneurial act and/or the performance of the process; however, the results have mostly led to different and sometimes contradictory conclusions. The diversity of entrepreneurial situations can explain this. Consequently, we may say that entrepreneurial individuals and their projects evolve in various environments, with multiple dimensions, perceived as being more or less hostile or conducive to the realisation of their business project (Bruyat 1993). Below we propose an analysis framework of the system's environments before examining the links between the system and its environments.

From a general level to a personal level

The entrepreneurial system is influenced by both the general environment (economic, social and cultural) and the environments specific to the project and the entrepreneurial individual.

The general environment

The general environment can be scaled on a global/local axis. At the most global level (which generally concerns a country, or region of the world), political stability, the status of private ownership and the free circulation of goods and people seem to be minimal requirements. However, there are other important factors, such as fiscal and social policies, accessibility and cost of finance, the state of the job market, general regulations, incitation and support measures, etc.

The local level is often of great importance, as most entrepreneurs want to develop their projects in locations where they have their bearings, their friends and their main networks. This propensity to undertake something in their current location is probably stronger for entrepreneurs who start up new businesses. Researchers have shown that this tendency concerned small businesses as well as high-growth technological companies (Myers and Hobbs 1985).

Creating broadcasting companies in major cities like Paris or London or in rural areas requires different methods of integration, and therefore different key factors of success according to the location. As a consequence the room for manoeuvre will vary depending on the local contexts. In their local environments, entrepreneurs will look for the main useful factors, such as incubation possibilities, entrepreneurial support structures, financing and venture capital agencies, a reasonably dynamic economy, the availability of suppliers, customers and a qualified workforce, and finally, good infrastructures. They will also favour the quality of life in terms of security, health, education and leisure potential.

The project's specific environment

This environment presents multiple characteristics that have received attention from industrial economists, and marketing and strategy specialists. These characteristics concern turbulence, uncertainty, initial difficulties, the potential of relevant markets, technologies, competition, the insertion possibilities of the project, etc. Concerning emerging sectors, which are often favoured by entrepreneurs, Porter (1980) highlighted the absence of known rules and argued that rules are defined by the actors and the competition as they go along. According to him, at the origin of emerging sectors (newly formed or reformed sectors) there are often technological innovations, modifications of relative costs, the emergence of new consumer needs, or other economic and social changes that lead to a product or service becoming a viable economic possibility. In this respect, during the elaboration phase of their project, entrepreneurs will be able to choose their specific environments to a certain extent.

The individual's environment

The individual's environment is undoubtedly a determining factor throughout the entrepreneurial process. For numerous entrepreneurs, the entrepreneurial project is also a personal project, or is (at least) compatible with their personal project. The entrepreneur's family and his or her social and professional networks will all play a significant role in his or her personal history. These environments are often where entrepreneurs find their role models, necessary resources, future partners, their first suppliers and customers, as well as advice and information (Smeltzer *et al.* 1991). Without the richness and diversity of the possibilities provided by personal environments, often things could not be done, and what could be done would not occur on the same scale. These resources, as well as the support from family and friends, constitute the primary source of energy of the entrepreneurial system.

Complex relations with multiple consequences

Empirical research has attempted to understand the impact of the environment on the entrepreneurial phenomenon, but without integrating the fact that these are interrelations that should be analysed from a systemic and therefore dynamic perspective.

We prefer to speak about interrelations between the environment and the individual/project system, as the entrepreneur does not only react to a state of the environment in a logic of adaptation. Entrepreneurs are capable of projecting themselves in a specific environment, starting from an initial vision, which turns into a project that organises and structures this vision. From a Schumpeterian perspective, the entrepreneur is liable to modify the environment, intentionally or not. By introducing new ways of doing things, he or she is going to change the rules of the game and create new ones. Reciprocally, some players of the environment may have their own ideas as regards business start-ups in or regarding one particular project.

The impact of these interrelations is also linked to time. One characteristic may have a positive impact at a given moment in the process, whereas it may have a different impact, or even be a factor of failure, at a different point in time. If the entrepreneur receives specific training in venture creation at the very beginning of the process, this will provide him or her with valuable knowledge, particularly regarding the strategic management of the process, whereas the same training received during the launch phase of the business will hardly have any effect at all. Entrepreneurs are also likely to change environments to a greater or lesser extent, as their status changes over time.

Relations are necessarily contingent, as one environment characteristic may be an opportunity or a favourable factor for a given project, but an obstacle for another, or it may have no impact whatsoever, and the same is true for entrepreneurs. For example, the implementation of strict norms and regulations in matters of environmental protection may be a difficult obstacle to overcome, but it could also be an opportunity of creation or development for entrepreneurs whose project is related to giving advice on environmental protection.

Finally, relations are paradoxical. For a specific case or type of company creation, the same environmental characteristic may impact simultaneously in a positive and negative manner on the venture creation process. Technological turbulence can be a source of opportunities as well as a source of risk that could make the success of the company more uncertain and the entrepreneurial act riskier, especially if the assets are specific and irreversible costs are high. This implies non-linear relations: no turbulence in the environment means little opportunity, too much turbulence generates too much risk.

In a word, the weight of the environment on the phenomenon is very significant. It will be all the more so if the local, personal and project-specific environments coincide. Industrial districts (Beccatini 1992) or clusters of competence (Courlet 1990) define closely knit networks that condition the emergence and the life of companies in a given sector. In this particular form of regional industrial organisation, cooperation and networks are pivotal, and in this context starting a company goes beyond the economic act and becomes an act of integration into a community. The industrial community overlaps with the social community along with the families and their social links.

A given environment may also have characteristics that prevent certain types or any types of entrepreneurial ventures. This is particularly true of political, social or religious environments prohibiting any kind of private enterprise, and this may also be true in the case of family constraints that are particularly heavy or in cases of extreme poverty of the populations involved.

9 | A generic model of the entrepreneurial process

Entrepreneurial processes are complex processes. They cannot be reduced to a few phases in a linear and predetermined sequence. Complexity also implies that it is difficult, given the diversity of situations, to identify regularities and cause–effect relations. In this respect, attempting to model the process is a perilous exercise that should be attempted with precaution. Aware of this pitfall, Bruyat (1993) carefully delimited the application scope of his model of new venture creation process. He also introduced the notion of canonical model, to distinguish his approach from other works with a more operational objective and that focus on more homogeneous types of creation. The process model we will develop in this chapter relies on a similar perspective. What we present here is a meta-model designed to be applicable to all the processes that support the entrepreneurial act.

An entrepreneurial process is made up of various decisions, actions and orientations based on how the individuals perceive and analyse situations, according to their goals, motivations, resources and environment. In the teleological perspective, it is the actor's perceived instantaneous strategic configuration that controls and pilots the process. Bruyat (1993) also examines these mechanisms in his approach to the business start-up process. His idea is above all to identify pivotal moments, changes in the activity or effort rhythm, and changes in the rhythm of important or irreversible intermediary decisions. While an arbitrary procedure, breaking down a process into elements is an interesting means better to apprehend and understand a complex process. In the following sections, I present the perspective that underlies our model and its validity scope before examining synchronic and diachronic approaches to the process.

Perspective and limitations of the model

I will first present the structuring aspects of our perspective, before examining the validity of our model depending on the type of situation, based on the individual/new value creation dialogic.

Our perspective

Two main ideas underlie the perspective I chose for our process-modelling attempt.

The idea of usefulness

The entrepreneur is at the heart of our preoccupations. However, the objective of this model is to be used by those who support and advise the entrepreneur in the context of business start-up and development support structures. The model is more particularly designed for venture creation stakeholders such as chambers of commerce and industry, regional and national administrations, large corporations, consulting and training organisations, etc.

One of the reasons behind designing a model that can be useful for support structures is that the entrepreneurial process, as far as the main actor is concerned, appears as a transitory, non-repetitive process. In addition, our own experience of supporting and following entrepreneurs throughout the process has led us to the conclusion that these activities and practices could be improved by the implementation of specific methods and tools.

The idea of complexity

Guiding an entrepreneur in his or her project implies that the dynamics and specificities of his personal character, know-how, project and resources should be taken into account in the context of multiple environments. Support structures may appear as an artificial means to facilitate and secure the entrepreneurial process, but we rather see them as structures favouring the success of entrepreneurs by helping them acquire, along the way, the situational intelligence that will enable them to deal with the various situations encountered while developing the

Table 9.1. *Complicated system and complex system*

TO UNDERSTAND and make sense of	
A COMPLICATED SYSTEM one can SIMPLIFY IT to discover its INTELLIGIBILITY (explanation)	A COMPLEX SYSTEM one must MODEL IT to build its INTELLIGIBILITY (understanding)
HOWEVER, BY SIMPLIFYING A COMPLEX SYSTEM, ONE DESTROYS A PRIORI ITS INTELLIGIBILITY	

Source: Le Moigne 1990.

project. In this light, it is clear that support cannot be reduced to providing natural statistical regularities to the entrepreneur.

The model I propose should enable us better to understand and act upon the phenomenon by taking its complexity into account. Table 9.1 illustrates the differences between the analytical and the systemic models of complexity.

Going for the complexity paradigm implies abandoning (at first) the idea of increasing the stock of local, empirical and contingent knowledge, while trying to develop tools that can be used in intervention situations. This also contributes to the research in line with the classic paradigm by proposing a synthetic vision and a qualitative theory of the entrepreneurial process.

My project is to build a model or a general canonical system as defined by Le Moigne[1] (1990: 38): 'to represent a complex phenomenon, it is necessary to represent it as a system, a general and stable enough system to account for all the types of complexity that may be considered; a canonical system in that it integrates the conjunctive axiomatic'. The purpose of this model is also to generate more instrumented models that could be applied to specific entrepreneurial processes in a perspective of intervention.

---

[1] We have extensively referred to and used Le Moigne's (1990) work in our modelling approach.

Table 9.2. *Validity of the model presented*

High validity of the model	Low validity of the model
Single actor	Group or partnership
Unique, single-occurrence act	Repeated operation
Strong personal commitment (low reversibility)	Little personal commitment (high reversibility)
The entrepreneur is an employee or job seeker	The entrepreneur owns a company
Independent company	Dependent company: subsidiary or profit centre
SME or larger	Micro-enterprise
New activity	Takeover of existing activity (no change)
Sustainability sought	Temporary operation ('one-off')
Private commercial sector	Non-profit sector (non-commercial)
Economic context	Political context

Source: Bruyat 1993.

The validity scope of our model

To define the validity scope of the model, we have used a number of criteria that individually and globally determine a zone of high (versus low) validity of the model. Table 9.2 presents these criteria.

It may be useful to clarify some of these criteria. The first four criteria concern the entrepreneur. The validity of our model is all the higher when the individual is a single actor (we also include teams, but exclude entrepreneurial acts without a leader), and is inexperienced as regards the entrepreneurial process. In most cases, this individual is an employee or a job seeker. The following criteria relate to the object of value creation. The new venture must be independent, as situations concerning creations of subsidiaries or profit centres, or even franchised companies, have less relevance with our model, as do job creations through micro-enterprises or takeovers of existing activities without major changes. Another important aspect is that of sustainability: the new value creation object must be viable in the long term. In conclusion, we could note that our work concerns specifically the creation, hopefully sustainable, of a new economic entity.

The time horizon considered is compatible with this last remark as well as with the usual support practices and tools. We consider as the starting point the moment when the individual envisages creating a new economic entity, and, as the end point, the moment when this entity is considered established, which generally corresponds to two to three years after its legal registration or the start of its commercial activities.

The entrepreneurial process from a synchronic perspective

The synchronic representation of the system may be formulated thus: at a given point in time, entrepreneurial individuals find information/decide/act influenced by their personal traits and mental patterns, and formulate one or several projects, more or less clear and definite, and the matrix of these projects is the representation they have of their strategic configuration (goals, skills and resources, characteristics of the environments). In the previous chapters, we presented the various elements in this representation: the entrepreneur or entrepreneurial individual, the new value creation object or entrepreneurial project, the perceived instantaneous strategic configuration, and finally the question of environments. In this section, we will present a generic form of entrepreneurial process, broken down into various 'positions' of the individual/new value creation dialogic system. These positions correspond to key events in the process, changes in the rhythm of the activity or efforts, and changes in the rhythm of important or irreversible intermediary decisions (see chapter 8). Figure 9.1 illustrates this approach.

> **Position 0** means that the possibility of venture creation is not perceived. This situation may be explained by insufficient information, resulting from the individual's education, personality or environment.
> **Position 1** means that the possibility of creating one's own company is perceived. Individuals in this situation have the necessary information to know and understand what starting up a business means, but this possibility is not acted upon and has not been thought through. In a study based on former students of Babson College who created their own businesses, Ronstadt (1982) wrote: 'most entrepreneurs in the sample did not purposely choose a career that would prepare them for their entrepreneurial

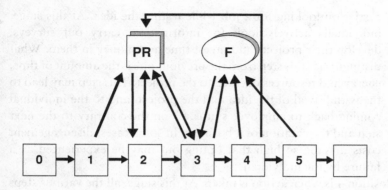

Step 0: the act of new venture creation is **not perceived**
Step 1: the act of new venture creation is **perceived**
Step 2: the act of new venture creation is **considered**
Step 3: the act of new venture creation is **desired**
Step 4: the act of new venture creation is **started**
Step 5: the act of new venture creation is **completed**
P   the act of new venture creation is **perceived**
R   the act of new venture creation is **refused**
F   **failure** of the action

Figure 9.1. A generic model of the entrepreneurial process (adapted from Bruyat 1993)

careers since they had no idea at the time that they would later pursue an entrepreneurial career'.

Position 2 means that the act of business creation is considered. In this case, individuals consider this as a possible alternative to their current situations. Individuals have a venture creation project in mind, but it is not yet very precise; it is more an intention than a project. Potential entrepreneurs try to identify a possible business idea, start to look for information, and pay attention to everything in the media that relates to venture creation or among their social network. However, at this stage, they devote little time and energy to this activity. This situation may last for a long time and stops when the individual goes to the next step or opts out.

Position 3 means the action is desired. Individuals are actively looking for an idea (if they have not found it yet), then will try to evaluate it, while continuing to work in their current job. If the entrepreneurial individual is a job seeker, he or she generally carries on looking for a job while testing the idea. At this stage, individuals actively look for information, carry out surveys, develop their projects and invest time and money in them. What distinguishes this step from the previous one is the amount of time, energy and resources devoted to the project. This step may lead to the withdrawal of the idea and the project, and to the individual coming back to employee status, or on the contrary to the next step and the creation of a business. In some cases, disengagement costs may be so high that opting out may be experienced as a failure by the individual.

Position 4 is when action is taken. At this stage, all the various steps required for the new economic entity to function are taken: leasing or buying premises and necessary production equipment, negotiation of deals with suppliers and customers, recruitment of staff, legal and financial procedures. The new organisation is ready to operate; it begins to produce and trade. At this point, going back is very difficult, even impossible, because the financial and psychological costs would be too high. The fledgling company, however, is still in a delicate position. It remains fragile and resource consuming, especially in terms of personal energy. It may reach its breakeven point, financial balance, and reach the fifth position, but it may also face difficulties that could, even at this stage, lead to failure or opting-out.

Position 5 means that the action is completed. The company has reached its operational balance. It has become an economic entity recognised by its external partners. The entrepreneur has succeeded. The entrepreneur has proved his or her project was a viable one, and is now a small (or medium-sized) company manager. The emergence phase is over, but in most cases the entrepreneur/fledgling firm dialogic remains.

In this vision of the process, the passage from one position to the other is not automatic. The actor may refuse to undertake an action (position 'PR' in the figure), opt out, go back to a previous position, or draw negative conclusions from the experience and decide to give up all idea of ever trying to start a business again. An action, once engaged, may also fail (position F). The actor may then go back to a former position or draw negative conclusions from this experience and decide to give up starting a business.

The company creation process we describe here implies that any individual who engages in it will have to accomplish a certain number of actions and will have numerous decisions to make. This breakdown shows key moments in the entrepreneurial process. Each step corresponds to a particular position of the entrepreneurial actor and to specific actions of business creation support. In practice, however, it is harder to determine whether the entrepreneur is still in one given position or if he or she has moved on to the next.

The entrepreneurial process from a diachronic perspective

In this section, we will highlight the key dynamics of creation and transformation of the entrepreneurial system. We will try to bring elements better to understand the evolutions and transformations of this system. The idea is to propose representations that can help anticipate several possible scenarios, identify configurations and determine key issues.

The process dynamics derive from the modifications of the perceived instantaneous strategic configuration, a notion we developed in chapter 5. This concept can be summarised as follows: the perceived instantaneous strategic configuration of the potential entrepreneur expresses goals and objectives perceived through the scope of his or her aspirations, skills and resources, and finally the possibilities of the environment. What we call the coherence zone of the perceived instantaneous strategic configuration corresponds to actions that are perceived by the individual as both desirable and possible. The potential entrepreneur considers he or she has the means and skills to succeed; he or she has a positive perception of his or her self-efficacy. It is within this zone that projects can develop and objectives can mature over time. Any evolution of the perceived instantaneous strategic configuration may trigger changes in the process.

The venture creation model we propose here in its diachronic dimension covers three phases: the **trigger of the process**, the **total commitment** of the entrepreneurial individual, the **survival of the company created** (abortion, success, possible expansion). We will develop in the three following subsections the dynamic of change and the conditions that lead the individual into each one of these phases. We will then conclude this chapter by addressing the concept of activity, which introduces the final part of this book.

How the process is triggered

The dynamics of evolution of the perceived instantaneous strategic configuration are both internal and external. They may be influenced by the individual or the environment and alter the coherence of the perceived instantaneous strategic configuration, which will consequently lead to the emergence of a new, more coherent configuration. Individuals' aspirations or skills may change, following a training course for instance. This change may lead the individual to consider that a venture creation, in this new light, is possible. The individual's environment may unsettle the zone of coherence of his or her perceived instantaneous strategic configuration, through the appearance of new threats, such as the threat of layoff, to name but one.

Below I consider in which conditions the process is triggered. These conditions are not independent, but work as a system. The first one seems to be the engine of the action, the second the real trigger event, whereas the third can potentially be a hindrance factor.

The act of creation must be perceived as both desired and possible

Intentions and aspirations are not sufficient to understand how the process is triggered; one essential condition is that the envisaged behaviour should be considered as possible by the individual. Shapero underlines that desire and the perception of feasibility are inseparable: 'perceptions of desirability and perceptions of feasibility necessarily interact. If one perceives the formation of a company as unfeasible, one may conclude it is undesirable. If one perceives the act as undesirable, one may never consider its feasibility' (Shapero and Sokol 1982: 86). This point of view is shared by many other authors in the field.

Thus the 'seeds' of creation may be already there, waiting for favourable circumstances in which to 'germinate', in which case the environment plays an essential part as a triggering element. Conversely, the perception of an opportunity or a constraint may trigger the desire to create.

The perceived instantaneous strategic configuration reveals important tensions and contradictions

These tensions and contradictions are linked to professional frustrations or the existence of rival and incompatible projects in the coherence zone of the perceived instantaneous strategic configuration. The individual will try to reduce these tensions and contradictions and consequently alter the project.

This idea that positive or negative factors of movement may encourage the entrepreneurial act was highlighted notably by Shapero, who wrote:

In the many studies of technical company formations, seldom is a case found in which a gradual, phased, carefully planned succession of actions and discussions leads to a company formation. The situation is better described as one in which the individual or group is subjected to a constantly interacting and dynamic field of forces that pushes him in all directions. These forces include both internal and external components and the individual is often balanced between internal pushes and external constraints, or vice versa. Usually the forces counterbalance each other so that there is some stability and continuity in an individual's occupational movements. When the forces are out of balance, the individual is pushed to act; if he is a potential entrepreneur, the act may be a company formation. (Shapero 1972: 79)

The individual needs time to work on the project

Without a little time set aside to engage in the primary search for information, and without a few resources to face compulsory expenses when required, it is hard to imagine how an individual could possibly enter the entrepreneurial process. This is how, for example, executives who seem to have all the required skills as well as a desire to set up their own business will not enter the creation process because, owing to their professional activities, they often lack the time to do so. Other situations, such as heavy debt or family responsibilities, may also crush any will to start a business. At this stage, the necessary energy to initiate the entrepreneurial project can only come from entrepreneurs themselves.

Total commitment/taking action

Total commitment is achieved when the potential entrepreneur devotes most of his or her time, and financial, intellectual and emotional investments, to his or her project. This commitment is a transitory phase, a phase of change: commitment increases progressively until it reaches a point of no return. Setting up a company represents a major strategic change for the individual. In this light, two conditions appear necessary for total commitment to be achieved. I present them below.

The act of venture creation is favoured and perceived as feasible

The first requirement for total commitment is that the act of venture creation or the creation project should be favoured over all alternatives of change (change of company for instance), and especially over the current situation (employee, job seeker, student). It must also be perceived as feasible.

Most theoretical models of venture creation put forward this dimension of preference as essential. It is generally presented as the result of the interaction with both personal and environmental factors.

Resistance to change must be overcome

Resistance to change stems from various factors and circumstances; it may come from habits and inertia in reasoning and behaviour. It is particularly important when an individual has spent most of his or her professional life as an employee, without ever considering the possibility of starting a business or developing other types of risk-taking behaviours. Another source of resistance is linked to the fear of the unknown. The uncertainty may be linked to a particular project or the general lack of knowledge about entrepreneurial situations. A third factor of resistance to change is linked to the perceived irreversibility of the newly created situation and the expected difficulties in case of failure (in finding another job as an employee for instance). Resistance to change also stems from the sacrifices implied, the financial and psychological costs: giving up a rewarding situation, leisure time, family time, cutting costs for a while (and maybe forever). Lastly, in some countries, like France, another factor of resistance to change is linked to the perceived hostility of the environment towards entrepreneurs and the obstacles which may stand in the entrepreneur's way.

As was the case for the triggering conditions, conditions for total commitment are interrelated. Strong resistance to change, for instance, may reduce the potential attractiveness of the entrepreneurial alternative.

Survival, failure or development

The act of venture creation does not always lead to the viability of the company, and the process may take different shapes: survival, failure or development. Here viability means whether a company can reach a breakeven point within a reasonable time span. The main conditions of success or failure are the actor's capacity to learn and the system's coherence.

Coherence between the entrepreneur's perceived instantaneous strategic configuration and the project

Here I argue that the coherence between the entrepreneur's perceived instantaneous strategic configuration and his or her project is an essential factor of success for the new venture creation project. In our opinion, there is no universal resource or skill applicable to all situations that would be required for the success of projects. Of course, some minimum skills in various fields are required, but the most important skill appears to be that of self-diagnosis. Self-diagnosis enables the actor constantly to check that the level of coherence between the perceived instantaneous strategic configuration and the project is adequate. Indeed, incoherencies generate unpredicted hidden costs and delays: delays in generating a turnover, higher supply and production costs, lower productivity, and increase in financial needs.

This factor is all the more important as the transformation of the individual/new value creation system almost always causes incoherencies and inadequacies. Moreover, the evolution of the system throughout the process changes the nature of required skills. The resources and skills that must be implemented are different, depending on the various phases of the process. For instance, if commercial skills are very important at start-up, they are far from being critical during the set-up phase of the project.

Learning can reinforce the coherence of the system

Learning is a key element of the success (or failure) of the process. Entrepreneurial individuals must learn as the system changes and incoherencies are generated; this will increase the coherence of the system and make it possible to balance it out. It will lead to the modification of the project and the acquisition of new resources and skills. This particular situation is well summed up in the following metaphor: 'to a certain extent, one finds oneself in the unbelievable situation of a pilot who must take off while still learning to fly, and while the plane is being built' (Massacrier and Rigaud 1984: 12).

Learning happens throughout the process, at different levels. In positions 2 and 3 (see synchronic perspective), the entrepreneur dominates the project and reality does not interfere with so much force. It is during this period that individuals can learn by transfer of knowledge in classic training courses (if, that is, they acknowledge that they need to learn). During the launch phase (position 4), time often becomes a rare resource for the entrepreneur, who therefore learns on the job, through action. Learning happens in an emergence context and will be particularly important in the first years of the fledgling company (Bouchikhi 1991). Following position 4, when the company has survived and the entrepreneur has learnt what needed to be learnt, the new organisation starts learning too.

The greater the change, the more the system needs quick learning and modification capacities. In this light, the entrepreneur's learning capacities appear as a key element to explain the success of a venture creation process. The earlier the learning, the earlier the company is able to avoid the weight of hidden costs due to incoherencies, and the better chances of success it will have.

The 'activities' in the process

The heterogeneity of situations and processes makes their analysis and the elaboration of universal models rather complicated. Some projects proceed rather linearly, others are clearly chaotic. The sequence of a project must be understood thus: the trigger and/or commitment may or may not happen, and the outcome may be positive or negative. This vision only partially covers the variety of cases and the potentially spiralling nature of the process. Sociologists from the Centre de Sociologie de l'Innovation (Centre for Sociology of Innovation) at the Ecole Nationale Supérieure des Mines de Paris have proposed a 'spiralling model'[2] of the innovation process. We could retain this idea, which is coherent with change and uncertainty situations, to address

---

[2] The French term coined by the CSI researchers is 'modèle tourbillonaire'.

the primary difficulty of linearity. The second problem is that the possible chain of events Trigger → Commitment → Outcome is too general to apply to processes of a very different nature. This is why we think it could be interesting to represent this chain of events, not at a global level (macroscopic), but at a finer level (microscopic), by adding another dimension or level, that of **activities** (that is to say the various activities that make up the entrepreneurial project). An activity could be triggered by the success or failure of a previous activity; commitment would be not commitment to the project, but total commitment to a given activity. We could also postulate that activities can occur simultaneously.

The introduction of the notion of activities also finds its justification in the fact that, in an entrepreneurial situation, there is permanent tension between the **resources necessary to accomplish the project** and the **resources available** (Stevenson and Jarillo 1990). These resources are insufficient at all levels (time, money, equipment, etc.). The permanence of these tensions implies specific behaviours and practices for the entrepreneur (including in terms of management). **The commitment of resources within an entrepreneurial process therefore happens gradually, activity by activity, not all at once.** This also means that after each activity, or during each activity, the project may be abandoned, or reformulated, resulting in taking a step back. By way of example, the activities considered in a new venture creation process could be the evaluation of the opportunity, the study and formulation of the project, the legal and financial set-up, and the launch of the trading activities.

Some activities, especially in technological and innovative projects, may require to be subdivided. Indeed, it could be necessary to identify separately activities such as testing technical feasibility and prototyping in order to give more credibility and tangibility to a technical idea or concept. All these activities, at different levels, and with more or less intensity, consume resources, in a context where they are scarce. These resources fuel the dialogic system that needs them to remain active.

PART IV

Entrepreneurial process dynamics

In the third part of this book, I defined and discussed the notion of entrepreneurial process and proposed a generic model in line with conceptual and epistemological choices. The foundations of the theoretical approach are based on the assumption that entrepreneurship is a subject/object dialogic, and my work revolves around the interacting individual/new value creation system.

'The process is a sequence of concomitant and/or successive configurations and interactions under the impact of compensating and amplifying regulations specific to the system concerned' (Jacquet-Lagreze *et al.* 1978). The process is a dynamic and evolving system in which time plays an essential role. The main engine of the process is teleological, which means that change is the consequence of the assignation of goals and the expression of a vision aspiring to a desired end state.

I proposed three distinct stages to describe the evolution of the system: the process trigger, the commitment to the process, and the process survival/development phase. The final three chapters of this book are devoted to developing these three phases. For each phase, I will propose and explore theoretical corpuses in order better to understand its dynamics. These theories should help us answer the following research questions: how can we better understand and model, in our chosen perspective, the trigger of the process, commitment to the process, and the survival/development of the project and the newly formed company.

Science is essentially anarchistic: theoretical anarchy is more humanitarian and likely to encourage progress than doctrines based on law and order (Feyerabend 1979). In view of this and encouraged by Van de Ven, I have looked not for one but for several explanatory theories borrowed from related fields. I consider these theories to be 'useful' in the sense given by Penrose (1989), as quoted by Bygrave and Hofer (1991: 16):

For the physical sciences, Penrose (1989) proposed three broad categories of theories: (1) Superb, (2) Useful, and (3) Tentative. Superb theories, such as Euclidean geometry, Newtonian mechanics, and Einsteinian special relativity, make predictions that are amazingly accurate. To date, however, all such theories fall exclusively in the province of the mathematical and physical sciences. According to Penrose, there are no basic theories in any other science that can be classified as 'Superb'. Darwinian natural selection comes closest, but it is still a good way off. Useful theories are rather more untidy than superb ones. Thus, while they generally make good predictions, their predictive power falls far short of the amazing accuracy of superb theories. Tentative theories, by contrast, are just that – tentative! Their predictions are, at best, vague and of limited accuracy, and they generally lack significant empirical support. Consequently, it seems for us that the very best we can hope for in the field of entrepreneurship is useful models and theories.

The theories we propose to use are specific neither to the object studied here, nor to the field of entrepreneurship in general; they were elaborated, proposed and tested in other contexts and other fields, but they nevertheless seem particularly relevant to the understanding of the various phases in our model. Because our field, entrepreneurship, is still in its early years, it does not have its own specific theories, although, as Lewin puts it, there is no better way to study a phenomenon than by resorting to a good theory. In light of this, and while waiting for the emergence of a theory specific to the entrepreneurial process, we have decided to use existing theoretical frameworks.

Chapter 10 will be devoted to the process trigger, the initial phase of the system. Shapero's work provided us with the useful theory of displacement and a model, that of the entrepreneurial event formation. Many years later, I can only commend these works in light of the many cases I have studied, and praise their accuracy and relevance. According to Shapero, the process trigger derives from a factor of displacement, often external, which calls into question the validity of previous choices and positions. Other authors adopted a different point of view and proposed intention models that rely on the intentionality of action and explain the trigger phase through internal dynamics. The theory of planned behaviour (Ajzen 1991) belongs to this second current of research and seems particularly relevant in understanding the process trigger.

Chapter 11 deals with the commitment phase. This is a very important phase, as the absence of strong commitment jeopardises projects and processes owing to a lack of motivation. We will show in this chapter that psychosocial theories of commitment are not sufficient in clarifying this issue. In light of this, we propose to use catastrophe theory as a metaphor to explain the multiplicity of commitment types.

The survival/development phase is examined in chapter 12. It distinguishes itself from the previous phases in that it lasts longer. To survive and develop, the fledgling company must acquire necessary resources at the right time. In order to do so, it is necessary to have allies who can allocate these resources. Allies may also be intermediaries who will facilitate access to the resources. To explain the mechanisms of identification, acquisition and utilisation of the resources necessary to the survival and development of the system, I propose using the theory of interest generation ('théorie de l'intéressement'), developed by researchers of the Centre de Sociologie de l'Innovation (CSI) of the Ecole Nationale Supérieure des Mines de Paris, social networks theory, and the structuration theory elaborated by Anthony Giddens.

10 | *Entrepreneurial process trigger phase*

The process is triggered by the conjunction of two factors: intention, which is an internal driving force, and displacement, which refers to an external force. These two elements should not be dissociated because they can both contribute to the evolution of the perceived instantaneous strategic configuration. I speak about 'conjunction' here, because, in my opinion, both factors are associated in triggering the process. However, these two factors do not always occur in the same order. In some cases, intention appears very early, and it can take a long time before a favourable occasion appears. In other situations, a displacement may trigger the formation of the intention, more or less progressively. I propose, in this chapter, two theoretical frameworks: the concept of displacement introduced by Shapero and the theory of planned behaviour that clarifies the notion of intention and proposes an intention model. I will start with Shapero's work, and then present some of the most famous intention models, before developing the theory of planned behaviour. In the final part of this chapter, I will attempt to combine both theoretical frameworks.

Shapero's entrepreneurial event and factors of displacement

In order to understand better the concept of displacement, I will present and discuss it from the perspective of Shapero and Sokol's model of the entrepreneurial event (1982). Shapero and Sokol's paper (1982) is based on the following question: what kind of social and cultural factors and environments result in entrepreneurial events?

Their aim is to describe the formation of the entrepreneurial event. The unit of analysis is the entrepreneurial event rather than the entrepreneur. The event becomes the dependent variable, while the individual or group that generates the event, as well as the social, economic, political and cultural contexts, become the independent variables (Shapero and Sokol 1982). According to these authors, higher

Table 10.1. *Variables at the root of the entrepreneurial event*

Displacements	Perceptions of desirability	Perceptions of feasibility
Negative displacements	Culture	Financial support
Forcefully emigrated	Family	Other support
Fired	Peers	Demonstration effect
Insulted	Colleagues	Models
Angered	Mentor	Mentors
Bored		Partners
Reaching middle age		
Divorced or widowed		
Between things		
Out of army		
Out of school		
Out of jail		
Positive pull		
From partner		
From mentor		
From investor		
From customer		

Source: Shapero and Sokol 1982: 83.

numbers of business start-ups are partially attributable to social and cultural variables.

In this perspective, the question concerning each entrepreneurial event is: 'how did group membership and social and cultural environments affect the choice of an entrepreneurial path?' (Shapero and Sokol 1982: 78).

It is important to understand that the new venture creation process is overdetermined, that is, that a number of factors are necessary, but no single factor is sufficient.

Shapero and Sokol express the key idea that the entrepreneurial event results from the interactions of situational, cultural and social variables. Table 10.1 presents these factors.

Shapero and Sokol suggest that individuals with no obvious reason for change sometimes opt for a major change in their life. The combination of a number of forces is necessary to lead to the change process.

It must also be noted that individuals are more likely to take action upon negative forces rather than positive ones. This change is called displacement. Negative displacements are found to result in far more business start-ups than do positive possibilities. However, it is the combination of both positive and negative forces that accounts for most major changes in life paths. In this perspective, displacement is a prevalent antecedent. Displacement can be internal or external. For instance, external displacements such as job-related displacements (layoff, boss sold the company, etc.) are rather frequent (Shapero 1975). Some other displacements are internal to the entrepreneur, in that they are not triggered by anything in particular, but mainly because of time passing by. For example, feeling out of place or being between things often precedes the creation of a company. Although negative displacements prevail, there are many positive pulls that lead to business start-ups: the offer of financial support, a contract proposal by a would-be customer, etc. In many instances, the subjects of both positive pulls and/or negative displacements report that they had no idea of going into business when the offer came.

Shapero and Sokol also answer the question of what helps determine which course of action (among all the possible and available alternatives for the individual) will be seriously considered and subsequently pursued. Perceptions of desirability and feasibility are two major factors influenced by the cultural and social environments. The perception of feasibility may influence the notion of what is desirable. This model suggests that two main requirements are necessary for the new venture event to appear. First, founders should perceive that starting a new venture is credible or desirable (i.e. they have intentions towards entrepreneurship). Starting a new venture must be a believable opportunity (Krueger 1993). Shapero defined perceived desirability as the extent to which one finds the prospect of starting a business to be attractive; in essence, it reflects one's feelings towards entrepreneurship. Second, founders should perceive that starting a new venture is feasible, that is to say, they believe that they are personally capable of starting a business (Krueger 1993).

Shapero and Sokol proposed several variables in order to measure these two factors (perceived desirability and feasibility). To measure the concept of desirability, data are collected within various contexts: the close family (which plays the most significant role in establishing the desirability and credibility of entrepreneurial action for the individual), the peer group (colleagues, relatives, classmates – the larger the number and variety of entrepreneurs in a particular culture, the greater the probability that the individuals in that culture will form companies), the ethnic group (it is no coincidence that entrepreneurship is highly identified with certain ethnic groups), and previous work experience (for example, a small firm provides a close view of the individual who founded it, so it becomes possible for the potential entrepreneur to consider a comparable role for himself). Two key factors that may influence feasibility and the 'propensity to act' are the availability of general or specific financial support for entrepreneurial activities, and would-be partners who can help transform vague possibilities into action.

The propensity to act as proposed by Shapero and Sokol (1982) concerns the disposition to act upon one's decisions. This reflects the volitional component of intention ('Will I actually do it?'). It seems difficult to imagine well-formed intentions without a significant propensity to act (Bagozzi and Yi 1989): one is unlikely to have serious intentions towards a behaviour without perceiving a likelihood of taking action. Moreover, propensity to act moderates other relationships in the model (Krueger 1993), which suggests that propensity to act might be better viewed as a moderating influence rather than a direct antecedent.

Intention-based models

Intention models have been used in an attempt to explain the emergence of entrepreneurial behaviour. In these approaches, career intentions depend on the attitude towards the behaviour considered, social standards and the level of perceived control (Ajzen 1991). For many authors (Shapero and Sokol 1982; Bird 1988; Krueger and Carsrud 1993; Autio *et al.* 1997; Tkachev and Kolvereid 1999), venture creation is a planned, hence intentional, behaviour. Intention therefore appears to be a better factor of predictability of the behaviour than attitudes, beliefs and other psychological or sociological variables (Krueger and Carsrud 1993). It means that attitudes and beliefs predict intention that in turn predicts behaviour (Ajzen and Fishbein 1980). Therefore we can say that intention serves as a mediator or catalyst for action.

Numerous models have been proposed in entrepreneurship literature, which can be a source of confusion, as Shook, Priem and McGee underline (2003: 386): 'With regard to theoretical limitations, the entrepreneurial intent literature has not resulted in cumulative knowledge because the various perspectives have been pursued in isolation from other perspectives . . . Future work on entrepreneurial intentions should attempt to integrate and reduce the number of alternative intention models.'

I have identified three interesting intention models proposed in the literature (see Krueger and Carsrud 1993 or more recently, Shook, Priem and McGee 2003). In the following sections, I will present Bird's and Shapero's models and then Ajzen's theory of planned behaviour.

Bird's intention-based model

This first model was proposed by Bird (1988; 1992), and was later modified, notably by Boyd and Vozikis (1994). The model is designed to represent the implementation of entrepreneurial ideas. In this model, entrepreneurial intentions are considered as the result of either rational, analytical and cause–effect thinking or intuitive, holistic and contextual thinking. Entrepreneurial intentions are considered as the link between the entrepreneur as an individual and the context within which a venture is created (Bird and Jelinek 1988).

The first postulate is that potential entrepreneurs start or buy existing businesses by choice; they choose this career alternative. Even though inspiration is the source of entrepreneurial ideas, sustained attention and intention are needed in order for them to surface (Bird 1988).

Bird and Jelinek (1988) define the concept of intentionality as 'a state of mind directing a person's attention, experience, and behavior towards a specific object or method of behaving'. Entrepreneurs' intentions tend to be directed towards goals, which are desired end-states, rather than towards the means to reach these goals, although both means and ends can be intentional (Bird 1988).

Bird and Jelinek (1988) break down the entrepreneur's intention-related skills into five key aspects:

Structuring resources: entrepreneurs dedicate existing resources (money, inventions, hard work, etc.) towards future outcomes by systematically organising, focusing and applying them to problems and dilemmas in the market or social system (Bird and Jelinek 1988). As resources are focused in this manner, rational entrepreneurial decisions are incremental and multistaged, with minimal exposure to risk at each stage (Stevenson 1985).

Flexible focus: the flexibility of strategic focus is necessary to ensure that current activities and decisions contribute to the organisation's future (Bird and Jelinek 1988). Hambrick and Crozier (1985) show how envisioning growth helps the entrepreneur to restructure and reposition the firm successfully.

Temporal agility: a plan requires ability to move comfortably between multiple future time horizons (Bird and Jelinek 1988). Long-term thinking is important to have a clear vision and to form long-term relationships (with bankers, strategic actors, etc.) while entrepreneurs are necessarily short-term actors. They must have a predisposition towards immediate action and a 'do it now' orientation to move from dreams into reality (the 'action bias' noted by Peters and Waterman 1982; cited by Bird and Jelinek 1988).

Behavioural flexibility: entrepreneurs need to be able to switch functions and roles, especially in the start-up situation when full-time staffing is limited (Bird and Jelinek 1988).

Influencing others: entrepreneurs must exercise substantial influence over others in order to implement their intentions (Bird and Jelinek 1988).

For Bird (1988), another dimension of entrepreneurial intention is that of rationality versus intuition. The individual's rational, analytical and cause–effect oriented processes structure intention and action (writing a formal business plan, opportunity analysis, etc.), while intuitive, holistic and contextual thinking also frame and structure the entrepreneur's intention and action.

While the model could be used for the purpose of our research, at least two objections can be raised: (a) this model has been designed mainly with the aim of better understanding the implementation of entrepreneurial ideas, while entrepreneurial intention, to my mind, could be formed and developed without the existence of such ideas, and (b) this model of implementing entrepreneurial ideas has apparently not yet been validated empirically.

Shapero's entrepreneurial event seen as an intention-based model

This second model is well known in the field and was proposed by Shapero and Sokol (1982). It is often presented as an intention model, especially in Krueger's works. However, as we have seen previously, Shapero and Sokol's goal was mainly to design a model to support the formation of the entrepreneurial event. The authors themselves talk about 'a possible frame of reference – a paradigm of entrepreneurial event formation' (Shapero and Sokol 1982: 76). They also propose an entrepreneurial event formation model (1982: 83) and highlight the key notion of displacement as a triggering element of the entrepreneurial process. The formation of the company depends on the perceptions of desirability and feasibility. This would suggest that, following a displacement, perceptions of desirability and feasibility lead to the formation of the entrepreneurial event. While these authors do not explicitly use the concept of intention, there appears to be a strong link between this concept and those of desirability and feasibility. Although this interesting framework (see Krueger 1993) has been tested and sometimes compared to other theories such as the theory of planned behaviour (see Krueger *et al.* 2000), it focuses exclusively on the issue of new venture creation and not on the evolution towards the adoption of an entrepreneurial behaviour in general.

The theory of planned behaviour

The theory of planned behaviour relies on the concept of reasoned action. It was elaborated by Ajzen (1991), who reformulated it in 2002. This theory gives the concept of intention a central and predominant role in the prediction and explanation of planned human behaviour. The theory postulates that planned human behaviour is entirely controlled by will and does not depend on any factor that would not be directly controllable by the individual concerned. This automatically limits the utilisation of the theoretical corpus, as the situations that meet all the requirements are scarce. This limitation concerns essentially the automatic nature of the relation between intention and behaviour. While intention can be, under certain circumstances, a good antecedent of behaviour, one cannot assume that intention is automatically followed by behaviour. This depends, naturally, on the type of

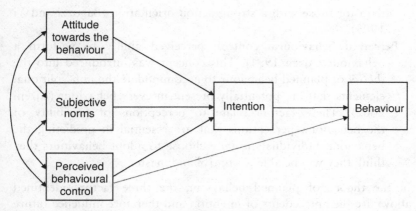

Figure 10.1. The theory of planned behaviour (Ajzen 1991)

behaviour. The examples used by Ajzen correspond, in most cases, to behaviours that are controllable by individuals in which personal will plays a great part: decision to stop smoking, election choices, or even choosing between breast-feeding and bottle-feeding. I am convinced of the importance of this theory for the field of entrepreneurship, especially regarding the role it may play in the trigger of the process, but I think that entrepreneurial behaviour is more complex (and therefore less predictable via the intention perspective) than the cases previously mentioned.

The central factor of the theory of planned behaviour is the individual intention to perform a given behaviour. The main postulate is that intention is the result of three conceptual determinants, as illustrated in Figure 10.1.

Attitude towards the behaviour: the degree to which the performance of the behaviour is positively or negatively valued (Ajzen 1991). When new issues arise requiring an evaluative response, people can draw on relevant information (beliefs) stored in their memories. Because each of these beliefs carries evaluative implications, attitudes are automatically formed.

Subjective norms: perceived social pressures to perform, or not, the behaviour (Ajzen 1991); i.e. the subject's perception of other people's opinions of the proposed behaviour. These perceptions are influenced by normative beliefs and are of less relevance for individuals with a strong internal locus of control (Ajzen 1991; 2002) than for those with a strong action orientation (Bagozzi and Yi 1989).

Perceived behavioural control: perceived ability to perform a behaviour (Ajzen 1991). This concept was introduced into the theory of planned behaviour to accommodate the non-volitional elements that are potentially present in every behaviour (Ajzen, 2002). These factors relate to perceptions of feasibility of the behaviour, perceptions that are essential in predicting the behaviour. Individuals usually choose to adopt behaviours they think they will be able to control and master.

In the theory of planned behaviour, the three factors identified above are the antecedents of intention and therefore influence future behaviours. Underlying the intention are perceptions, which are developed gradually from beliefs.

Among these three factors, perceived behavioural control plays a significant part in Ajzen's theory. The concept of perceived behavioural control is rather similar to Bandura's notion of perceived self-efficacy (1977; 1982). Perceived self-efficacy refers to 'people's beliefs about their capabilities to exercise control over their own activities and over events that affect their lives' (Bandura 1991). From my point of view, the distinction is that perceived behavioural control focuses more particularly on the ability to perform one particular behaviour. In 2002, Ajzen redefined his concept of perceived behavioural control to avoid errors in interpretation: 'perceived control over performance of behaviour'.

Intention or displacement

In the following subsection, I will show that the model developed by Krueger and Carsrud (1993) can be used as a theoretical framework to explain how the process is triggered. I will close this chapter by presenting two real situations that were triggered in very different circumstances.

A model combining intention and displacement

Krueger and Carsrud (1993) were the first to apply the theory of planned behaviour to the field of entrepreneurship by adapting Ajzen's

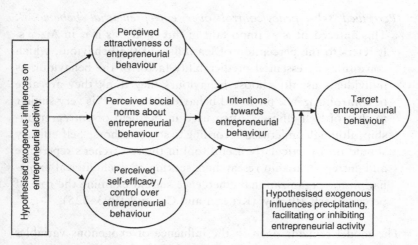

Figure 10.2. The theory of planned behaviour applied to entrepreneurship (Krueger and Carsrud 1993)

model to make it compatible with other theoretical frameworks, notably Shapero and Sokol's (1982). The final model they propose (see Figure 10.2) combines the two notions that we consider as the most relevant to explain the trigger of the process: 'intention' through the theory of planned behaviour, and the concept of 'displacement' derived from Shapero's works.

In this model, the three antecedents of intention are:

'*Perceived attractiveness of entrepreneurial behaviour*'. This factor corresponds to the attitudes towards the behaviour. They depend on beliefs as regards the behaviour in terms of positive or negative consequences. We also can find in this antecedent the notion of perceived desirability (or undesirability) that is one of the components of Shapero and Sokol's model (1982).

'*Perceived social norms about entrepreneurial behaviour*'. This criterion deals with how influential people or groups of people (peer group, friends and family, etc.) perceive the behaviour considered. These perceptions are influenced by normative beliefs and are less relevant for individuals with a more internal locus of control and a strong action orientation. This factor also overlaps with the notions of desirability and feasibility included in Shapero and Sokol's model (1982).

'*Perceived self-efficacy/control over entrepreneurial behaviour*'. This antecedent is as important in this model as it is in Ajzen's. It refers to the perception of feasibility of the behaviour, which constitutes an essential predictability factor of the behaviour, as individuals usually choose behaviours they think they are able to control. Ajzen's 'perceived behavioural control' is very similar to that of 'self-efficacy' often used in the field of entrepreneurship, although underused according to some authors: 'Self-efficacy should be a particularly useful tool in the researcher's repertoire and entrepreneurship researchers seeking a psychological explanation for organizational emergence should examine the role of perceived self-efficacy' (Krueger and Carsrud 1993: 325).

The model remains open to the influence of exogenous variables that may play a part in the evolution of beliefs and attitudes. It relies on some of Shapero and Sokol's conceptual inputs (1982), notably the notion of external trigger to explain the passage from intention to behaviour. These inputs are not limited to this role, however, as push or pull factors of displacement may also affect the antecedents of the intention and contribute to its formation or development.

According to intention models, for a new venture to appear (entrepreneurial behaviour), there must be the formation of an intention resulting from a change of attitude regarding the behaviour concerned.

In my opinion, intention and/or displacement can, at best, only explain how the process is triggered, as the actual behaviour, that of starting a business, concerns a longer-term process during which numerous events may happen that may unsettle the project.

Keeping this in mind, the trigger may occur as a consequence of a displacement (professional dissatisfaction, layoff or threat of a layoff, meeting with a potential partner, etc.), without the intention being high. It is even possible that the individual may not be perfectly aware of his or her entrepreneurial intention. The process may also be triggered under the pressure of a very strong intention that will lead to planning the first operations, such as finding an idea or opportunity. As a conclusion, it appears to me that the process is often triggered by the combination of an intention and a factor of displacement, without it being possible to assert whether the intention preceded the displacement or not.

Two illustrations of process triggers

The CH case

CH was bored. By the age of 35, he had reached his objectives. Coming from a working-class background, he had completed technical studies, then climbed up the ladder in his profession. For about fifteen years, he had been learning his trade in various small and medium-sized companies. For the last five years, he had been the head of purchasing and production in a family business in the sector of leather goods and accessories. He considered, and rightly so, that his career so far was a success, but had the impression he had no more to learn. The job he had found so exciting at first had become a mere routine. Although he had good relations with his employer, he could not face the idea of working in the same conditions until retirement. He could not see a way out. He had considered changing jobs, but with his professional and educational background, he did not think it possible to find a better situation, all the more so since, because of family constraints, he wanted to continue working in the same region. Little by little, the idea of creating his own business became obvious.

In this particular case, nothing came from the outside and the environment did not change. Favourable conditions emerged from the internal evolution dynamics of his perceived instantaneous strategic configuration. Dissatisfactions sometimes appear and lead to boredom and professional frustration. This is an example of negative displacement that triggered the new venture creation process.

The RC case

In 1995, RC was 28 and had just finished an MBA programme in a major French School of Management. RC was an engineering graduate and came from a university background that did not predispose him to the career of entrepreneur. After completing technical studies, he worked for a large American company in France for a few years. During the MBA programme, RC enrolled in an optional business creation class and discovered a world that was totally new to him. He recognises himself that this course generated rather quickly within him the intention to create a business. However, he decided to complete his MBA programme in an English university and graduated with a double degree, following which he was all set to find, without too much effort, a good and well-paid job corresponding to his new qualifications. RC therefore started looking for a job, while at the same time becoming interested in the idea of creating a company. He became particularly keen on a rather crazy, passionate idea in the wine sector. He started talking about it, to his fellow students, his teachers, and especially to the teacher who was in charge of the company creation elective. The wine trade, whatever the quality of the concept developed, is a very tough sector with low margins and intense competition, and therefore the first reactions were rather discouraging. However, RC decided to hold onto his idea, and for three months led his job search in parallel with his study of a venture creation project in the wine sector. He was going to recruitment interviews while meeting wine professionals to refine his project. This could have gone on forever, but RC started realising he was diluting his time and energy into two projects of a contradictory nature. He had to choose. He decided to stop his job search for a while and devote all his time and energy to his new venture creation project.

In this second case, it was the intention to create, which did not exist before his training course, which pushed RC to trigger a business start-up process. Intention preceded the search for an idea and project; it was the driving force at the very beginning of the process. There was neither a change in his life, nor a professional or personal dissatisfaction that could explain the first steps of the creation process here. If there was a displacement, then it may be materialised through his discovering a previously unknown world, that of entrepreneurship. This input of new knowledge, through a training course, contributed to the formation of an intention strong enough, on its own, to trigger the process.

11 | *Entrepreneurial process commitment phase*

I consider the individual's commitment to be a determining variable in understanding the entrepreneurial act and the actual emergence of a company.[1] I see in the individual's commitment a synonym of motivation and implication, and a source of internal energy. Commitment may be partial or total. It is total when it has reached a stage in the process that makes going back all but impossible. The individual, after reaching this point, will go all the way, as the costs of disengagement would be too high. How does commitment start, develop, and evolve throughout the process? How can we model and explain an individual's commitment to a new venture creation process?

This chapter addresses the issue of commitment in the context of new venture creation by an individual who does it for the first time, without any specific experience. My definition of commitment corresponds to the stage when the individual devotes most of his or her time and energy, and financial, intellectual, relational and affective means, to the project or the enterprise. Once committed, the individual does not consider the possibility of going back, which, incidentally, given the investments made, would be far too difficult and would be experienced as a failure.

I will first examine the notions of commitment and escalation of commitment from a more general point of view, before addressing them in the context of entrepreneurship. I will then introduce a theoretical framework presenting the multiple forms of commitment to venture creation processes in order better to understand the dynamics involved.

Commitment and commitment theories

A review of the literature reveals the existence of numerous works that have led to the elaboration of theories on commitment in the

---

[1] I would like to thank warmly my colleague Christian Bruyat for his help in writing this chapter.

fields of social psychology (Joule and Beauvois 1989; 2002; Kiesler and Sakumara 1966; Kiesler 1971) and cognitive psychology (Festinger 1957; Staw 1981). These concepts have been applied to the fields of management and company administration, especially in the contexts of commitment to work (Mowday 1998; Meyer and Allen 1997), new product development projects (Royer 1996; Schmidt and Calantone 2002) or software development projects (Keil 1995; Abrahamsson 2002). However, few researchers have explicitly used the concept of commitment in the field of entrepreneurship. We can note in particular Bruyat's works (1993; 2001) and Gaillard-Giordani's (2004) in the francophone literature, and the article by McCarthy *et al.* in the English-language literature, published in the *Journal of Business Venturing* (1993).

To develop the concept of commitment, I will first explore the various meanings it has been attributed in the existing research works devoted to it. I will then present in more detail a few perspectives of particular interest.

Semantic approach and definition

In the *American Heritage Dictionary*, 'commitment' is 'A pledge to do [something] . . . the state of being bound emotionally or intellectually to a course of action.' Commitment is related to decision and action. Moreover, Festinger (1964) defines commitment as a decision that directly influences future behaviours.

In 1971, Kiesler laid the foundations of the social psychology of commitment. For Kiesler, commitment is what 'binds the individual to his or her behavioural acts'. It relies on the notion of perseverance with a decision. People are only committed through their actions, and only the decisions made with a certain degree of freedom (we could also speak about freely consented decisions) lead to perseverance.

Most psychologists define commitment as the force that stabilises the behaviour of individuals (Brieckman 1987; Kiesler 1971), a force that gives individuals the strength to pursue whatever course of action they have undertaken, despite the obstacles met and whatever the attractiveness and potential of alternative options (Dubé, Jodoin and Kairouz 1997).

According to Beauvois and Joule (1981), in any given situation, the more the individual acts, the more he or she commits himself or herself.

They also consider that the likelihood of an activity leading to the individual's commitment is directly linked to the individual's feeling of freedom. Individuals must feel they have a certain amount of freedom when making a decision for the ensuing actions to lead to commitment. In a nutshell, the notion of commitment relates to a process that develops over time and forces individuals to preserve the consistency of their actions or the consonance of their decisions.

Commitment corresponds to a position that it is difficult to opt out of (Becker 1960); we can even say it corresponds to an irrevocable choice (Secord and Backman 1974), or a constraint that prevents any change in behaviour (Gerard 1965).

Commitment refers to a decision/action process. In this light, the works on commitment can be linked to those on decision. Since March and Simon (1964) and Simon (1983), we have known that the rationality of decisions is bounded. It is bounded by the individual's cognitive biases, and lack or absence of useful skills, habits or even values. Giddens (1984a) also underlines the limitations in the actors' competence: according to him, the structured properties of social systems extend over space and time way beyond the control that the actor may exercise. Unintended consequences constitute, therefore, along with the subconscious, one of the main limits of the social actor's competence. Unwanted consequences constantly arise from the course of action pursued and, retroactively, may subconsciously condition future actions. This is an essential aspect that should be considered in the works on commitment.

The notion of escalating commitment completes the notion of commitment and often overlaps with it. The escalation of commitment corresponds to the propensity of individuals to persist, sometimes in an excessive manner, with a decision or a course of action, despite negative feedback and the existence of a halo of uncertainty that affect the plausibility of a future success (Staw 1981). Sabherwal *et al.* (1994) even speak about being 'too committed'. Escalation of commitment may concern the individual, the group or the organisation (Caldwell and O'Reilly 1982). Commitment escalation has been studied in various fields of application: researchers have used this perspective to address subjects such as the war in Vietnam, urban planning policies and software development projects (Staw 1981; Simonson and Staw 1992).

Beauvois and Joule (1981) attempt to explain the reasons for the escalation 'We are only committed through our actions. We are not committed through our ideas, our feelings, but by our actual behaviour. The individual rationalises his or her behaviours by endorsing, retroactively, ideas designed to justify them.' This type of retroactive discourse to justify the individual's behaviour will be progressively internalised and contribute to convince the individual that his or her new opinion is founded.

Theoretical approaches

There are several analysis frameworks that can help us better understand the notion of commitment. Drawing on my review of the literature, I retain three main approaches.

The theory of cognitive consistency and dissonance

This theory originated with the precursor works of Festinger (1957), who at the time spoke of 'simultaneous existence of elements of knowledge (cognition) which, in one way or another, are conflicting (dissonance), which motivates the individual to make efforts to make them concordant (reduction of dissonance)'.

The central postulate is based on the stability of individuals' cognitive systems. When individuals behave in a way that does not fit with their system of beliefs, the imbalance induced is such that they will do anything in their power to restore the balance of the system. In this case, individuals have a choice of two alternatives: they alter either their behaviour or their attitude.

Dissonance results from internal conflicts that occur between discordant acquired opinions and new elements. Festinger (1957) notes four types of cognitive dissonance: the first type results from prior decisions, the second stems from action, the third is linked to the amount of effort required, and the last type arises from temptations.

This theory also relates to self-justification which results from individuals' desire to appear rational in their every act or decision: 'individuals will bias their attitudes on the experimental task in a positive direction so as to justify their previous behaviour' (Festinger and Carlsmith 1959).

Brockner (1992) confirms that, for him, the theory of self-justification explains, to a great extent, the escalation of commitment.

Beauvois and Joule's theory of commitment[2]

These two leading French researchers distinguish, first of all, what they call the 'decision traps', which translate into three phenomena.

The **'freezing effect'**: the decision freezes out the system of possible alternatives by making the individual focus exclusively on what is directly linked to his or her decision.

The **'escalation of commitment'**: a behavioural tendency of the individual to stick to his or her initial decision even though this decision is clearly questioned by the facts. The individual shows the need and the will to persist in his or her actions in order to prove the rational character of the initial decision(s) taken.

The **'unnecessary expenditure'** and **'dead end'**:[3] it is an 'unnecessary expenditure' to the extent that individuals put themselves through an unnecessary and unproductive course of action because they have committed themselves to doing it (financially, materially, etc.); and a 'dead end' because individuals voluntarily put themselves through tough situations in which the goals set are no longer achievable.

In this perspective, all goes to show that individuals, committed through their initial choices, would rather sink with the ship than admit an initial error of assessment, judgement or appreciation. This is when the idea of self-justification appears. This behaviour leads to useless actions and costs and may lead the individual to continue with a process whatever the consequences and whatever the costs.

The commitment theory developed by these authors relies heavily on the individual's feeling of freedom and the nature of the acts accomplished or to be accomplished. According to Beauvois and Joule, the feeling of freedom accounts for the perseverance in a decision. Two main types of action are considered: 'non-problematic' actions that are compatible with our ideas and beliefs and induce a greater resistance to change and a strong commitment, and the constrained or 'problematic' actions. These often lead people to alter their decisions, except if they have been very difficult to make. In the latter case, positions are more rigid and commitment is rather weak. When an individual has

[2] See especially Beauvois and Joule (1981) and Joule and Beauvois (1989; 2002).
[3] Beauvois and Joule refer to 'dépense gâchée' and 'piège abscons' in French.

been forced to make a decision, indeed, there is a boomerang effect that goes against the desired effect.

Escalation of commitment

The escalation of commitment theory owes a great deal to the works published by Staw and his team (Staw 1976; 1981; Staw and Ross 1987; Simonson and Staw 1992).

Staw considers global action processes, not isolated actions: 'many most difficult decisions an individual must make are choices not about what to do in an isolated instance but about the fate of an entire course of action'. He also underlines the fact that individuals have a tendency to persist in a given course of action, which provokes the escalation of commitment. This phenomenon can be explained by the need of all individuals to rationalise their behaviours. Staw (1980) distinguishes two types of rationalisation, retrospective and prospective: 'the individual seeks to appear competent in previous as opposed to future actions', and the behaviour models based on the subjective expected utility theory examine the principle of prospective rationality. The combination of these two rationalisation factors brings an added difficulty to the understanding of decision-making processes.

Staw (1981) highlights four factors of escalation:

internal justification (self-justification) or external justification that he explains thus: 'to prove to others that they were not wrong in an early decision and the force for such external justification could well be stronger than the protection of self-esteem'
persistence of the action
perceived probability of result
perceived value of the result.

For Staw (1981), commitment is a complex process, subjected to multiple and sometimes conflicting forces. His theoretical model based on the four types of determinants presented above is still often used in empirical research.

Entrepreneurship and commitment

As previously mentioned, commitment theories have been little used in entrepreneurship research. The notion of commitment itself is not perceived homogeneously. Bruyat (1993; 2001) puts it explicitly at the centre of his thesis. I agree with this author's idea that commitment is a set of actions/decisions that are spread over time. Actions and decisions are joined in the process, and it is difficult to identify a traditional sequence of events (collection of data, analysis and deliberation, decision, and action). The new business founder described by Bruyat has a bounded rationality and progressively commits himself or herself to the process until total commitment. This escalation of commitment leads to a stage of near irreversibility (except if the individual opts out) and leads individuals to focus increasingly on their projects. Going back therefore becomes very difficult, even impossible, given the costs of disengagement (financial resources consumed, social costs through the partners involved, costs in terms of career, psychological costs and cognitive dissonance). This commitment process that leads to full commitment may be incremental or revolutionary, depending on the resistance to change in particular. It is therefore important to distinguish several forms of commitment.

Gaillard-Giordani (2004) addresses the question of commitment within the context of the relation between investors and entrepreneurs. The perspective adopted is financial and the approach focuses mainly on the mutual commitment of the actors of the entrepreneurial process. The perspective developed by this author relies on the exchange of mutual and credible commitment; and these exchanges participate in the sense-making and realisation of the project. The types of commitment examined in this work are represented by process-specific knowledge and resources. While Bruyat considers commitment as an individual variable, it appears mainly in its collective dimension in Gaillard-Giordani's doctoral research. Both authors nevertheless concur on the importance they give to the issue of commitment.

In the anglophone literature, commitment theories seem to be applied to the field of entrepreneurship in a totally different perspective. Commitment is perceived no longer as an essential element (phase or act) of the process, but as a psychological factor susceptible to diverting the entrepreneur from the right decision paths, considering that the right decision paths should be dominated by the – often economic – rationality of the actor. The reduction of cognitive dissonances and the escalation of commitment are considered as possible cognitive biases. This appears more particularly in the work of McCarthy *et al.* (1993), which attempts to analyse to what extent the decisions of financial reinvestment are influenced by rational processes or variables of commitment escalation. The results show that entrepreneurs who started their own business are more prone to commitment escalation than entrepreneurs who took over an existing business. Moreover, entrepreneurs who have too much self-confidence are those who exhibit the most significant escalation of commitment.

In a recent work (Fayolle, Degeorge and Aloulou 2004), we examined the possibility and desirability of resorting to psychological and social commitment theories to answer our research questions. 'How does the individual's commitment start, develop, transform and proceed throughout a new venture creation process?' 'How can we represent and explain the individual's commitment during this process?'

Through these questions and the case studies we conducted, it appears clearly that what we are really trying to understand is more the process that leads to the total commitment of the individual than the process through which he or she remains committed despite (and whatever) the costs. For us, escalation of commitment relates to the increasing commitment from the moment when individuals start looking for information until their total commitment to the project (and near irreversibility). This includes all the conscious as well as subconscious processes that lead to the total commitment. The psychosociologists' preoccupation, however, is upstream from our conception and refers to the propensity of individuals (once they are committed) to persevere with their initial decisions, to rationalise and justify them. To illustrate our remark, we would like to refer to Beauvois and Joule: when they speak about resistance to change, they mean the resistance individuals must overcome to leave the path on which they were previously engaged (following their initial decision) to change direction. In our own research, resistance to change is applied to the passage from a given situation (employee, student, researcher, job seeker) to an entrepreneurial situation. This type of resistance to change therefore occurs before any committing decision, and therefore before any total commitment.

We may note here that our initial questions remain, and while I believe that cognitive and social psychology theories may be applied to understand better one aspect of the commitment escalation, I believe that their scope is more limited when it comes to explaining the other aspect (the escalation process that leads to total commitment). In view of this conclusion, in the following section I present a commitment model based on Thom's catastrophe theory.[4]

A metaphorical model of entrepreneurial commitment

In our model, commitment is a period of transition or a change of phase. It is during this period that ambiguity, paradox and tension are at their highest. My intention here is to contribute to the subject, not to address it in its entirety.

Escalation of commitment leading to irreversibility (where a termination of the process would be a failure for the entrepreneur) occurs at different stages of the venture creation process: before the company is legally established, when the project may still be fairly vague; during legal establishment or afterwards, if the entrepreneur has kept a paid job. In some cases, escalation of commitment is gradual, spread over a fairly long period, with no particular critical moment. In other cases it occurs as a sudden rupture. In this section, we will try to understand the phenomenon of commitment escalation and its different forms. Giving up paid employment to create a business is not only a strategic change, but also an extremely important career choice for an individual.

Conditions of the entrepreneurial commitment

As is frequently the case in a process of change, two conditions will be considered essential for commitment to occur. First, the venture creation action must be preferred, and second, resistance to change must be overcome. In both cases, of course, these are individual perceptions, and there may be some significant cognitive biases in estimating the risks, among other things. The desirability of entrepreneurial action involves psychological and social aspects as well as financial ones.

The act (or project) of new venture creation is favoured and perceived as achievable

Some projects abort because the entrepreneur is unable to gather the necessary means – e.g. financial resources, permits, means of

---

[4] René Thom was a French mathematician who received the prestigious Fields Medal. He died in October 2002.

production, support from a partner, etc. The project must therefore be abandoned, even though it was what the entrepreneur preferred.

If the individual is not forced to abandon the project, commitment occurs when the act of venture creation (a specific project, whether detailed or not) is perceived as being preferable to the current situation (employee, unemployed, student, etc.) or to any other alternative course of action (e.g. change of employer). Most theoretical models of venture creation retain this aspect as essential. They describe the formation of this preference as the result of environmental factors and factors specific to the entrepreneur. We will not, however, be considering these factors in further detail at this point. Instead, the preference, resulting from a push–pull situation, is assessed on the basis of criteria relating to the desirability and feasibility of the act of venture creation. The individual's cognitive limitations must also be considered. The emergence of the preference is a complicated process, made even more complex by:

the potential diversity of the criteria to be considered
the fact that the criteria are not independent from one another
the difficulty of measuring them (they are perceptions, not 'objective' facts)
the dynamic evolution of the perceptions over time
the non-linearity of the functions linking some of the criteria to the preference (sigmoidal curves, parabolic curves, etc.)
the fact that it is impossible to formalise these links by a classical preference function (additive model), as one single factor may trigger opting-out. In other words, it is a system.

For our model, we will assume that the entrepreneur's full commitment does not occur unless the venture creation project is preferred over the status quo or any other alternative option.

Resistance to change

The preference for a venture creation project, translated by a need and desire for change, will only lead to actual change if the actor is able to overcome his or her resistance to change. Strangely enough, this is not discussed as such in entrepreneurship literature, probably because entrepreneurs are often considered to have different attitudes to risk from the general public. However, empirical research does not appear to have produced key findings in support of this.

Consideration of resistance to change adds to the complexity of analysing commitment processes but, as we shall see later, also helps to explain their diversity. Without going into detail, and without claiming to cover every possibility, we propose to analyse resistance to change as follows:

resistance to change due to habits and inertia in reasoning and behaviour: this is particularly important where individuals have devoted most of their past commitment to a salaried position without ever considering venture creation (cognitive dissonance, family role model)

resistance to change due to fear of the unknown: uncertainty may be related to a specific project or a lack of knowledge of what creating and managing a small business actually involves

resistance to change due to the perceived irreversibility of the new situation: in some cases, individuals believe (accurately) that if their projects should fail, it would be impossible for them to go back to their previous job or indeed to any other job; failure, even if not immediate, would therefore be disastrous

resistance to change due to the perceived opportunity costs and/or significant irreversible costs: the potential entrepreneur withdraws from an enjoyable situation, devotes less time to family and leisure activities, commits most of the family heritage, cuts back his or her life style, and so on

resistance to change due to a lack of resources or advice and, more generally, environmental hostility to venture creation.

Here again, the hiding hand[5] plays a significant role in dissimulating or exaggerating certain problems. Entrepreneurs who take action often overestimate their chances of success and underestimate the problems they are likely to encounter. Resistance to change in the venture creation process varies in intensity. For example, it is weaker if:

the individual has been exposed early in life to the idea of venture creation (parents or entrepreneurial role models)

---

[5] Hirschman (1967) explains that one of the motors for action is the individual's ignorance of what awaits him or her when action is taken. The term *hiding hand* is a play on words with Smith's *hidden hand*.

   the individual has a social network and lives in an environment (family, friends, education) which is relevant and conducive to venture
   creation
   the individual's current situation is unsatisfactory
   the project involves only a low degree of uncertainty for the individual (duplicate creation, broad experience of the sector and of
   management)
   the project can be implemented gradually, without engaging significant irreversible costs.

These various points are not independent, but overlap to some extent
and form part of an overall system. Accordingly, resistance to change
and the preference for venture creation are not independent. Because of
the complexity of the system, we have attempted to highlight a thread
that could eventually be further formalised for specific applications.

   In our model, total commitment occurs only when the founder is
able to overcome his or her resistance to change.

The dynamics of entrepreneurial commitment

By observing or supporting entrepreneurs throughout the venture creation process, we have been able to identify many different types of
commitment. Some people, even though they seem to have both a suitable project and the necessary expertise, may suddenly abandon their
venture creation project and go back to paid employment. Others, who
appear to be less well prepared, go on to create businesses. Sometimes
the process seems fragile, able to be upset by minor incidents, while
in other cases it is much more powerful and nothing seems to get in
its way. The classical explanation of this phenomenon is that the people who abandon are not really entrepreneurs, and those who persist
are the ones who have the 'right stuff' (tolerance for risk, high need
for achievement, etc.). The explanation is a convenient one, but in my
opinion it does not appear to be supported by empirical findings, nor
does it correspond to what I have observed in the field. Particular attitudes and skills are no doubt required for venture creation. People with
no self-confidence, no tolerance for risk and no desire to be in charge
probably have very little chance of going into businesses or being successful as entrepreneurs. However, we can postulate that the minimal

attitudes and features required for venture creation are by no means exceptional.

Evolution or revolution?

The behaviour of I↔NVC is potentially chaotic. Only three order parameters or three degrees of freedom are required for a system to become chaotic. Explaining[6] the entrepreneurial act appears to involve (where possible) constructing a model probably containing more than two non-linear differential equations. In recent years, the 'hard' sciences have developed theories and models to help understand innovation, phase changes, turbulence and unpredictability. Chaos, bifurcation and catastrophe theories have, in some cases, called into question the practicality of the deterministic conception of the classical mechanism, already damaged by quantum physics. Since entrepreneurship involves change, innovation and emergence, and is also a complex phenomenon, these new approaches cannot be ignored. Total commitment on the part of the entrepreneur can be regarded as a change of phase, since the system (considered to be dissipative) shifts over time to a new and relatively stable state if the process is successful. This has already been pointed out by some well-known authors in the field (Stevenson and Harmeling 1990; Bygrave 1989b; Lichtenstein 2002). However, the use of these theories in the social sciences runs up against three basic difficulties:

   the large number of variables to be considered, and the difficulty of measuring them
   the speed of the changes affecting the system's operations and its links to a changing environment (artificial world paradigm)
   the fact that the 'objects' observed are self-restructuring systems likely to have a conscious impact on their operations (the observer is no more intelligent than the system being observed).

It is therefore not surprising that references to chaos have never been more than simple observations. Given the current state of knowledge, we do not believe chaos theory can be used because of the complexity of the phenomenon being studied. Bygrave (1989a) agrees that chaos

---

[6] In the sense of building an explanatory, hence predictive, model.

theory cannot be supported by data, but regards it as a good metaphor. In my view, it is useless if not downright dangerous, especially where the reference is deterministic chaos – useless, because it is difficult to go beyond a simple assertion that the phenomenon is likely to involve chaotic behaviour. How would it be possible to build a (deterministic) model that is both simple and operational enough to represent a system sensitive to small variations in the initial conditions, while ignoring (through simplification) many of its determinants? Chaos theory is not suitable for qualitative modelling. We believe it is also dangerous, in that it involves a deterministic vision of the world where the individual/ venture creation project system is regarded as an object incapable of impacting consciously on its own future. This is a direct contradiction of the fundamental basis of both entrepreneurship and management, and calls into question their legitimacy as independent research fields.

Instead, we will be using Thom's (1980) idea of morphogenesis and catastrophe theory as metaphors. Thom, in his work, states that catastrophe theory is a qualitative modelling approach that has very little chance of producing a rigorous (wholly predictive) quantitative model, especially in the social sciences. According to Thom, it operates as an analogy that may help in understanding certain phenomena and anticipating unexpected situations. Clearly, if quantitative models existed that both explained and predicted the phenomenon, they would have been our first choice. This, however, is not the case in the social sciences in general, and in entrepreneurship in particular. Catastrophe theory has the advantage that it can be used as a heuristic to provide a visual (topographical) representation of a qualitative model from which consequences can be deduced. Our use of it will be more metaphorical than analogical, and we will be taking some liberties with its mathematical design, using only its topographical or geometrical aspects.

A topographical representation

We consider the I↔NVC system to be a dissipative system. According to Ekeland (1984; 1990), dissipative systems, as they relate to catastrophe theory, are those whose dynamics are extremely simple: movement abates over time, tending towards neutral positions. The handful of neutral positions available are known as equilibrium. A simple example would be a marble thrown onto a flat surface with a few

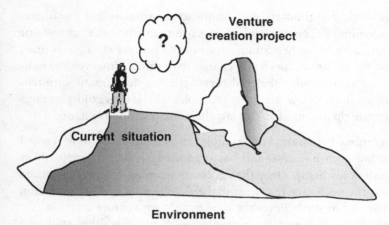

Venture
creation project

?

Current situation

Environment

Figure 11.1. Topographical metaphor: pseudo-attractors in a specific case

depressions. The marble will end up in one of the depressions, because of the effects of friction. Our system, however, is somewhat more complex, in that the topography changes over time, owing in large part to the entrepreneur. Instead of the notion of equilibrium, we have therefore preferred Atlan's (1979) notion of pseudo-attractors, i.e. meaningful virtualities that are created only in the movement from which they originate, and that cannot be said to have been 'already there' before the singular events leading to their creation actually occurred. In our model, the pseudo-attractors are the situation of the individual and the projects the individual perceives as being both desirable and possible. Figure 11.1 clarifies this rather abstract description. It is a metaphorical illustration of the situation of a specific entrepreneur at a given point in time – in other words, a topography.

In this 'mountain' metaphor, the height of the mountains represents the desirability of the situations envisaged by the individual (pseudo-attractors). In this case, the venture creation project is clearly preferable to the current situation, and the individual is not seriously considering any other alternatives. The height of the pass between the two peaks, compared to the height of the current situation, represents resistance to change. In this case, there is very little resistance to change. Where there is no pass (resistance to change) between two pseudo-attractors, the system naturally gravitates towards the one with the highest gradient. Where there is a pass, the system must overcome the resistance to change in order to attain the pseudo-attractor with the highest gradient. The individual's decisions and actions are then somewhat chaotic or determined by his or her commitment to the process (at a given time, because the situation can clearly change over time). However, the individual can act to modify the gradients of the pseudo-attractors[7] (intentionally or not). Below are some examples of classical configurations to illustrate these remarks. The last three are potentially chaotic.

Programmed creation: For example, an individual has long wanted to launch a business, and has organised his or her employment path accordingly. Once the necessary learning has been acquired and the necessary resources gathered, the individual takes action when he or she believes the time is right for venture creation.

Inevitable opting-out: The entrepreneurial individual has studied a project that turns out to be unattractive and riddled with uncertainty. Resistance to change is significant. For the individual, it becomes more reasonable to opt out of the project, especially if the current situation is interesting or satisfactory.

The opting-out dilemma: In this case, an attractive but somewhat uncertain (vision) project competes with a current situation (paid employment) that is comfortable. Resistance to change is high. Here, as in the following situations, the perception of risk combines with the attraction of the venture creation project to undermine escalation of commitment.

The competing project dilemma: This would be the classic case of someone recently laid off who identifies two opportunities, namely finding another satisfactory job or launching a business. Both possibilities are of interest. Here, the decision/action situation is much more complex. In such a potentially chaotic situation, time pressures (from the project or from the entrepreneur) are of key importance. Chance also plays a role, in that the individual may not explore the various possibilities in a 'rational' way owing to lack of time.

Multiple projects: Here, the topography is even more convoluted because the individual has generated a number of different projects. The individual's current situation is satisfactory and he

---

[7] In concrete terms, the creator will try to improve the value of the project by applying a skimming strategy, limiting the risks by subcontracting and forging alliances.

or she could change jobs fairly easily, but could also launch a business too. The situation should incite the individual to change, but it is virtually impossible to establish what the final choice will be. The situation is extremely dynamic and chance (the timing of windows of opportunity) is crucial.

Catastrophe theory as a heuristic

Catastrophe theory offers a metaphor for understanding the links between individual behaviour and the two aspects we have retained as conditions for commitment within a synchronic vision. Of the different types of elementary catastrophe proposed by Thom, I will be using the 'cusp catastrophe', which is simple and particularly well suited to phenomena that have a creative element.[8] It does, however, require a certain amount of simplification. I will use the representation proposed by Bigelow (1982), linking three variables to a catastrophic type surface containing points of rupture:

a normal variable that will serve as the creation's attractiveness (the pseudo-attractor's gradient)

a breakdown variable, resistance to change

a dependent variable, venture creation or opting-out (total commitment of the entrepreneur).

According to catastrophe theory, there is an ongoing relationship between the dependent variable and the normal variable where the value of the breakdown variable is low (path 1 in Figure 11.2); this relationship is discontinued where the variable values are high. For low normal variable values, the dependent variable also has a low value; for high normal variable values, the dependent variable also has a high value; and for intermediate normal variable values, the dependent variable is bimodal (path 2).

---

[8] Thom, using catastrophe theory in linguistics, states that the cusp-type elementary catastrophe applies to a subject–verb–object sentence structure. He submits that this is the classical type of transitive sentence, in that the subject is the actant that survives and triumphs over the catastrophe; the object generally suffers the catastrophe and is damaged or completely destroyed by it. For example, Eve eats the apple. Clearly a transitive verb does not always express the capture or creation of the object, but creating and destroying are typical transitive actions whose structural mould has attracted and captured the structure from less simplistic geometric actions (Thom 1980: 181).

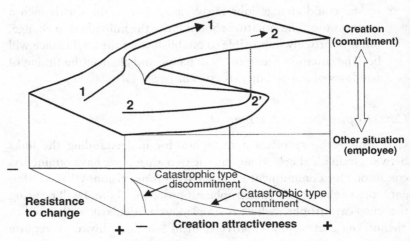

Figure 11.2. Venture creation: a cusp-type catastrophe surface

Where resistance to change is low, commitment occurs as soon as the venture creation pseudo-attractor gradient becomes greater than the gradients of the current situation and other projects. Commitment occurs incrementally; it is a progressive process (path 1).

Where resistance to change is high, commitment occurs only if the venture creation pseudo-attractor gradient is significantly higher than the others, i.e. where there is hysteresis. Around the rupture zone (in 2' in Figure 11.2), commitment occurs in a revolutionary (catastrophic) manner and is sensitive to weak variations in the normal variable and/or the breakdown variable. The same applies to opting-out. Projection of the rupture zones onto the basic surface reveals the fracture or bifurcation lines.

This form is a simplified representation of a commitment process in a venture creation project. It highlights the different paths available and the different forms of commitment (evolution or revolution). It clarifies the conditions of commitment, to help individuals reach their goals, and is also useful in understanding opting-out where it occurs. Although it cannot accurately predict commitment, it can help identify possible scenarios (logic of possibilities) and the conditions for their application.

Having said this, I will illustrate these remarks with a brief commentary. Figure 11.3 shows the trigger and commitment zones.

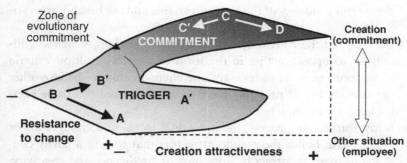

Figure 11.3. Trigger and commitment zones

In A and D, the system is highly stable. Point D corresponds to the case of an entrepreneur whose project has been completely successful, and point A to a situation in which venture creation is not envisaged. Time is required for these situations to be called into question, usually by means of a major 'displacement' event. The productive configurations are situated in A′, and are therefore highly unstable.

For points B and C, there is only one pseudo-attractor, with a low gradient. These configurations are extreme cases that have very little chance of achieving stability. They will evolve naturally towards C′ or B′, or towards A or D.

This form represents and helps explain the different dynamics leading to venture creation. The use of animated images would illustrate speed of change.

Final comments on the metaphorical model

The model does have some limitations, in that the metaphor used does not take into account:

the possibility of multiple modes in decision/action situations; in other words, an individual's situation may include more than two pseudo-attractors at any one time, whereas the form used (cusp) is bimodal

the fact that an individual can, at any one time, be situated in two pseudo-attractors at once[9]

[9] For example, someone who has created and manages a firm while continuing to hold paid employment (sometimes part-time). Universities that create technology or consulting firms often fall into this category.

the interdependency of the normal variable and the breakdown variable

the fact that there are only two composite variables, which are difficult to operationalise in the form of classical multiple criteria functions in order to 'explain' the phenomenon; we believe other variables would probably have to be considered too (time pressures, for example)

lastly, during the process, the individual learns and changes his or her goals; builds the pseudo-attractors that will, in a partly conscious manner, attract by appealing to intelligence and creativity; and creates pseudo-attractors that are completely new both to the individual and to the individual's advisers.

However, the model does provide a methodological framework for future research. To be productive, a model must reflect the facts as they may be observed through empirical research, and must also help understand facts that may, at first sight, appear to be contrary to common sense. I believe this model of commitment meets these criteria.

The first step would be to add elements in support of the model. The model can, of course, be used directly as a theoretical framework for qualitative research. On the other hand, it cannot be confirmed quantitatively, in that we will never be able to measure accurately the gradients of the individual's different career prospects or resistance to change. To be predictive, catastrophe theory requires very accurate measurements. It would probably be possible to add factual empirical elements that would statistically contradict or support the model. However, this would not be easy in practice, since the measurements must be taken at the time the entrepreneurs make their career choices, not afterwards. What counts is the entrepreneur's perception at the time of the action, not the facts as reported or perceived by the researcher after the event.

In its current state, the model does help show why research into entrepreneurs' attitudes towards risk is so disappointing[10] (generally speaking, entrepreneurs are not (or are only slightly) more likely to take risks). The diagrams presented in this chapter suggest that the ability to take risks is only a key factor when the number of situations is limited (basically the opting-out dilemma where the gradients of the venture creation project and the current situation are similar and resistance to

---

[10] See Ray (1986) who presented at the 1986 Babson Conference an excellent paper showing us the complexity of the risk notion.

change is high). If we assume that this type of situation accounts for only a small percentage of venture creations, however, the empirical results are not surprising. In addition, commitment depends on the actor's perceptions, not on objective facts (the role of the hiding hand). How, then, can entrepreneurs' attitudes to risk be separated from their internal locus of control or self-confidence (hiding hand)? The notion of risk can only really be understood in light of the project and the actor's perceptions of its desirability and feasibility at the time the action takes place. Such a perception is not objective, nor is it dependent solely on intra-individual characteristics. While, for an observer (usually not an entrepreneur), venture creation involves taking a risk, it may also, in some cases, be a way for the venture creator to limit uncertainty.

12 | *Entrepreneurial process survival/development phase*

As soon as the individual or the small team is totally committed to the process, they are embarked in the entrepreneurial system and have to deal with questions related to the survival/development of the fledgling company. These questions arise from activities that are indispensable to the progression of the project and which are accomplished in specific conditions and contexts depending on the situation. As noted previously, there is permanent tension between available resources and the resources required for the project to succeed (Stevenson and Jarillo 1990). These resources are insufficient at all levels, and the permanence of these tensions implies specific behaviours and practices for the entrepreneur. The commitment of resources within an entrepreneurial process therefore happens gradually, which also implies that after each activity, or during each activity, the project may be abandoned, or reformulated, resulting in a step back.

In this chapter, we will first examine the main questions raised during this survival/development phase. Secondly, we will present three perspectives from the field of sociology that provide theoretical frameworks better to understand the issues and dynamics at work during this phase. These three perspectives are the 'théorie de la traduction et de l'intéressement' (interest generation and translation theory), the theory of social networks in section, and finally, Anthony Giddens' structuration theory. These theories are complementary, and can be used either independently or combined, given the variety and heterogeneity of situations and research questions.

Three key issues: generating interest, socialising and structuring

The activity considered here is the survival/development phase. The system must be fed from both the inside and the outside for this activity to proceed. The nascent entrepreneur can feed the process with his own energy (vitality, dynamism, creativity, initiative, etc.), but it is not sufficient. During the entire process the entrepreneur will have to learn. He or she will also need to transform information and observed or experienced situations and practices into useful knowledge for action. The aim of acquiring key resources and knowledge is to boost the system as well as reinforce its internal and external coherence. Incoherencies cause delays and hidden costs, and they also hinder the credibility and attractiveness of the project. The notion of coherence in the individual/new value creation system is therefore pivotal. Without this coherence, it could prove difficult to acquire new resources, to arouse the interest of stakeholders, to build networks and/or integrate the project into existing networks, and to build successive organisation configurations.

We could summarise the questions raised by this survival/ development phase as follows:

how to acquire (rare) resources in a context characterised by asymmetric information and uncertainty
how to use, build or integrate social networks
how to organise and structure, in the course of action, a new emerging organisation.

These issues depend on the nature of entrepreneurial projects, their dynamics, their new value creation potential, the concrete situations they generate and the stakes they raise. However, I consider that these issues exist (to a greater or lesser extent) whatever the case, as soon as the situation is entrepreneurial (entrepreneurial in the sense we have defined). Figure 12.1 shows the interrelations between these questions and the concepts we use to answer them.

The first question – 'how to acquire (rare) resources in a context characterised by asymmetric information and uncertainty' – is probably the most crucial question. Without the acquisition of the 'right' resources at the 'right' time, the process has small chances to develop. Although financial resources are important and often regarded as 'unique' in the literature (Shane 2003), I am of the opinion that they only represent a fraction of the necessary resources. During the process, the entrepreneur needs knowledge, information, social capital, material equipment, etc., and it is the efficient assimilation and utilisation of these resources that will condition the process survival and development. These resources are generally difficult to acquire given the project's uncertainty and the asymmetry of information between the

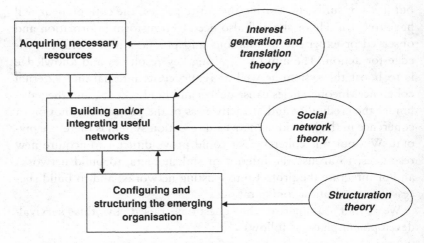

Figure 12.1. Three issues raised during the entrepreneurial process survival/development phase

entrepreneur and his or her potential partners at all levels. Difficulties often stem from resource allocation modes based on the evaluation and competition between projects. In these conditions, knowing how to generate interest becomes a key condition for the entrepreneur to have access to the resources he or she needs. Access to resources is facilitated if the actors have a good knowledge of support structures as well as a sufficient understanding of their objectives and practices. This means that entrepreneurs must be able to gain access to support networks adapted to their projects. It is not uncommon for nascent entrepreneurs to have to create their own specific networks; this is particularly the case with high-value creation projects. Integrating and using existing networks as well as building specific networks therefore constitute important activities without which the project's chances of success would be greatly reduced. Consequently, social network theories seem particularly relevant in understanding this phase and helping us answer our second question: 'how to use, build or integrate social networks'.

Entrepreneurs are embedded in both general and specific social networks that will play a role in the configuration and structuring processes of the emerging company. Organisational choices appear to be the consequence of interactions between the entrepreneurs' projects in the etymological sense and the responses/reactions of their environments and networks in particular during the various steps and phases of the project. In this light, Anthony Giddens' theory seems to provide a possible answer to our third question: 'how to organise and structure, in the course of action, a new emerging organisation'.

I will develop in subsequent sections each one of these theoretical frameworks.

The theories of interest generation and translation (*théories de la traduction et de l'intéressement*)

This first theoretical body of knowledge comes from the Centre de Sociologie de l'Innovation (CSI – Centre for Sociology of Innovation) of the Ecole Nationale Supérieure des Mines de Paris. This theory was developed in the context of research on innovation processes and draws on the sociotechnical approach elaborated by the researchers of the Tavistock Institute in London. Sociotechnical theory posits that the organisation is an open system composed of both a technical and a social system, the combined optimisation of which conditions the efficacy of the whole. CSI researchers who applied this perspective to innovation issues have shown that the success of innovations depends on the success of a new association between several actors. New dynamics of production as well as a new sociotechnical network will emerge from this association through the involvement and cooperation of all the actors, which will lead to the efficiency and success of the process. During the process, the innovators will constantly have to perform translations to present the innovation intelligibly to the stakeholders, in order for them to perceive fully the interest of this innovation for them.

CSI researchers summarise their input as follows:

The fact that a [an innovation] project should depend on the alliances formed and the interest generated explains why no criterion or no algorithm makes it possible to ensure its success *a priori*. Rather than the rationality of decisions, one should talk about the aggregation of interest(s) they may or may not induce. Innovation is the art of arousing the interest of an increasing number of potential partners who make you stronger and stronger. (Akrich, Callon and Latour 1988)

In this perspective, innovation is constantly altered under the effect of the various obstacles encountered and through the various attempts to generate interest. This is a spiralling process that is characterised by the anticipation of constraints, successive experimentations and socio-technical transformations. Each newly found equilibrium materialises into a prototype or a new project that makes it possible to test the feasibility of the compromise (Akrich *et al.* 1988: 21).

If we apply this approach to the field of entrepreneurship, we can see how, to acquire key resources and build a network of committed partners, one would simply have to generate the interest of as many stakeholders as possible, by translating the project, if necessary, to make it intelligible and align it with these actors' expectations. Of course, not all entrepreneurial projects correspond to the type of innovation projects studied by the CSI, but most of them are likely to contain elements of novelty or differentiation. An entrepreneurial project has little chance of success, for instance, if it is impossible or very difficult to show how it could contribute to creating new value for its stakeholders. Finally, for any type of entrepreneurial project, it is indispensable to attract at least one type of partners: customers. And this can only be achieved by anticipating constraints, experimenting, and transforming the offer accordingly.

This theoretical framework seems well adapted to the issue of resource acquisition in a context characterised by asymmetry of information (necessity of a translation) and uncertainty (project novelty). In this line of thought, the empirical works led for more than twenty years by the French National Institute for Economic Statistics (Institut National de la Statistique et des Etudes Economiques – INSEE) show significant correlations between company survival probabilities after the first five years, and both the number of experts involved (informational and relational resources) and the number of partners granting facilities (financial and relational resources).

The theories of interest generation and translation are also very useful to understand how it is possible to build specific networks that will support a project in which stakeholders have identified an interest.

Social networks theory

The interest generation and translation theory shows just how important social networks can be for projects and nascent entrepreneurs. It is obvious that entrepreneurship, whatever the situation considered, is more and more a collective business. A successful creation implies a team and a network of individuals. There is no doubt about the fact that the actions of nascent entrepreneurs are deeply embedded into social structures (Reynolds 1991; Starr and MacMillan 1990). Research regularly shows that the utilisation of social networks in a venture creation process is essential in obtaining resources (Greve and Salaff 2003).

To build, use or integrate networks, it is necessary to have a good understanding of what a network is, and what its main structure and functioning patterns are. We will first address these elements, then distinguish two types of network that can be very useful to emerging entrepreneurs: support networks and specific social networks. To conclude, we will examine the notion of social capital that relates to both types of network.

Elements for the structural analysis of social networks

The structural analysis of social networks is closely related to graph theory. This theory makes it possible to analyse relations between actors, their orientation and density, and the actors' positions and connections (Lemieux and Ouimet 2004). Numerous research works on social networks have attempted to test the influence of these parameters on activity and performance variables.

Orientation and density of relations

Connections between different actors may be oriented or non-oriented. In the first case, there is transmission from one actor to the other (of information or other types of resources). In the second case, a relationship is non-oriented when there is no 'transmission' (for instance, friendly relations are considered as non-oriented). The density of relationships within a network is the ratio of existing relations to the number of possible relations.

Connections between actors

The notion of connection draws on graph theory. In graph theory, the term 'directed path' or 'directed route' is used to designate a sequence of oriented links (or connections), and 'path' or 'route' to refer to a series of undirected (non-oriented) links. Using the term 'connection' seems more appropriate to the field of social networks, in which it designates either directed or undirected routes composed of more than one relation.

The actors' positions in the network(s)

Actors may have different positions within a network, depending on their weight in this network, which is assessed via their number of connections. This is how, for example, an actor is in a dominant position in a network when this actor is the initiator of connections with all the other actors in the network. The actor or agent is 'dominated' if he or she is the initiator of no one-way connection with another actor, in a network where there is at least one dominant actor. An actor is isolated when he or she is the initiator or recipient of no one-way connection with any of the other actors in the network.

The role of the various actors may also be assessed using the notion of centrality, a notion that is used in non-oriented networks. There are various types of centrality that measure either the actors' relational activity, their capacity for autonomy or independence, or the importance of their intermediary positions.

Support networks

Support networks consist of individuals (nascent entrepreneurs) who receive help and actors who provide the help (training and orientation structures, support structures, public institutions, etc.). Supporting entities give their support, in the shape of goods or services, information, networking and other resources. Support is all the more efficient if the benefiting individuals have a good understanding of the potential supporting entities, and if they have significant social capital.

These support networks exist and are organised differently according to the entrepreneurial situation. Nascent entrepreneurs may rely on networks that are situation specific (company takeovers, creations of innovative businesses, or social organisations, etc.). These specifically segmented networks add to the existing institutional support structures, which include, in France for instance, the Chambers of Commerce and Industry, local administrations, the Agence pour la Création d'Entreprise (APCE – business start-up agency).[1]

---

[1] This French state institution plays a key role in France in the diffusion of useful information for entrepreneurs and their initiatives.

The main problem for nascent entrepreneurs is therefore to know how to locate these networks in order to be able to use them. They must first map them out, then learn how to navigate them in order to locate and access the resources they need. Nascent entrepreneurs have an isolated position in these networks and only use them in a temporary manner.

Specific social networks

While this type of network is better adapted to political analysis and competition between opposed coalitions, I am of opinion that their utilisation in the field of entrepreneurship is as relevant as that of support networks. The constitution of these networks also relies on the social capital of the actors in need of support, but contrarily, to support networks, they are generally built from scratch around one specific project and team. We can see here an application of the theory of interest generation and translation that we addressed in the previous section.

Individuals who benefit from this support are also nascent entrepreneurs, but the supportive actors are not just any actors. They are stakeholders with a strong interest in the project who behave as close partners of the nascent entrepreneurs on a long-term basis. In specific social networks, entrepreneurs occupy a dominant and central position and give the network all its coherence and reason to be.

Social capital

Social capital is essential in accessing and navigating support networks, and it is just as crucial in building specific social networks. This notion is often defined in terms of the resources an individual has access to according to the quality and scope of his or her social relations. Pierre Bourdieu (1980) gives the following definition of social capital: 'social capital is the aggregate of the actual or potential resources which are linked to the possession of a durable network of more or less institutionalised relationships of mutual acquaintance and recognition'.

Despite its increasingly widespread use, the notion of social capital remains rather polysemous depending on the specialist who uses it. Among the numerous works devoted to this concept, two main generic approaches may be distinguished. Social capital becomes for some people a significant resource only if they possess a great number of 'strong ties'. Granovetter (1983) established this distinction between strong ties (husband/wife, relatives, friends) and weak ties (other relationships). For other authors, an actor's social capital is constituted of low-intensity relations and structural holes (Burt 1992). In other terms, extracting all the advantageous resources of social capital depends mainly on low-intensity relationships (weak ties) and the actor's intermediary position: indeed, original information flows may circulate when the actor knows other actors who do not know one another.

Social capital is made up of social relations that enable nascent entrepreneurs to reach their goals and satisfy their needs (Burt 1992). These contacts can be found in the professional, friendly or family sphere of relations and may be formal or informal.

The utilisation of social networks varies during the entrepreneurial process (Greve and Salaff 2003). At the very beginning, the closest relations (strong ties) are the most called upon. Later on, entrepreneurs extend their networks and devote a lot of time and energy to activities of construction and 'maintenance' of these relationships. In the ultimate phases of the process, entrepreneurs concentrate on the most important and useful contacts while reducing the amount of time they invest in the management of their social networks (Greve and Salaff 2003).

Structuration theory

Structuration theory is the theory elaborated by Anthony Giddens in the mid-1980s. This theory is well adapted to analysing processes in an individual/new value creation dialogic. Indeed, the structuration concept as elaborated by Giddens (1984a; 1987) is an invitation to go beyond the traditional approach that often opposes actors to structures and their constraints. Structuration is presented as 'the structuring of social relations across time and space, in virtue of the duality of structure'. Individuals and structure are therefore considered as interdependent components of one same dialectic duality. The notion of duality of structure refers to the idea that structure is both enabling and constraining. In this light, structural constraints and the actors' skills take a central role. The actors' social competence relies on their reflexive capacity to understand, while engaged in day-to-day activities, what they are doing and why.

In his structuration model, structural constraint can explain the actors' behaviour only when their actions conform to it. The notion of social competence accounts for why actors act the way they do. Social action therefore stems from a dynamic dialectic: between individual (endowed with social skills) and structure (constraining the individual).

I will first examine the key concepts of this theory, then some research works that have applied it to entrepreneurship, before developing my own views about its use in the context of this research.

Key concepts of structuration theory

Structuration theory has been used and still is very much in use in the field of management, to analyse situations of organisational change (Bouchikhi 1990; Rouleau 2002), or explore entrepreneurial situations (Bouchikhi 1993; Sarason *et al.* 2002; 2006). This theory particularly applies to the dynamic evolution of social structures through interactions between individuals and the social institutions within which they evolve. To understand better the essence of this theory, it is important to come back to three fundamental notions: social interaction, the duality of structure and the actor.

Duality of structure

In his theory, Giddens identified a fundamental dualism in social theory opposing 'objectivism' and 'subjectivism' (Giddens 1987: 31). Indeed, objectivism is assigned to functionalist and structuralist perspectives which privilege structure over action and grant importance to its constraining dimension, whereas subjectivism, in line with interpretative sociologies, gives importance to action and its significance in explaining human conduct (1987: 50). To overcome this dualism, Giddens proposes the idea of 'duality of structure' as a new approach to human action and mutual dependence of structure and agency. He conceives structure as consisting of 'rules' and 'resources' recursively organised and reproduced through social interaction. The idea of duality supposes that the structure is both the means and the result of human interaction, both constraining and enabling (1987: 74–5). It emerges and is maintained through action (Bouchikhi 1993: 557).

Actor and action

According to Giddens, actors are competent agents who have their (sub)conscious reasons for interacting with their social system. The agents' competence is assessed on the basis of their capacity for reflexivity and rationalisation of their actions and considered as their capacity to explain what they do while they are doing it (Rojot 1998: 8). This reflexivity is conceived as the condition and consequence of the continuity of social practice. The rationalisation of action is considered as the main basis on which actors evaluate the general competence of others (Giddens 1987: 52).

Action is contextual and inseparable from the actor, performed in a continuous stream of conduct and embedded in contexts that shape it (Rojot 1998: 6). Every course of action produces a new act, and every action exists in continuity with the past, which provides the means of its initiation (1998: 13).

Considering action in space and time brings Giddens to identify some limits to the competence of actors (1987: 62): the unintended consequences of one initial action may condition future actions.

Social interaction

Giddens defines the structure as the development, in space and time, of regulated models of social relations engaging in the reproduction of practices. To clarify the main dimensions of the duality of structure, Giddens considers three interrelated structural properties of the social system: 'signification', 'domination', 'legitimation'. With these properties, structures include resources (command over people or material goods) and rules (recipes for action), which, combined, provide a social system with power (structures of domination to control actors), norms/routines (structures of legitimation) and meaning (structures of signification).

Entrepreneurship and structuration theory

Structuration theory provides a different outlook on the entrepreneurial process (Bouchikhi 1993: 557). It could also provide a new representation of its commitment phase. For example, drawing on this theory, Bouchikhi suggests implicitly that the entrepreneurial process and its outcome emerge from complex interactions between entrepreneurs and their context (1993: 557). Bypassing the subject/object duality, structuration theory rejects any dichotomy between synchronicity and diachronicity (Rojot 1998) and separation between contexts of interaction and structure. Through its actions, the entrepreneurial system is at the centre of action and structure. The trigger of the entrepreneurial process is assured by a competent actor (knowledgeable entrepreneur) capable of being reflexive. Structuration theory considers the recursive dimension of the system in interaction with its environment. This recursive dimension allows the system as well as its space-time actors to learn, act, rationalise their actions and perform new actions.

Recently, Sarason *et al.* (2004) suggested that: 'Since both structuration theory and the domain of entrepreneurship focus on the nexus of individuals and social systems, the insights of the intricacies of structuration theory are particularly applicable to the nature of the entrepreneurial process.' The authors consider the business start-up process as a recursive process that evolves when actors interact with their social context. Actors are both the means and the result of the process. Their idiosyncratic (and cognitive) characteristics enable them to make sense of (subjective) interpretations of information (and opportunities) in their social system and to give sense to their actions.

Structuration theory and the survival/development phase

Structuration theory can provide valuable insight into understanding the formation and evolution of the organisation as well as the structures which will support, facilitate and constrain the project and the company's activities during its survival/development phase. The application of structuration theory to the venture creation process leads us to consider that while nascent entrepreneurs create their organisations, they are also constrained and transformed by it. This mechanism of co-creation implies a reflexive interaction (a dialogic) between the nascent entrepreneur and his or her creation project through space and time. The concepts of reflexivity and social competence are coherent and compatible with an actor pushed by a teleological force generated by the vision of a desired future and goals to reach. Nascent entrepreneurs act upon structures and contribute to shaping and transforming them, while their reflexive capacity leads them to take into account their current actions to decide upon further action in order to create, alter or reinforce the value creation potential of their projects.

The survival/development process may, in these conditions, be considered as a co-construction in which the emerging organisation is at the same time both the means and the result of the nascent entrepreneur's conduct. Nascent entrepreneurs produce structures while being guided by them at the same time.

Conclusion

The currents of research grounded in the classic American paradigm of management run up against two main difficulties that both limit and weaken their results. The first difficulty is linked to the validity and accuracy of the measurement. How do you measure the performance of the companies created? Can the entrepreneur's goals be put aside? The second one relates to the notion of process and temporal non-homogeneity. When should performance be measured, for instance? To a certain extent, the ambition of this book is to answer some of these questions, thanks in particular to our model of the entrepreneurial process. However, I would like to go further and conclude by proposing a particular research approach that may help us better take into account the various points previously mentioned.

Conducting research on processes faces numerous problems

Within our perspective,[1] the main problem is linked to the support of entrepreneurial projects, this being all the more necessary in cases of innovative and technological activities. This type of business start-up is a heterogeneous, complex and dynamic phenomenon, characterised by uncertainty. In France, the bearers of innovative activity creation projects[2] have at their disposal easily accessible information, through the Internet in particular, thanks to the work accomplished by the Agence pour la Création d'Entreprise (APCE – business start-up agency). There are also support structures and incubators that may provide them with help and guidance (Albert, Fayolle and Marion 1994). Various tools exist that enable project bearers to carry out financial simulations, clarify the legal aspects of the project or formalise business

---

[1] Davidsson (2005) proposes quite an exhaustive list of the theoretical and methodological difficulties encountered when studying entrepreneurial processes.

[2] Individuals or small teams working for themselves or a company.

211

plans. However, numerous surveys indicate that the bearers of such projects are far from satisfied. Their main difficulty lies in the fact that they are piloting a process in which goals will be modified, in which new actors will get involved while others will opt out, etc. Scientific and technological aspects too often take precedence over economic aspects, which is coherent with this type of entrepreneurial profile. These types of entrepreneurs go from a vision of the world based on scientific references to a representation integrating other dimensions and characterised by uncertainty (linked to innovation and the market), which is bound to unsettle and alter their decision-making processes. This issue is particularly linked to the initial training and background of the project bearers, and the complexity and uncertainty inherent in such projects make this transition all the more difficult. Today, only experienced advisers can understand all the decision-making levers and help them, but there are not enough of them. Indeed, many years of practice are required to achieve a relevant and useful level of expertise in this field. We must also keep in mind that in matters of entrepreneurship the responsibility of the project lies with the entrepreneur only. The entrepreneur is the real initiator and driving force of the venture creation project, therefore the control of the project cannot be blindly entrusted to his or her advisers, as skilled and experienced as they may be. This is all the more so as the technical aspect is important, because consultants cannot be expected to have the necessary scientific and technical skills fully to understand the economy of the project.

A second problem to solve lies with the type of research that should be favoured to produce useful knowledge with a practical impact on helping entrepreneurs through these support processes. As we have recurrently noted, the phenomenon is complex and dynamic. It seems difficult, therefore, to observe this phenomenon in its dynamic, adaptive and evolving dimensions by adopting perspectives and tools that are mainly intended for the measurement of what is static. In other words, research relying on a positivist paradigm does not seem appropriate here. The positivist paradigm is compatible with the equilibrium theory while entrepreneurship should only be approached, according to a number of researchers, from the perspective of change[3] (Van de Ven 1992; 1999).

---

[3] A presentation of the theories of equilibrium and of change is proposed by Stevenson and Harmeling (1990).

Traditional descriptive research has enabled us to document the phenomenon. In it we have found a number of results and statistical regularities that can be used for defining policies or even guiding the actions of potential entrepreneurial partners. However, these are not of much use for the main actors concerned: the entrepreneurs themselves. The necessity for researchers who want to produce useful knowledge is therefore to enter the 'black box' of the entrepreneurial process, by integrating the complexity and dynamics of the situations studied. Observations must be made longitudinally to monitor closely the creation processes of the innovative activities concerned. Van de Ven (1999) advances that, to acquire in-depth knowledge of an activity or situation, it is necessary to observe it by being in close contact with those who are involved, and to reflect extensively upon the manner in which the situations are being handled. This type of research, however, runs up against numerous practical and methodological difficulties. A longitudinal study of an innovative business start-up project requires time and availability, which means that, in current conditions, observable cases are scarce. Moreover, it is necessary to follow the whole process until its completion before being able to produce any results. This may take years and thus give this type of research a counter-productive image, in the publish-or-perish world of academic research. Another difficulty lies in the fact that observation is not always accepted, which, combined with the risk of not being present at the right moment, may prevent the researcher from gathering data on essential events.

The type of research we would like to develop should bring appropriate answers to these issues. The research method we are thinking about would enable us to enter the black box of entrepreneurial processes, to take into account the complexity and dynamics of the situations studied and make real-time observations in a longitudinal approach, while helping nascent entrepreneurs and their partners through a new type of action research.

Research of a new kind

This new type of research innovates in that it is linked to an unusual epistemological positioning and specific tools. The research method relies on a model of the entrepreneurial process that uses information and communication technologies (ICT) as tools to ensure the monitoring of entrepreneurial projects. I think it is essential to create suitable tools that would enable entrepreneurs to improve their representations of the complex situations in which they are engaged, directly or through the people who support them. To help them better perceive the risks and stakes of a decision or orientation, to suggest possible orientations likely to ensure better performance of the future activity or its better coherence with their goals and skills, to avoid failure by diagnosing earlier the weaknesses of a given project, are but a few impacts of this set of tools intended to help the actors pilot the processes in which they are engaged.

Of course, our objective is not to ensure the success of every venture creation project and eliminate the uncertainty inherent in this type of activity. Our aim is simply to provide the actors with decision-making and analysis support tools, to help them reach their objectives by facilitating the combination of the technological, economic, commercial and human perspectives during the process. These tools are also meant to provide entrepreneurs and their teams with opportunities to acquire or reinforce their management skills – indispensable to the conduct and development of the project. They are intended for joint use by entrepreneurs and those who support them. The aim is not to replace support structures or advisers, but to make their actions more effective and more efficient. In the future, however, some of these tools may be used autonomously by nascent entrepreneurs.

Chief among the obstacles to entrepreneurial research is the difficulty of observing the process throughout its evolution. Data are too often collected *ex post* following the creation of the new venture, with all the biases and rationalisations this implies (those who have a practical experience of venture creation support will certainly recognise the phenomenon). Longitudinal studies are long and complicated to conduct, as well as resource consuming. For obvious practical reasons, they only concern a few cases. The tools we propose to develop should enable us to collect data in real-time – with the agreement of the entrepreneurs and their partners, of course.

These tools will be not only decision-making and analysis support tools for the entrepreneurs and their advisers, but also invaluable research tools for researchers by enabling them to collect data in real-time on a large number of innovative venture creation processes, and whether or not they actually lead to the creation of a (sustainable) venture. This would constitute a major innovation for the field of

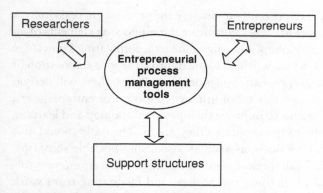

Figure C.1. Multifunctional and complementary tools

entrepreneurship. This type of research should considerably increase our knowledge of entrepreneurial processes and therefore contribute to improving the set of tools available to entrepreneurs. The development of this set of tools relies mainly on the theoretical models of the venture creation process presented in this book, as well as on research on particular populations of entrepreneurs (scientists and engineers). However, numerous obstacles must still be overcome in order to make the tools operational and develop adapted and attractive interfaces. They will be first intended for specific phases of innovative start-up processes and will only concern specific populations and projects.

This research system (Figure C.1) involves three types of actors who are involved in the processes studied: 'researchers', entrepreneurs and support entities. Researchers belong to cross-disciplinary research teams with experts in the support of specific projects. The word 'entrepreneurs' here designates project bearers, nascent entrepreneurs or individuals at different stages of commitment to the process. 'Support structures' include support entities such as institutional incubators, centres for entrepreneurs, technical centres, large corporations if the innovative venture takes place within an existing organisation, and individual advisers (experts, business angels, etc.). These support entities all provide help for entrepreneurs in a more or less organised and structured manner. The 'entrepreneurial process management tools' represent the interface between the various actors, a sort of common language with various applications. For researchers, they represent a unique opportunity to observe the processes in real-time (as opposed to *a posteriori*). They constitute the supporting elements of an experimental methodology and contribute to accumulating knowledge on multiple cases, which will lead to the improvement or elaboration of theories on the entrepreneurial phenomenon. Researchers will design, improve and maintain this set of interactive tools. For entrepreneurs, these tools are a means to improve their personal training and learning experience specific to the situations they are in. The tools should also have other useful applications such as visualising possible scenarios, identifying critical situations according to the configuration, monitoring, refining and formalising the project, and facilitating team work and decision-making. The diversity of situations observed should make it possible to improve the configurations of innovative ventures, and entrepreneurs could adjust the set of tools according to their assessment of the relevance and efficiency of the system. Concerning the support entities, the entrepreneurial management tools could be used to train new advisers, to capitalise on knowledge via the constitution of a library of cases, and, finally, to improve project selection, evaluation and monitoring. Just like entrepreneurs, the advisers have a role to play as regards the relevance of this system and the expansion of the case library. Finally, the tools would lead to the improvement of the support provided by dedicated structures, and even enable, partially or totally, distance support services.

To conclude

The research system presented above is based on a constructivist approach and implements a new method of action research that implies three types of actors: researchers, entrepreneurs and advisers. They interact mainly through an ICT-based set of tools which have a dual function: to enable entrepreneurs, through simulations, evaluations of coherence, representations of situations and decision-making devices, to become more 'intelligent' in complex situations and help them in piloting the process. They also enable researchers to keep track of numerous cases of entrepreneurial projects, to collect data over the whole duration of the process, while lifting some of the limitations of qualitative longitudinal approaches, especially in relation to the size of available samples.

This type of research is new in management science, and the method could be applied to other fields beyond the scope of this project. This new perspective for entrepreneurial research concludes this book that offers a renewed vision of the field, a synchronic and diachronic model of the entrepreneurial process and perhaps the beginnings of a possible theory of the venture creation process.

References

Abrahamsson, P. (2002), The role of commitment in software process improvement, dissertation, University of Oulu, Finland.

Ajzen I. (1991), The theory of planned behaviour, *Organizational Behavior and Human Decision Processes* 50: 179–211.

(2002), Perceived behavioral control, self-efficacy, locus of control, and the theory of planned behavior, *Journal of Applied Social Psychology* 32: 1–20.

Ajzen, I. and Fishbein, M. (1980), *Understanding Attitudes and Predicting Social Behaviour*, Englewood Cliffs, NJ: Prentice Hall.

Akrich, M., Callon, M. and Latour, B. (1988), A quoi tient le succès des innovations: l'art de l'intéressement et l'art de choisir les bons porte-paroles, *Gérer et Comprendre* 11 and 12: 4–29.

Albert, P., Fayolle, A. and Marion, S. (1994), L'évolution des systèmes d'appui à la création d'entreprises, *Revue Française de Gestion* 101: 100–12.

Aldrich, H. (1999), *Organizations Evolving*, Newbury Park, CA: Sage Publications.

Aldrich, H. and Baker, T. (1997), Blinded the cities? Has there been progress in entrepreneurship research?, in Donald L. Sexton and Ray W. Smilor (eds.), *Entrepreneurship: 2000*, Chicago, IL: Upstart Publishing Co., 377–400.

Aldrich, H. and Martinez, M. (2001), Many are called, but few are chosen: an evolutionary perspective for the study of entrepreneurship, *Entrepreneurship Theory and Practice* 25, 4: 41–56.

Amit, R., Glosten, L. and Mueller, E. (1993), Challenges to theory development in entrepreneurship research, *Journal of Management Studies* 30, 5: 815–34.

Ancona, D. G., Okhuysen, G. A. and Perlow, L. A. (2001), Taking time to integrate temporal research, *Academy of Management Review* 26, 4: 512–29.

Ansoff, I. (1989), *Stratégie de développement de l'entreprise*, Paris: Les Editions d'Organisation; trans. of *Corporate Strategy: An Analytic*

Approach to Business Policy for Growth and Expansion, New York: McGraw Hill.

Atlan, H. (1979), *Entre le cristal et la fumée*, Paris: Editions du Seuil.

Audretsch, D. B. and Thurik, A. R. (2004), A model of the entrepreneurial economy, *International Journal of Entrepreneurship Education* 2, 2: 143–66.

Autio, E., Keeley, R. H., Klofsten, M. and Ulfstedt, T. (1997), Entrepreneurial intent among students: testing an intent model in Asia, Scandinavia and USA, in *Frontiers of Entrepreneurship Research*, Babson Conference Proceedings, Wellesley, MA: Babson College.

Bagozzi, R. and Yi, Y. (1989), The degree of intention formation as a moderator of the attitude–behavior relationship, *Social Psychology Quarterly* 52: 266–79.

Bandura, A. (1977), Self-efficacy: toward a unifying theory of behavioral change, *Psychological Review* 84: 191–215.

(1982), Self-efficacy mechanism in human agency, *American Psychologist* 37: 122–47.

(1986), *The Social Foundations of Thought and Action*, Englewood Cliffs, NJ: Prentice Hall.

(1991), Social cognitive theory of self-regulation, *Organisational Behaviour and Human Decision Processes* 50: 248–87.

Barreyre, P. Y. and Lentrein, D. (1987), La participation des services achat à l'innovation dans les grandes entreprises industrielles: approche organisationnelle et problématique managériale, in *Futur et Gestion de l'Entreprise*, Poitiers: IAE de Poitiers, 29–41.

Bartlett, C. A. and Ghoshal, S. (1993), Beyond the M-Form: toward a managerial theory of the firm, *Strategic Management Journal* 14 (winter 1993, special issue): 23–46.

Batsch, L. (1997), Temps et gestion, in *Encyclopédie de gestion*, Paris: Economica, 3303–9.

Baumol, W. J. (1993), Formal entrepreneurship theory in economics: existence and bounds, *Journal of Business Venturing* 3: 197–210.

Beauvois, J. L. and Joule, R. V. (1981), *Soumission et idéologies: psychosociologie de la rationalisation*, Paris: Presses Universitaires de France.

Beccatini, G. (1992), Le district marshallien: une notion socio-économique, in G. Benko and A. Lipietz (eds.), *Les regions qui gagnent. Districts et réseaux: les nouveaux paradigmes de la géographie économique*, Paris: PUF, 35–55.

Béchard, J. P. and Grégoire, D. (2005), Entrepreneurship education research revisited: the case of higher education, *Academy of Management, Learning and Education* 4, 1: 22–43.

(2007), Archetypes of pedagogical innovation for entrepreneurship education: model and illustrations, in A. Fayolle (ed.), *Handbook of Research in Entrepreneurship Education*, vol. 1, Cheltenham: Edward Elgar, 261–84.

Becker, H. S. (1960), Notes on the concept of commitment, *American Journal of Sociology* 66: 32–40.

Becker, T. E. and Sexton, D. E. (1989), *The Entrepreneurial Spirit as a Profile of Commitment: An Explication of the Propensity for Growth*, 34th ICSB Conference, Québec: University of Quebec, 333–48.

Berthier, C. and Parent, M. C. (1994), Créations, disparitions et restructurations d'entreprises: les effets dur l'emploi des PME, *Economie et Statistique* 271–2: 13–23.

Bhave, M. P. (1994), A process model of entrepreneurial venture creation, *Journal of Business Venturing* 9, 3: 223–42.

Bigelow, J. (1982), A catastrophe model of organisational change, *Behavioral Science* 27: 26–42.

Bird, B. (1988), Implementing entrepreneurial ideas: the case for intention, *Academy of Management Review* 13, 3: 442–54.

(1992), The operation of intention in time: the emergence of the new venture, *Entrepreneurship Theory and Practice* 17, 1: 11–20.

Bird, B. and Jelinek, M. (1988), The operation of entrepreneurial intentions, *Entrepreneurship Theory and Practice* 13, 1: 21–9.

Boncler, J. and Hlady-Rispal, M. (2003), *Caractérisation de l'entrepreneuriat en économie sociale et solidaire*, Les Editions de l'ADREG, www.editions-adreg.net.

Bonneau, J. (1994), La création d'entreprises source de renouvellement du tissu des PME, *Economie et Statistique* 271–2: 25–36.

Borne, P. (1992), *Modélisation et identification des processus*, Paris: Tecnip.

Bouchikhi, H. (1990), *Structuration des organisations: concepts constructivistes et étude de cas*, Paris: Economica.

(1991), Apprendre à diriger en dirigeant, *Gestion*, novembre: 56–63.

(1993), A constructivist framework for understanding entrepreneurship performance, *Organization Studies* 14, 4: 549–70.

(1994a), Structuration des organisations: un point de vue constructiviste, Cahiers du CERESSEC, Paris: ESSEC.

(1994b), *Entrepreneurs et gestionnaires*, Paris: Les Editions d'Organisation.

(2003), Entrepreneurship professors and their constituencies: manifesto for a plural professional identity, paper presented at *IntEnt Conference 2003*, Grenoble, 5–7 September.

Boulding, K. (1956), General system theory: the skeleton of science, *Management Science* 2: 197–208.

Bourdieu, P. (1980), Le capital social: notes provisoires, *Actes de la Recherche en Sciences Sociales* 31: 2–3.

Boutillier, S. and Uzunidis, D. (1999), *La légende de l'entrepreneur: le capital social, ou comment vient l'esprit d'entreprise*, Paris: Editions La Découverte et Syros.

Boyd, N. G. and Vozikis, G. S. (1994), The influence of self-efficacy on the development of entrepreneurial intentions and actions, *Entrepreneurship Theory and Practice* 18, 4: 63–77.

Brand, M., Wakkee, I. and Van Der Veen, M. (2007), Teaching entrepreneurship to non-business students: insights from two Dutch universities, in A. Fayolle (ed.), *Handbook of Research in Entrepreneurship Education*, vol. 2, Cheltenham: Edward Elgar.

Brazeal, D. V. and Herbert, T. T. (1999), The genesis of entrepreneurship, *Entrepreneurship Theory and Practice* 23, 3: 29–45.

Bréchet, J. P. and Desreumaux, A. (1998), Le thème de la valeur en sciences de gestion: représentations et paradoxes, in J. P. Bréchet (ed.), *Valeur, marché et organisation*, Actes des 14èmes journées des IAE 1, Nantes: Presses Académiques de l'Ouest, 27–52.

Brieckman, P. (1987), *Commitment, Conflict and Caring*, Englewood Cliffs, NJ: Prentice Hall.

Brockhaus, R. H. (1980), Risk taking propensity of entrepreneurs, *Academy of Management Journal* 23, 3: 509–20.

(1982), The psychology of the entrepreneurs, in C. A. Kent *et al.* (eds.), *Encyclopedia of Entrepreneurship*, Englewood Cliffs, NJ: Prentice Hall, 39–57.

Brockner, J. (1992), The escalation of commitment to a failing course of action: toward theoretical progress, *Academy of Management Review* 17, 1: 39–61.

Bruyat, C. (1993), Création d'entreprise: contributions épistémologiques et modélisation, Thèse de doctorat, Université Pierre Mendés France de Grenoble.

(1994), Contributions épistémologiques au domaine de l'entrepreneuriat, *Revue Française de Gestion* 101: 113–25.

(2001), Créer ou ne pas créer? Une modélisation du processus d'engagement dans un projet de création d'entreprise, *Revue de l'Entrepreneuriat* 1, 1: 25–42.

Bruyat, C. and Julien, P. A. (2001), Defining the field of research in entrepreneurship, *Journal of Business Venturing* 16, 2: 165–80.

Burgelman, R. A. (1983), Corporate entrepreneurship and strategic management: insights from a process study, *Management Science* 29: 1349–64.

(1986), Stimuler l'innovation grâce aux intrapreneurs, *Revue Française de Gestion* 56–7: 128–39.

Burgelman, R. A. and Sayles, L. R. (1986), *Inside Corporate Innovations: Strategy, Structure and Managerial Skills*, New York: Free Press.

(1987), *Les intrapreneurs*, Paris: McGraw Hill (French trans. Florence Herbulot).

Burt, R. S. (1992), *Structural Holes: The Social Structure of Competition*, Cambridge, MA: Harvard University Press.

Bygrave, W. D. (1989a), The entrepreneurship paradigm (I): a philosophical look at its research methodologies, *Entrepreneurship Theory and Practice* 14, 1: 7–26.

(1989b), The entrepreneurship paradigm (II): chaos and catastrophes among quantum jumps?, *Entrepreneurship Theory and Practice* 14, 2: 7–30.

(1994), *The Portable MBA in Entrepreneurship*, New York: John Wiley and Sons.

Bygrave, W. D. and Hofer, C. W. (1991), Theorizing about entrepreneurship, *Entrepreneurship Theory and Practice* 16, 2: 13–22.

Caldwell, D. F. and O'Reilly, C. (1982), Response to failure: the effects of choice and responsibility on impression management, *Academy of Management Journal* 25, 1: 121–36.

Cantillon, R. (1755) *Essai sur la nature du commerce en général*, London: Henry Giggs (rev. edn London: Macmillan, 1931).

Carland, J. W., Hoy, F., Boulton, W. R. and Carland, J. A. C. (1984), Differentiating entrepreneurs from small business owners: a conceptualisation, *Academy of Management Review* 9, 2: 354–9.

Carland, J. W., Hoy, F. and Carland, J. A. C. (1988), Who is an entrepreneur? is a question worth asking, *American Journal of Small Business* 12, 4: 33–9.

Carree, M. A. and Thurik, A. R. (2003), The impact of entrepreneurship on economic growth, in D. B. Audretsch and Z. J. Acs (eds.), *Handbook of Entrepreneurship Research*, Boston and Dordrecht: Kluwer Academic Publishers, 437–71.

Carrier, C. (1992), L'intrapreneuriat dans la PME: une étude exploratoire du phénomène à partir des représentations des principaux acteurs concernés, Thèse de doctorat, Université de Montpellier I.

(1997), *De la créativité à l'intrapreneuriat*, Sainte-Foy: Presses de l'Université du Québec.

(2007), Strategies for teaching entrepreneurship: what else beyond lectures, case studies and business plan? in A. Fayolle (ed.), *Handbook of Research in Entrepreneurship Education*, vol. 1, Cheltenham: Edward Elgar, 143–59.

Carsrud, A. L., Gaglio, C. M. and Olm, K. W. (1986), Entrepreneurs-mentors, networks and successful new venture development: an exploration, in *Frontiers of Entrepreneurship Research*, Babson Conference Proceedings, Wellesley, MA: Babson College, 229–35.

Carter, N. M., Gartner, W. B. and Reynolds, P. D. (1996), Exploring start-up event sequences, *Journal of Business Venturing* 11, 1: 51–66.

Casson, M. (1982), *The Entrepreneur: An Economic Theory*, Oxford: Martin Robertson.

Chandler Gaylen, N. and Lyon Douglas, W. (2001), Issues of research design and construct measurement in entrepreneurship research: the past decade, *Entrepreneurship Theory and Practice* 26, 2: 101–13.

Christensen, P. S., Madsen, O. and Peterson, R. (1989), Opportunity identification: the contribution of entrepreneurship to strategic management, paper presented at *9ème Conférence de la Société de Management Stratégique, San-Francisco, 11–14 octobre*.

Churchill, N. C. (1983), Entrepreneurs and their enterprises: a stage model, in *Frontiers of Entrepreneurship Research*, Babson Conference Proceedings, Wellesley, MA: Babson College, 1–22.

Churchill, N. C. and Lewis, V. L. (1983), Les cinq stades de l'évolution d'une P.M.E., *Harvard l'Expansion*, Automne: 51–63.

Collins, O. F. and Moore, D. G. (1964), *The Enterprising Man*, East Lansing, MI: Michigan State University.

Conti, S., Malecki, E. J. and Oinas, P. (1995), *The Industrial Enterprise and Its Environment: Spatial Perspectives*, Aldershot: Avebury.

Cooper, A. C. (1971), The founding of new, technology-based firms, unpublished paper, Center for Venture Management, Milwaukee.

—— (1973), Technical entrepreneurship: what do we know? *R&D Management* 3, 2: 59–65.

Cooper, A. C., Folta, T. B. and Woo, C. (1995), Entrepreneurial information search, *Journal of Business Venturing* 10, 2: 107–20.

Courlet, C. (1990), Industrialisation et territoire: les systèmes productifs territorialisés, paper presented at Conference on Industrial Districts and Inter-Firm Cooperation: Lessons and Policies for the Future, Université du Québec à Trois-Rivières, Québec.

Covin, J. G. and Miles, M. P. (1999), Corporate entrepreneurship and the pursuit of competitive advantage, *Entrepreneurship Theory and Practice* 23, 3: 47–63.

Covin, J. G. and Slevin, D. P. (1991), A conceptual model of entrepreneurship as firm behavior, *Entrepreneurship Theory and Practice* 16, 1: 7–25.

Crozier, M. and Friedberg, E. (1977), *L'acteur et le système*, Paris: Editions du Seuil.

Cunningham, J. B. and Lischeron, J. (1991), Defining entrepreneurship, *Journal of Small Business Management* 29, 1: 45–61.

Danjou, I. (2002), L'entrepreneuriat: un champ fertile à la recherche de son unité, *Revue Française de Gestion* 138: 109–25.

Daval, H. (2002), L'essaimage: vers une nouvelle rationalité entrepreneuriale, *Revue Française de Gestion* 28, 138: 159–73.

D'Aveni, R. A. (1994), *Hypercompetition: Managing the Dynamics of Strategic Maneuvering*, New York: Free Press.

Davidsson, P. (1989), Continued entrepreneurship and small business growth, Doctoral dissertation, Stockholm School of Economics.

——— (1995), Determinants of entrepreneurial intentions, paper presented at the *RENT IX Conference*, Workshop in Entrepreneurship Research, Piacenza, Italy, 23–4 November.

——— (2005), Method issues in the study of venture start-up processes, in A. Fayolle, P. Kyrö and J. Ulijn (eds.), *Entrepreneurship Research in Europe: Outcomes and Perspectives*, Cheltenham: Edward Elgar, 35–54.

Davidsson, P., Low, M. B. and Wright, M. (2001), Editor's introduction: Low and MacMillan ten years on: achievements and future directions for entrepreneurship research, *Entrepreneurship Theory and Practice* 25, 4: 5–15.

Deeds, D. L., DeCarolis, D. and Coombs, J. E. (1998), Firm-specific resources and wealth creation in high-technology ventures: evidence from newly public biotechnology firms, *Entrepreneurship Theory and Practice* 22, 3: 55–73.

de la Ville, V. I. (1996), Apprentissages collectifs et structuration de la stratégie dans la jeune entreprise de haute technologie, Thèse de doctorat, Université de Lyon 3.

——— (2001), L'émergence du projet entrepreneurial: apprentissages, improvisations et irréversibilités, *Revue de l'Entrepreneuriat* 1, 1: 43–60.

Delmar, F. (2001), The pre-organizing and organizing of the new firm: an activity based approach, working paper, Stockholm School of Economics.

——— (2002), Entrepreneurial process: emergence and evolution of new firms in the knowledge intensive economy, paper presented at First European Summer University on Entrepreneurship Research, 19th–22nd September, INPG-ESISAR, Valence, France.

Delmar, F., Shane, S. and Smith, R. H. (2001), Legitimating first: organizing activities and the survival of new ventures, paper presented at 11th Global Conference on Entrepreneurship Research, EM Lyon, Lyon, France.

Deschamps, B. (2002), Les spécificités du processus repreneurial, *Revue Française de Gestion* 28, 138: 175–87.

Desreumaux, A. (1993), *Stratégie*, Paris: Dalloz.

Drucker, P. (1985), *Les entrepreneurs*, Paris: L'Expansion–Hachette.
Dubé, L., Jodoin, M. and Kairouz, S. (1997), Development and validation of three-factor model of commitment: from dynamic process to personal disposition, unpublished paper, Université de Montréal.
Eisenhardt, K. M. and Schoohoven, C. B. (1990), Organizational growth: linking founding team, strategy, environment and growth among US semiconductor ventures, 1978–1988, *Administrative Science Quarterly* 35: 506–39.
Ekeland, I. (1984), *Le calcul, l'imprévu*, Paris: Editions du Seuil.
—— (1990), Le roi Olav lançant les dés, in S. Amsterdamski *et al.* (eds.), *La querelle du déterminisme*, Paris: Gallimard, 163–72.
European Commission (2002), *Making Progress in Promoting Entrepreneurial Attitudes and Skills through Primary and Secondary Education*, Report from the Expert Group on Entrepreneurship Education.
—— (2004), *Helping to Create an Entrepreneurial Culture*, Luxemburg: Office for Official Publications of the European Communities.
Fayolle A. (1997), L'enseignement de l'entrepreneuriat: réflexions autour d'une expérience, Cahiers de recherche, EM Lyon 9705.
—— (2003a), *Le métier de créateur d'entreprise*, Paris: Editions d'Organisation.
—— (2003b), Research and researchers at the heart of entrepreneurial situations, in C. Steyaert and D. Hjorth (eds.), *New Movements in Entrepreneurship*, Cheltenham: Edward Elgar, 35–50.
—— (2004a), Entrepreneuriat, de quoi parlons-nous? *L'Expansion Management Review* 114, September: 67–74.
—— (2004b), *Entrepreneuriat: apprendre à entreprendre*, Paris: Dunod, collection Gestion Sup.
—— (2005), Evaluation of entrepreneurship education: behaviour performing or intention increasing, *International Journal of Entrepreneurship and Small Business* 2, 1: 89–98.
—— (2007a), *Handbook of Research in Entrepreneurship Education*, vol. 1, *A General Perspective*, Cheltenham: Edward Elgar.
—— (2007b), *Handbook of Research in Entrepreneurship Education*, vol. 2, *A Contextual Perspective*, Cheltenham: Edward Elgar.
Fayolle, A., Degeorge, J. M. and Aloulou, W. (2004), Entre intention et création d'une entreprise nouvelle: le concept d'engagement, Cahiers de recherche du CERAG, 2004–10, Université Pierre Mendès France de Grenoble.
Fayolle, A. and Filion, L. J. (2006), *Devenir entrepreneur: des enjeux aux outils*, Paris: Pearson Education France.
Fayolle, A. and Klandt, H. (eds.) (2006a), *International Entrepreneurship Education: Issues and Newness*, Cheltenham: Edward Elgar.

(2006b), Issues and newness in the field of entrepreneurship education: new lenses for new practical and academic questions, in A. Fayolle and H. Klandt. *International Entrepreneurship Education: Issues and Newness*, Cheltenham: Edward Elgar, 1–17.

Fayolle, A., Kyrö, P. and Ulijn, J. (2005), *Entrepreneurship Research in Europe: Outcomes and Perspectives*, Cheltenham: Edward Elgar.

Festinger, L. (1957), *A Theory of Cognitive Dissonance*, Stanford, CA: Stanford University Press.

(1964), *Conflict, Decision and Dissonance*, Stanford. CA: Stanford University Press.

Festinger, L. and Carlsmith, J. M. (1959), Cognitive consequences of forced compliance, *Journal of Abnormal and Social Psychology* 58: 203–10.

Feyerabend, P. K. (1979), *Contre la méthode: esquisse d'une théorie anarchiste de la connaissance*, Paris: Editions de Seuil.

Fiet, J. O. (2001a), The theoretical side of teaching entrepreneurship, *Journal of Business Venturing* 16, 1: 1–24.

(2001b), The pedagogical side of teaching entrepreneurship, *Journal of Business Venturing* 16, 2: 101–17.

Filion, L. J. (1990), Vision and relations: elements for an entrepreneurial metamodel, in *Frontiers of Entrepreneurship Research*, Babson Conference Proceedings, Wellesley, MA: Babson College, 57–71.

(1991), Vision and relations: elements for an entrepreneurial metamodel, *International Small Business Journal* 9, 2: 26–40.

(1997), Le champ de l'entrepreneuriat: historique, évolution, tendances, Cahiers de recherche 97.01, HEC Montréal.

Ford, C. M. (1996), A theory of individual creative action in multiple social domains, *Academy of Management Review* 24, 1: 1112–42

Gaglio, C. M. and Taub, R. P. (1992), Entrepreneurs and opportunity recognition, *Frontiers of Entrepreneurship Research*, Babson Conference Proceedings, Wellesley, MA: Babson College.

Gaillard-Giordani, M. L. (2004), Les modalités transactionnelles et relationnelles de la création et du financement des nouvelles organisations: la dynamique des engagements et des désengagements, Thèse pour le doctorat, Université de Nice Sophia Antipolis.

Gartner, W. B. (1985), A framework for describing the phenomenon of new venture creation, *Academy of Management Review* 10, 4: 696–706.

(1988), 'Who is an entrepreneur?' is the wrong question, *American Journal of Small Business* 12, 4: 11–31.

(1989), Some suggestions for research on entrepreneurial traits and entrepreneurship, *Entrepreneurship Theory and Practice* 14, 1: 27–38.

(1990), What are we talking about when we talk about entrepreneurship? *Journal of Business Venturing* 5, 1: 15–28.

(1993), Words lead to deeds: towards an organizational emergence vocabulary, *Journal of Business Venturing* 8, 3: 231–9.

(1995), Aspects of organizational emergence, in I. Bull, H. Thomas and G. Willard (eds.), *Entrepreneurship Perspectives on Theory Building*, Oxford: Pergamon, 67–90.

(2001), Is there an elephant in entrepreneurship? Blind assumptions in theory development, *Entrepreneurship Theory and Practice* 25, 4: 27–39.

Gélinier, O. (1978), Renaissance de l'esprit d'entreprise, *Revue Française de Gestion* 16: 9.

Gerard, H. B. (1965), Deviation, conformity and commitment, in R. P. Steiner and M. Fishbein (eds.), *Current Studies in Social Psychology*, New York: Holt, Rinehart and Winston, 263–77.

Gibb, A. A. (1993), The enterprise culture and education. Understanding enterprise education and its links with small business, entrepreneurship and wider educational goals, *International Small Business Journal* 11, 3: 11–37.

(1996), Entrepreneurship and small business management: can we afford to neglect them in the twenty-first century business school? *British Journal of Management* 7, 4: 309–24.

Giddens, A. (1979), *Central Problems in Social Theory*, London: Macmillan.

(1984a), *The Constitution of Society*, Cambridge: Polity Press.

(1984b), Elements of the theory of structuration, in *The Polity Reader in Social Theory*, Cambridge: Polity Press.

(1987), *La constitution de la société*, Paris: Presses Universitaires de France.

Gomez, P. Y., Volery, T. and Sangupta, M. (2000), How do organizations come into existence? Towards an evolutionary theory of entrepreneurship, working paper, EM Lyon.

Graham, J. B., Long, W. A. and McMullan, E. W. (1985), Assessing economic value added by university based new venture outreach programs, in *Frontiers of Entrepreneurship Research*, Babson Conference Proceedings, Wellesley, MA: Babson College, 489–520.

Granovetter, M. (1983), The strength of weak ties: a network theory revisited, in R. Collins (ed.), *Sociological Theory*, San Fransisco, CA: Jossey-Bass, 201–33.

Greiner, L. E. (1972), Evolution and revolution as organizations grow, *Harvard Business Review* 50: 37–46.

Greve, A. and Salaff, J. W. (2003), Social networks and entrepreneurship, *Entrepreneurship Theory and Practice* 28, 1: 1–22.

Gumpert, D. E. (1996), *How To Really Create a Successful Business Plan*, Boston: Goldhirst Group, Inc.

Guth, W. D. and Ginsberg, A. (1990), Guest editor's introduction: corporate entrepreneurship, *Strategic Management Journal* 11: 5–15.

Hambrick, D. C. and Crozier, M. (1985), Stumblers and stars in the management of rapid growth, *Journal of Business Venturing* 1, 1: 31–45.

Harrison, R. T. and Leitch, C. M. (1994), Entrepreneurship and leadership: the implications for education and development, *Entrepreneurship and Regional Development* 6, 2: 111–25.

Hernandez, E. M. (1999), *Le processus entrepreneurial: vers un modèle stratégique d'entrepreneuriat*, Paris: L'Harmattan.

(2001), *L'entrepreneuriat: approche théorique*, Paris: L'Harmattan.

Hills, G. E. (1995), Opportunity recognition by successful entrepreneurs, a pilot study, in *Frontiers of Entrepreneurship Research*, Babson Conference Proceedings, Wellesley, MA: Babson College.

Hills, G. E. and Laforge, R. W. (1992), Marketing and entrepreneurship: the state of the art, in D. L. Sexton and J. D. Kasarda (eds.), *The State of the Art of Entrepreneurship*, Wellesley, MA: Babson College.

Hindle, K. (2007), Teaching entrepreneurship at the university: from the wrong building to the right philosophy, in A. Fayolle (ed.), *Handbook of Research in Entrepreneurship Education*, vol. 1, Cheltenham: Edward Elgar, 104–26.

Hirschman, A. (1967), *Development Projects Observed*, Washington, DC: Brookings Institution.

Hisrish, R. D. and O'Brien, M. (1981), The woman entrepreneur from a business and sociological perspective. Their problems and needs, in *Frontiers of Entrepreneurship Research*, Babson Conference Proceedings, Wellesley, MA: Babson College, 21–39.

Hlady-Rispal, M. (2002), *La méthode des cas: applications à la recherche en gestion*, Brussells: De Boeck Université.

Hornaday, J. A. (1982), Research about living entrepreneurs, in C. A. Kent, D. L. Sexton and K. L. Vesper (eds.), *Encyclopedia of Entrepreneurship*, Englewood Cliffs, NJ: Prentice Hall, 281–90.

Jacot, J. H. (1994), *Formes anciennes, formes nouvelles d'organisation*, Lyons: Presses Universitaires de Lyon.

Jacquet-Lagreze, E., Roy, B., Moscarela, J. and Hirsch, G. (1978), Description d'un processus de décision, Cahiers du LAMSADE 13, Université de Paris IX Dauphine.

Johannisson, B. (1991), University training for entrepreneurship: a Swedish approach, *Entrepreneurship and Regional Development* 3, 1: 67–82.

Johansson, B., Karlsson, C. and Westin, L. (1994), *Patterns of a Network Economy*, London: Springer Verlag.

Joule, R. V. and Beauvois, J. L. (1989), Une théorie psychosociale: la théorie de l'engagement, *Recherche et Applications en Marketing* 4, 1: 79–90.

(2002), *Petit traité de manipulation à l'usage des honnêtes gens*, Grenoble: Presses Universitaires de Grenoble.

Julien, P.-A. and Marchesnay, M. (1996), *L'entrepreneuriat*. Paris: Economica, Collection Gestion/Poche.

Kaisch, S. and Gilad, B. (1991), Characteristics of opportunities search of entrepreneurs versus executives: sources, interests, general alertness, *Journal of Business Venturing* 6, 1: 45–61.

Katz, J. A. (2003), The chronology and intellectual trajectory of American entrepreneurship education, *Journal of Business Venturing* 18, 3: 283–300.

Katz, J. and Gartner, W. B. (1988), Properties of emerging organizations, *Academy of Management Review* 13, 3: 429–41.

Kazanjian, R. K. and Drazin, R. (1990), A stage-contingent model of design and growth in technology based new ventures, *Journal of Business Venturing* 5, 3: 137–50.

Keil, M. (1995), Pulling the plug: software project management and the problem of project escalation, *MIS Quarterly* 19, 4: 421–47.

Kets de Vries, M. F. R. (1977), The entrepreneurial personality, *Journal of Management Studies* 14: 34–57.

Kiesler, C. A. (1971), *The Psychology of Commitment*, New York: Academic Press.

Kiesler, C. A. and Sakumara, J. (1966), A test of a model of commitment, *Journal of Personality and Social Psychology* 3, 3: 349–53.

Kirchhoff, B. A. (1994), *Entrepreneurship and Dynamic Capitalism: The Economy of the Business Firm Formation and Growth*, New York: Praeger Publisher.

(1997), Entrepreneurship economics, in W. D. Bygrave (ed.), *The Portable MBA in Entrepreneurship*, New York: John Wiley and Sons.

Kirzner, I. M. (1973), *Competition and Entrepreneurship*, Chicago: University of Chicago Press.

(1983), *Perception, Opportunity and Profit: Studies in the Theory of Entrepreneurship*, Chicago, IL: University of Chicago Press.

Knight, F. H. (1971), *Risk, Uncertainty and Profit*, Chicago, IL: University of Chicago Press.

Krueger, N. F. (1993), The impact of prior entrepreneurial exposure on perceptions of new venture feasibility and desirability, *Entrepreneurship Theory and Practice* 18, 1: 5–17.

Krueger, N. F. and Carsrud, A. L. (1993), Entrepreneurial intentions: applying the theory of planned behaviour, *Entrepreneurship and Regional Development* 5, 4: 315–30.

Krueger, N. F., Reilly, M. D. and Carsrud, A. L. (2000), Competing models of entrepreneurial intentions, *Journal of Business Venturing* 15, 5–6: 411–32.

Kuratko, D. F. (2005), The emergence of entrepreneurship education: development, trends and challenges, *Entrepreneurship Theory and Practice* 29, 5: 577–97.

Landström, H. (1998), The roots of entrepreneurship research: the intellectual development of a research field, paper presented at Conférence RENT XII (Research in Entrepreneurship and Small Business), Lyon, 26–27 novembre 1998, 18 p.

(2005), *Pioneers in Entrepreneurship and Small Business Research*, New York: Springer.

Langley, A., Mintzberg, H., Pitcher, P., Posada, E. and Saint-Macary, J. (1995), Opening up decision making: the view from the black stool, *Organization Science* 6, 3: 260–79.

Learned, K. E. (1992), What happened before the organization? A model of organization formation, *Entrepreneurship Theory and Practice* 17, 1: 39–48.

Lee, J. H. and Venkataraman, S. (2002), Aspiration, market offerings and the decision to become an entrepreneur, Working Paper, Darden School of Business, University of Virginia.

Leibenstein, H. (1979), The general X-efficiency paradigm and the role of entrepreneurship, in M. J. Rizzio (ed.), *Time, Uncertainty and Disequilibrum*, Lexington, MA: D. C. Heath, 127–39.

Lemieux, V. and Ouimet, M. (2004), *L'analyse structurale des réseaux sociaux*, Brussells: De Boeck.

Le Moigne, J. L. (1984), *La théorie du système général: théorie de la modélisation*, Paris: Presses Universitaires de France, 2nd edn.

(1990), *La modélisation des systèmes complexes*, Paris: Dunod.

Lichtenstein, B. M. (2002), Entrepreneurship as emergence: insights and methods from philosophy and complexity science, Working Paper, University of Hartford.

Lichtenstein, B. M., Carter, N. M., Dooley, K. J. and W. B. Gartner (2007), Complexity dynamics of nascent entrepreneurship, *Journal of Business Venturing* 22, 3: 238–61.

Liles, P. (1974), Who are the entrepreneurs?, *MSU Business Topics* 22: 5–14.

Long, W. A. and McMullan, W. E. (1984), Mapping the new venture opportunity identification process, in *Frontiers of Entrepreneurship Research*, Babson Conference Proceedings, Wellesley, MA: Babson College, 567–91.

Lorino, P. (1995), Le déploiement de la valeur par les processus, *Revue Française de Gestion* 104: 55–71.

McCarthy, A. M., Schoorman, F. D. and Cooper, A. C. (1993), Reinvestment decisions by entrepreneurs: rational decision-making or escalation of commitment? *Journal of Business Venturing* 8, 1: 9–24.

McClelland, D. C. (1961), *The Achieving Society*, Princeton, NJ: Van Nostrand.

March, J. G. (1991), Exploration and exploitation in organisational learning, *Organization Science* 2, 1: 71–87.

March, J. G. and Simon, H. A. (1964), *Les organisations: problèmes psychologiques*, Paris: Dunod.

Marchesnay, M. and Julien, P. A. (1989), Small business as space of transaction, *Entrepreneurship and Regional Development* 2, 3: 267–77.

Marion, S. (1999), L'évaluation de projets de création d'entreprises dans le contexte d'une intervention financière, Thèse de doctorat, Université Jean Moulin de Lyon.

Martin, M. J. C. (1984), *Managing Technological Innovation and Entrepreneurship*, Reston, VA: Reston Publishing Co.

(1994), *Managing Innovation and Entrepreneurship in Technology-Based Firms*, New York: John Wiley and Son.

Martinet, A. C. (1990), *Epistémologies et sciences de gestion*, Paris: Economica.

Massacrier, G. and Rigaud, G. (1984), Le démarrage des activités nouvelles: aléas et processus, *Revue Française de Gestion* 45: 5–18.

Meredith, G. G., Nelson, R. E. and Neck, P. A. (1982), *The Practice of Entrepreneurship*, Geneva: Bureau International du Travail.

Meyer, J. P. and Allen, N. J. (1997), *Commitment in the Workplace: Theory, Research, and Application*, London: Sage Publications.

Miller, D. and Friesen, P. H. (1982), Innovation in conservative and entrepreneurial firms: two models of strategic management, *Strategic Management Journal* 3: 1–25.

Millier, P. (1997), *Stratégie et marketing de l'innovation technologique*, Paris: Dunod.

Mintzberg, H. (1991), *Le management*, Paris: Les Editions d'Organisation.

Moore, C. F. (1986), Understanding entrepreneurial behavior, in J. A. Pierce II and R. B. Robinson Jr. (eds.), *Academy of Management Best Papers Proceedings*, Forty-sixth Annual Meeting of the Academy of Management, Chicago, 66–70.

Moreau, F. (2003), Proposition d'une typologie des modes de développement des jeunes entreprises technologiques innovantes à fort potentiel de croissance, Thèse de doctorat, Université Paris X Nanterre.

Morgan, G. (1989), *Images de l'organisation*, Laval: Les Presses de l'Université Laval.

Morin, E. (1986), *La méthode III: connaissance de la connaissance*, Paris: Editions du Seuil.

(1989), Diriger dans la complexité, paper presented at Colloque du 9 mars 1989, Entreprise et Progrès.

Mowday, W. H. (1998), Reflections on the study and relevance of organizational commitment, *Human Resource Management Review* 8, 4: 387–401.

Mustar, P. (1997), Spin-off enterprises. How French academics create high-tech companies: the conditions for success or failure? *Science and Public Policy* 24, 1: 37–43.

Myers, D. D. and Hobbs, D. J. (1985), Profile of location preferences for non-metropolitan high-tech firms, in *Frontiers of Entrepreneurship Research*, Babson Conference Proceedings, Wellesley, MA: Babson College, 358–82.

Naman, J. L. and Selvin, D. P. (1993), Entrepreneurship and the concept of fit: a model and empirical tests, *Strategic Management Journal* 14: 137–53.

Nystrom, H. (1995), Creativity and entrepreneurship, in C. M. Ford and D. A. Gioia (eds.), *Creative Action in Organizations*, London: Sage Publications.

Osborn, A. F. (1988), *Créativité: l'imagination constructive*, Paris: Bordas.

Penrose, R. (1989), *The Emperor's New Mind: Concerning Computers, Minds and the Laws of Physics*, New York: Oxford University Press.

Peters, T. J. and Waterman, R. H. Jr. (1982), *In Search of Excellence*, New York: Harper and Row.

Pettigrew, A. (1992), The character and significance of strategy process research, *Strategic Management Journal* 13: 5–16.

Pinchot, G. (1985), *Intrapreneuring: Why You Don't Have to Leave the Organization to Become an Entrepreneur*, New York: Harper and Row.

Pleitner, H. J. (1985), Entrepreneurs and new venture creation: some reflections of a conceptual nature, Working paper, St Gall Graduate School of Economics, Law, Business and Public Administration.

Porter, M. (1980), *Competitive Strategy*, New York: The Free Press.

(1985), *Competitive Advantage*, New York: The Free Press.

Ray, D. R. (1986), Perceptions of risk and new enterprise formation in Singapore: an exploratory study, in *Frontiers of Entrepreneurship Research*, Babson Conference Proceedings, Wellesley, MA: Babson College, 119–45.

Reynolds, P. D. (1991), Sociology and entrepreneurship: concepts and contributions, *Entrepreneurship Theory and Practice* 16, 2: 47–70.

Reynolds, P. D., Hay, M. and Camp, S. M. (1999), *Global Entrepreneurship Monitor*, Kansas City: Kauffman Center for Entrepreneurial Leadership.

Reynolds, P. and Miller, B. (1992), New firm gestation: conception, birth and implications for research, *Journal of Business Venturing* 7, 4: 405–17.

Risker, D. C. (1998), Toward an innovation typology of entrepreneurs, *Journal of Small Business and Entrepreneurship* 15, 2: 27–41.

Roberts, E. B. and Wainer, H. A. (1968), Entrepreneurship and technology: a basic study of innovators, *Research Management* 11, 4: 249–66.

Rojot, J. (1998), La théorie de la structuration, *Revue de Gestion des Ressources Humaines* 26–27: 5–19.

Ronstadt, R. C. (1982), Does entrepreneurial career path really matter? in *Frontiers of Entrepreneurship Research*, Babson Conference Proceedings, Wellesley, MA: Babson College, 540–67.

(1984), *Entrepreneurship*, Dover: Lord Publishing.

Rouleau, L. (2002), La formation des stratégies sous microscope, *Revue Canadienne des Sciences de l'Administration* 19, mars: 1.

Royer, I. (1996), L'escalade de l'engagement dans le développement de produits nouveaux, *Recherche et Applications en Marketing* 11, 3: 7–22.

Sabherwal, R. *et al.* (1994), Why organizations increase commitment to failing information systems projects? Working paper, Miami, FL, Department of Decision Science and Information Systems.

Sammut, S. (1998), *Jeune entreprise: la phase cruciale du démarrage*, Paris: L'Harmattan.

Sandberg, W. R. and Hofer, C. W. (1987), Improving venture performance: the role of strategy, industry structure, and the entrepreneur, *Journal of Business Venturing* 2, 1: 5–28.

Sapienza, H. J., Herron, L. and Menendez, J. (1991), The founder and the firm: a qualitative analysis of entrepreneurial process, in *Frontiers of Entrepreneurship Research*, Babson Conference Proceedings, Wellesley, MA: Babson College, 254–70.

Sarason, Y., Dean, T. and Dillard, J. F. (2006), Entrepreneurship as the nexus of individual and opportunity: a structuration view, *Journal of Business Venturing* 21, 3: 286.

Sarason, Y., Dillard, J. F. and Dean, T. (2002), Structuration theory as a framework for exploring the entrepreneurship domain. Paper presented at the Academy of Management Meeting, August 9–13, Denver, CO.

Say, J.-B. (1803), *Traité d'économie politique*, Paris: Déterville.

Schmidt, J. B. and Calantone, R. J. (2002), Escalation of commitment during new product development, *Journal of the Academy of Marketing Science* 30: 103–18.

Schoonhoven, C. B. and Romanelli, E. (2001), *The Entrepreneurial Dynamics: Origins of Entrepreneurship and the Evolution of Industries*, Stanford, CA: Stanford Business Books.

Schumpeter, J. A. (1928), Unternehmer, in L. Elster, A. Weber and F. Wieser (eds.), *Handwörterbuch der Staatswissenschaften*, Band 8, Jena: Verlag von Gustav Fisher, 476–87.

(1934), *The Theory of Economic Development*, Cambridge, MA: Harvard University Press.

(1939), *Business Cycles*, vol.1, New York: McGraw Hill.

Secord, P. F. and Backman, C. W. (1974), *Social Psychology*, New York: McGraw Hill.

Sfez, L. (1986), Lettre Martiniquaise, *Sciences de l'intelligence, sciences de l'artificiel*, Lyons: Presses Universitaires de Lyon.

Shane, S. (2003), *A General Theory of Entrepreneurship: The Individual Opportunity Nexus*, Cheltenham: Edward Elgar.

Shane, S. and Venkataraman, S. (2000), The promise of entrepreneurship as a field of research, *Academy of Management Review* 25, 1: 217–26.

Shapero, A. (1972), The process of technical company formation in local area, in A. C. Cooper and J. L. Komives (eds.), *Technical Entrepreneurship*, Milwaukee, WI: Center for Venture Management, 546–62.

(1975), The displaced uncomfortable entrepreneur, *Psychology Today* 7, 11: 83–8.

(1984), The entrepreneurial event, in C. A. Kent (ed.), *The Environments of Entrepreneurship*, Lexington, MA: Lexington Books, 21–40.

Shapero, A. and Sokol, L. (1982), The social dimensions of entrepreneurship, in C. Kent, D. Sexton and K. Vesper (eds.), *Encyclopedia of Entrepreneurship*, Englewood Cliffs, NJ: Prentice Hall, 72–90.

Sharma, P. and Chrisman, J. J. (1999), Toward a reconciliation of the definitional issues in the field of corporate entrepreneurship, *Entrepreneurship Theory and Practice* 23, 3: 11–28.

Shaver, K. G. and Scott, L. R. (1991), Person, process, choice: the psychology of new venture creation, *Entrepreneurship Theory and Practice* 16, 1: 23–45.

Shook, C. L., Priem, R. L. and McGee, J. E. (2003), Venture creation and the enterprising individual: a review and synthesis, *Journal of Management* 29, 3: 379–99.

Simon, H. (1983), *Administration et processus de décision*, Paris: Economica.

(1986), Commentaires, in *Sciences de l'intelligence, sciences de l'artificiel*, Lyons: Presses Universitaires de Lyon, 577–600.

Simon, H. et al. (1986), *Decision Making and Problem Solving*, Washington, DC: National Academy Press.

Simonson, I. and Staw, B. M. (1992), De-escalation strategies: a comparison of techniques for reducing commitment to losing courses of action, *Journal of Applied Psychology* 77, 3: 419–26.

Smeltzer, L. R., Van Hook, B. L. and Hutt, R. W. (1991), Analysis of the use of advisors as information sources in venture start-ups, *Journal of Small Business Management* 29, 3: 10–19.

Smith, N. R. (1967), The entrepreneur and his firm: the relationship between type of man and type of company, East Lansing: Bureau of Business and Economic Research, Michigan State University.

Starr, J. and Fondas, N. (1992), A model of entrepreneurial socialization and organization formation, *Entrepreneurship Theory and Practice* 17, 1: 67–76.

Starr, J. and MacMillan, I. C. (1990), Resource cooptation via social contracting: resource acquisition strategies for new ventures, *Strategic Management Journal* 11, Summer: 79–92.

Staw, B. M. (1976), Knee-deep in the Big Muddy: a study of escalating commitment to a chosen course of action, *Organizational Behavior and Human Performance* 16: 27–44.

(1980), Rationality and justification in organizational life, in B. M. Staw and L. Cummings (eds.), *Research in Organizational Behavior*, vol. 2, Greenwich, CT: JAI Press, 45–80.

(1981), The escalation of commitment to a course of action, *Academy of Management Review* 6, 4: 577–87.

Staw, B. M. and Ross, J. (1987), Understanding escalation situations: antecedents, prototypes, and solutions, in B. M. Staw and L. L. Cummings (eds.), *Research in Organizational Behavior*, vol. 9, Greenwich, CT: JAI Press, 39–78.

Steinmetz, L. L. (1969), Critical stages of small business growth, *Business Horizons*, February: 29–36.

Stevenson, H. H. (1985), A new paradigm for entrepreneurial management, in J. Kao and H. Stevenson (eds.), *Entrepreneurship: What It Is and How To Teach It*, Boston, MA: Harvard Business School, 2–24.

Stevenson, H. H. and Gumpert, D. E. (1985), The heart of entrepreneurship, *Harvard Business Review* 62, 2: 85–92.

Stevenson, H. H. and Harmeling, S. (1990), Entrepreneurial management's need for a more 'chaotic' theory, *Journal of Business Venturing* 5, 1: 1–14.

Stevenson, H. H. and Jarillo, J. C. (1990), A paradigm of entrepreneurship: entrepreneurial management, *Strategic Management Journal* 11: 17–27.

Thiétart, R. A. (ed.) (1999), *Méthodes de recherche en management*, Paris: Dunod.

Thom, R. (1980), *Modèles mathématiques de la morphogénèse*, Paris: Bourgeois.

Thomson, J. L. (2004), The facets of the entrepreneur: identifying entrepreneurial potential, *Management Decision* 42, 2: 243–58.

Thornberry, N. (2001), Corporate entrepreneurship: antidote or oxymoron? *European Management Journal* 19, 5: 526–33.

Thornton, P. H. (1999), The sociology of entrepreneurship, *Annual Review of Sociology* 25: 19–46.

Timmons, J. A. (1978), Characteristics and role demands of entrepreneurship, *American Journal of Small Business* 3, 1: 5–17.

(1994), *New Venture Creation*, New York: McGraw Hill.

Timmons, J. A. and Spinelli, S. (2004), *New Venture Creation: Entrepreneurship for the 21st Century.* New York: McGraw Hill.

Tkachev, A. and Kolvereid, L. (1999), Self-employment intentions among Russian students, *Entrepreneurship and Regional Development* 11, 3: 269–80.

Tornikoski, E. (1999), Entrepreneurship through constructivist lenses: visionary entrepreneurship process – a conceptual development, Licentiate thesis, University of Vaasa.

Ucbasaran, D., Westhead, P., Wright, M. and Binks, M. (2003), Does entrepreneurial experience influence opportunity recognition, *Journal of Private Equity* 17: 7–14.

Van de Ven, A. H. (1992), Longitudinal methods for studying the process of entrepreneurship, in D. L. Sexton and J. D. Kasarda (eds.), *State of the Art of Entrepreneurship*, Boston, MA: PWS-Kent Publishing Company, 214–42.

(1999), Interview d'Andrew Van de Ven, *Revue Française de Gestion* 125: 58–63.

Van de Ven, A. H., Angle, H. L. and Poole, M. S. (eds.) (1989), *Research on the Management of Innovation,* New York: Ballinger/Harper and Row.

Van de Ven, A. H. and Poole, M. S. (1990), Methods for studying innovation development in the Minnesota innovation research program. *Organization Science* 1: 313–35. Reprinted in G. Huber and A. Van de Ven (eds.), *Longitudinal Field Research Methods: Studying Processes of Organizational Change*, Thousand Oaks, CA: Sage, 1995, 155–85.

(1995), Explaining development and change in organizations, *Academy of Management Review* 20, 3: 510–40.

Van de Ven, A. H., Poole, M. S., Dooley, K. and Holmes, M. E. (2000), *Organizational Change and Innovation Processes: Theory and Methods for Research*, New York: Oxford University Press.

Van der Veen, M. and Wakkee, I. (2002), The entrepreneurial process, an overview, unpublished Proceedings, First European Summer University on Entrepreneurship Research, 19th-22nd September, Valence, France.

Van Stel, A. J., Carree, M. A. and Thurik, A. R. (2005), The effect of entrepreneurial activity on national economic growth, Working Paper 405, Max Planck Institute for Research into Economic Systems.

Venkataraman, S. (1997), The distinctive domain of entrepreneurship research: an editor's perspective, in J. Katz and R. Brockhaus (eds.), *Advances in Entrepreneurship: Firm, Emergence, and Growth*, vol. 3, Greenwich, CT: JAI Press, 119–38.

Venkataraman, S. and Van de Ven, A. H. (1998), Hostile environmental jolts, transaction set and new business development, *Journal of Business Venturing* 13, 3: 231–55.

Vérin, H. (1982), *Entrepreneurs/entreprise: histoire d'une idée*, Paris: PUF.

Verstraete, T. (1999), *Entrepreneuriat: connaître l'entrepreneur, comprendre ses actes*, Paris: L'Harmattan.

——— (2002), *Essai sur la singularité de l'entrepreneuriat comme domaine de recherche*, Les Editions de l'ADREG, www.editions-adreg.net.

——— (2003), *Proposition d'un cadre théorique pour la recherche en entrepreneuriat*, Editions de l'ADREG, www.editions-adreg.net.

Verstraete, T. and Fayolle, A. (2005), Paradigmes et entrepreneuriat, *Revue de l'Entrepreneuriat* 4, 1: 33–52.

Vesper, K. (1989), When's the big idea, in *Frontiers of Entrepreneurship Research*, Babson Conference Proceedings, Wellesley, MA: Babson College, 334–43.

Watkins, D. (1976), Entry into independent entrepreneurship: toward a model of the business initiation process, Working Paper 24, Manchester Business School and Center for Business Research.

Weick, K. E. (1979), *The Social Psychology of Organizing*, Reading, MA: Addison-Wesley.

Wennekers, S., Van Stel, A., Thurik, R. and Reynolds, P. (2005), Nascent entrepreneurs and the level of economic development, Working Paper 1405, Max Planck Institute for Research into Economic Systems.

Wicklund, J., Dahlqvist, J. and Havnes, P. A. (2001), Entrepreneurship as new business activity: empirical evidence from young firms, in *Frontiers of Entrepreneurship Research*, Babson Conference Proceedings, Wellesley, MA: Babson College.

Woo, C. Y., Cooper, A. C., Nicholls-Dixon, C. and Dunkelberg, W. C. (1990), Adaptation by start-up firms, in *Frontiers of Entrepreneurship Research*, Babson Conference Proceedings, Wellesley, MA: Babson College, 132–43.

Index

Printed in the United States
By Bookmasters